Transmitting Rights

Transmitting Rights

International Organizations and the Diffusion of Human Rights Practices

BRIAN GREENHILL

OXFORD
UNIVERSITY PRESS

OXFORD
UNIVERSITY PRESS

Oxford University Press is a department of the University of
Oxford. It furthers the University's objective of excellence in research,
scholarship, and education by publishing worldwide.

Oxford   New York

Auckland   Cape Town   Dar es Salaam   Hong Kong   Karachi
Kuala Lumpur   Madrid   Melbourne   Mexico City   Nairobi
New Delhi   Shanghai   Taipei   Toronto

With offices in

Argentina   Austria   Brazil   Chile   Czech Republic   France   Greece
Guatemala   Hungary   Italy   Japan   Poland   Portugal   Singapore
South Korea   Switzerland   Thailand   Turkey   Ukraine   Vietnam

Oxford is a registered trademark of Oxford University Press
in the UK and certain other countries.

Published in the United States of America by
Oxford University Press
198 Madison Avenue, New York, NY 10016

Library of Congress Cataloging-in-Publication Data
ISBN 978-0-19-027163-3 (hbk.); 978-0-19-027164-0 (pbk.)

1 3 5 7 9 8 6 4 2
Printed in the United States of America
on acid-free paper

CONTENTS

LIST OF FIGURES AND TABLES

Figures

Tables

ACKNOWLEDGMENTS

This book emerged out of the PhD dissertation I wrote in the Political Science department at the University of Washington between 2005 and 2010. Dealing with the ups and downs of dissertation research can be an emotionally exhausting experience, but I was lucky enough to have two of the most supportive dissertation advisors I could have wished for, Aseem Prakash and Mike Ward. Aseem and Mike jointly chaired my committee and played an extremely important role in shaping the ideas and analysis in what would become this book. I am also very grateful for the help that the other members of my dissertation committee—Jim Caporaso, Rachel Cichowski and Peter Hoff—were able to give me in developing these ideas and sharpening the argument.

At Dartmouth I have benefited greatly from many lengthy discussions on this project with my colleagues in the Government Department. I would especially like to thank Steve Brooks and Ben Valentino not only for their help with developing the arguments in the book, but also for spending so much time guiding me through the many steps involved in bringing this project to completion. In the spring of 2014, Dartmouth's Dickey Center for International Understanding sponsored a workshop on my manuscript that came to play a crucial role in bringing this project to completion. Jon Pevehouse and Beth Simmons generously agreed to serve as my external discussants, while the Dartmouth delegation included Steve Brooks, John Carey, Jeff Friedman, Josh Kertzer, Jennifer Lind, Daryl Press, Ben Valentino, Bill Wohlforth, and Chris Wohlforth. All of the participants took the time to carefully read an early draft of the manuscript and provided me with extremely useful comments and suggestions.

I am also grateful for the very useful feedback I have received in the course of various discussions over the past few years, and when presenting parts of this project at seminars and at conferences. Among those I would especially like to thank are Leonardo Bacinni, Dan Berliner, Zoltan Buzas, John Campbell, Xun Cao, Christina Davis, Bud Duvall, John Freeman, Fabrizio Gilardi, Ryan Goodman, Julia Gray, Seva Gunitsky, Jeremy Horowitz, Paul Ingram, Adam Kleinbaum, Ron Krebs, Yon Lupu, Jamie Mayerfeld, Jon Mercer, Alex Montgomery, Brendan Nyhan, James O'Malley, Magnus Thor Torfason, Fabio Wasserfallen, and Andreas Wimmer. I would also like to thank a number of Dartmouth under-graduates who provided valuable research assistance with this project–specifically, Feyaad Allie, Sebastian DeLuca, Irvin Gomez, Alejandro Gomez-Barbosa and Kali Montecalvo.

My work on this project has been made possible in part by the financial support I received in the form of a faculty research grant from the Nelson A. Rockefeller Center for Public Policy at Dartmouth College, and by the funding I received for my final year of graduate school through a DARPA-IPTO subcontract to the University of Washington (Dr. Ward, PI) for the investigation of international crisis early warning systems (ICEWS).

Finally, I would like to express my heartfelt appreciation to my family. The support I received from my parents, Kenneth and Vivian, and from my brothers, Paul and Jonny, was absolutely essential in giving me the confidence to leave my previous profession, head to graduate school and eventually succeed in reinventing myself as a political scientist. And in that time my family has grown to include my wife, Claire, and our two young children, Tali and Adam. They are the ones who have given me so much day-to-day support while I spent long hours working on this project, and it is to them that this book is dedicated.

1

Introduction

1.1 Globalization and Human Rights

Is globalization good or bad for human rights? Human rights activists tend to be pessimistic about the longer-term effects of globalization, and often for good reason. In recent years we have been exposed to stories about well-respected global brands using sweatshop labor in their overseas manufacturing plants and of the sometimes devestating consequences that rapid exposure to global markets has had on vulnerable populations in the developing world. Yet, it is also easy to think of globalization success stories—for example, those of South Korea or Taiwan—where economic openness appears to have served as an "engine of development," helping to lift large segments of their populations out of poverty and facilitate major political and social reforms. Clearly, the relationship between globalization and human rights is more complex than the rhetoric of activists on either side of the globalization debate would lead us to believe.

Recently, scholars have come to realize that making sense of the globalization debate depends upon unpacking some of the complexity associated with the term "globalization." In its most general sense, globalization implies that things that happen in one society are now highly dependent on things that happen in other parts of the world (Baylis, Smith, and Owens, 2014: 9). But this general definition obviously fails to distinguish among many different forms of interdependence—for example, international trade, foreign investment, exposure to foreign media sources—each of which could have very different consequences for human rights. In this book I shall consider one important but often overlooked actor in the globalization and human rights story: Intergovernmental Organizations (IGOs). Most people have some familiarity with prominent IGOs such as the United Nations (UN) or the European Union (EU), and, to a lesser

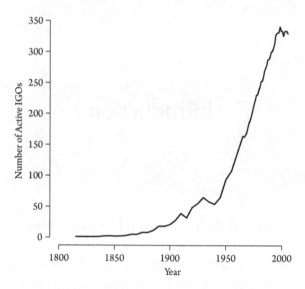

Figure 1.1 Total number of IGOs by year, 1815–2005.
Note: Data from the Correlates of War dataset.

degree, with the work that these organizations have done to promote human rights. Yet very few people have any familiarity with the hundreds of other less prominent IGOs such as the European Space Agency or the International Coral Reef Initiative—most of which, in any case, have no obvious connection to human rights issues.

As the graph in Figure 1.1 shows, the number of active IGOs has undergone an enormous expansion in recent decades. Political scientists, however, remain divided as to what effect, if any, they are having on international politics. The debates so far have tended to focus on the question of whether these organizations actually achieve their stated goals—for example, whether the World Trade Organization (WTO) increases trade among its member states, or whether the North Atlantic Treaty Organization (NATO) makes much of a contribution to interna- tional security. But in the midst of these important debates about the efficacy of certain high-profile IGOs, political scientists have only recently begun to think more holistically about the ways in which membership in larger numbers of IGOs could be affecting state behavior.[1]

This book advances the discussion of the role of IGOs in international politics by encouraging us to move beyond the relatively narrow—albeit very important—discussions of the efficacy of particular organizations. It offers a more sociological perspective on international institutions that conceives of IGOs as constituting a tightly woven fabric of ties between states. I argue that this network, though often obscured by our tradition-ally state-centric view of international relations, provides an important channel through which states can influence, and be influenced by, the behavior of others. In some cases this influence is explicit and direct—for example, when the EU issues directives that require its member states to achieve a particular policy outcome. But in other cases the influence takes on much more subtle forms of pressure to conform to the prevailing norms of the group. I argue that this second, more subtle, form of IGO influence plays a surprisingly important role in promoting convergence among states' human rights practices.

The central finding to emerge from the empirical chapters that follow is that, even after accounting for a wide array of domestic and international influences, states' human rights practices tend to become more similar to those of their fellow IGO member states. Finding evidence of this con-vergence effect challenges us to think differently about the consequences that IGO membership has for states. But in addition to demonstrating convergence using broad measures of IGO membership, I am also able to show that the effect is not significantly larger when the analysis is restricted to only the IGOs with an obvious connection to human rights issues. I argue that these results are most consistent with a process in which states become socialized into the norms that prevail within the IGOs to which they belong. Moreover, I also find evidence to suggest that convergence in human rights practices is a two-way street: not only do IGOs enable states with exemplary human rights standards to inspire other states to improve their own standards, but they also enable the states with poorer human rights standards to negatively influence the standards of others. As a result, the IGO-based diffusion story is not necessarily a positive one.

We can begin to get some sense of how IGOs have influenced the development of human rights practices by looking at trends among the states of Central and Eastern Europe. In the years following the end of the Cold War, many of these states joined IGOs that significantly increased their exposure to Western influences. For instance, Poland entered the 1990s belonging to 53 IGOs, but by the end of the decade belonged to 79. During the 1990s Poland left the by-then defunct Council for Mutual Economic Assistance (COMECON) and Warsaw Pact and instead joined a raft of more Western-oriented IGOs that included NATO, the Organization for Economic Cooperation and Development (OECD), and the Council of Europe. Very early in the decade Poland began the long process of applying for EU membership. It became an associate member in

1994 and was finally admitted as a full member as part of the EU's dramatic eastward expansion in 2004.

By the end of the 1990s Poland, along with many other former members of the Soviet bloc, was showing significant improvements in its human rights practices. Although many different factors were in play, a strong case can be made for the role that membership (or prospective membership) in these Western IGOs played in facilitating the reforms. This consisted of a mixture of material incentives—as is expressed most clearly by the EU's ability to effectively link improvements in human rights to the promise of membership in the organization—as well as a number of "softer" forms of social influence. For instance, Schwellnus (2005) notes that Poland's adoption of more progressive policies with respect to minority groups can be better explained by the influence of norms promoted by the Council of Europe than by the imposition of firm conditions by the EU. Similarly, Gheciu (2005a,b) explains how NATO—an organization that tends to be viewed by International Relations (IR) scholars as simply a military alliance—engaged in a long series of courses, workshops and seminars aimed at socializing the elites of its new member states into Western-style norms concerning democracy, human rights, and civil-military relations.

Of course, the process through which participation in IGOs can lead states to internalize the human rights norms that prevail among their fellow member states is not straightforward. One might expect that certain IGOs are more effective than others in transmitting human rights norms—a point I explore more closely in Chapter 4. At the same time, the domestic politics of each state obviously matters a great deal not only to the internal development of human rights practices in that state, but also to its receptiveness to external influences. Some states may be strongly influenced by the human rights cultures of the IGOs in which they participate, whereas others may be more resistant to these influences. As I shall explain in Chapter 2, a state's ability to translate the signals it receives from its fellow IGO members into measurable changes in its human rights practices is contingent upon a number of different factors that include its level of engagement with IGOs as well as the extent to which its diplomats are able to exert meaningful influence over the policymaking process.

Taken together, the findings presented in the empirical chapters have important implications not just for the politics of human rights, but also for how we think about the role played by IGOs in the international system. Adopting a network perspective on IGOs will allow us to see that what makes them such important actors is not so much the work implied by their formal mandates (e.g., increasing trade or providing security) but rather the additional opportunities that IGOs provide for states to influence one another over a much wider range of social and political issues.

1.2 IGOs: Some Background

Before embarking on a discussion of IGO networks and the more subtle consequences they have for the states that constitute them, we ought to take a step back and consider some background on IGOs—specifically, what IGOs actually are and what they do. This section sketches out some basic answers to these questions, so readers who are already familiar with the literature on IGOs might want to skip past this section and move straight to the beginning of Section 1.3 on page 10.

What Exactly Are IGOs?

IR scholars generally take the view that IGOs exist to solve problems that states face. Many of these problems—for example, regulating the emission of greenhouse gases or dealing with threats to international security—are issues that by their very nature depend upon multiple states acting in concert. Most of this cooperation takes place within IGOs, the formal organizations that states have created to deal with these international problems. There are literally hundreds of different IGOs in operation today, but examples of some of the more prominent ones include the UN, the EU and NATO. As Figure 1.1 had shown, the number of IGOs has undergone a massive increase in recent decades. As a result, political scientists and sociologists are becoming increasingly interested in studying their effects.

IGOs differ from other types of international organizations in two main respects. First, IGOs are by definition organizations that are comprised of representatives of different governments. In that sense they are different from other well-known international organizations whose membership consists of non-governmental actors. For instance, international advocacy groups such as Amnesty International or Greenpeace represent the interests of their individual members, rather than the governments that represent them, and are therefore usually referred to as international *non*-governmental organizations (INGOs). Similarly, multinational corporations (MNCs) such as the Exxon Mobil Corporation also represent a type of international organization that does not consist of states and is therefore excluded from the IGO category.[2]

Second, IGOs need to have some minimal level of organizational structure that distinguishes them from less formal gatherings of states. In practice, this means that these organizations must have what is known as a secretariat—that is, a permanent office staffed by people who work for the IGO itself rather than for its member states. NATO, for example, employs over 1000 people at its secretariat in Brussels. Less formal groups of states that lack a secretariat—for example, the Non-Aligned Movement (NAM) or the Group of 8 (G-8)—are generally not recognized as IGOs. (In cases like these, the member states will usually have opted for a less formal, more flexible type of governance structure.) Moreover, while all IGOs are established by an international treaty, not all international treaties give rise to IGOs. International agreements such as the Kyoto Protocol or the Convention Against Torture do not involve establishing new organizations with their own secretariats and are therefore not recognized as IGOs.[3]

What Do IGOs Do, and What Does IR Theory Tell Us About Them?

IGOs are designed to deal with many different types of cooperation problems in IR. For example, consider the problem of ensuring that all states agree on a common protocol for recognizing internet addresses. This represents a relatively simple coordination problem: few states will have an interest in which particular method is chosen, but all will share a strong interest in ensuring that some sort of universal standard exists for sending information over the internet. In this sense it is similar to, say, deciding whether cars should drive on the left- or right-hand side of the road, or deciding on a common railroad gauge for international rail transport. States often deal with problems like these by delegating the task of managing an agreement to an IGO—in this particular case, the International Telecommunications Union (ITU) headquarted in Geneva. Although the ITU was originally established in 1865 to coordinate telegraph communications between states, it continues to provide a forum in which representatives of all of its member states (which currently consists of all 193 members of the United Nations) can come together and, through consultation with various panels of experts, develop common standards for internet and other forms of communication.

But IGOs are about much more than just setting standards. (To be fair, even the ITU performs many other functions unrelated to standardization, such as assisting poorer countries to develop their information infrastructure.) Many IGOs enable states to overcome much more difficult cooperation problems, allowing member states to exchange information, assess compliance with international agreements, and resolve disputes among their member states. For instance, cooperation problems that resemble the structure of the classic Prisoners' Dilemma—that is, those in which each party fears that its cooperative efforts will be taken advantage of by the other side—can be solved by institutions that provide public information about member states' compliance. As Keohane (1984) demonstrates in his classic text *After Hegemony*, institutions can solve these types of problems by facilitating repeated interactions, thereby making the long-term costs of non-cooperation more costly than they might otherwise be. (This is what Axelrod (1984) refers to as "enlarging the shadow of the future.") Institutions established to monitor compliance with free trade agreements, such as the WTO or the EU, are able to assure their member states that their trading partners are complying with their obligations under international agreements, and, when required, have the power to sanction states that violate the terms of their agreements.

As Keohane (1984) also notes, one of the most important ways in which institutions can facilitiate cooperation stems from their ability to lower the transaction costs associated with reaching international agreements. If IGOs did not exist, these transaction costs would often be prohibitively high; states would have to rely entirely on their bilateral diplomatic ties to collect information about other states' preferences. While this might work well for negotiations involving very small groups of states (e.g., in the case of arms control agreements between the United States and Russia), it would be an extremely inefficient way of negotiating agreements that are more global in scope. With their permanent headquarters, agreed-upon rules of procedure and clearly defined delegations from their member states, IGOs provide a forum in which these agreements can be hashed out significantly more efficiently than would be possible through a series of bilateral negotiations. IGOs therefore provide an efficient way of aggregating the preferences of their member states.

Once provided with information about other states' positions on an issue, a state's own position on the issue will often change. It might discover an opportunity to build a coalition among other like-minded states, or it might find opportunities for logrolling that would otherwise not have been apparent. Or it might come to realize that it is in a much smaller minority on a particular issue than it had previously thought, and, as a result, decide to drop its efforts to advance its favored position. Thus, from the perspective of information exchange, IGOs can bring about behavioral change as a simple result of the very practical opportunities they provide to facilitate the process of international negotiation.

But the benefits of institutions in facilitating international cooperation do not stop there. As Keohane (1984) explains, institutions create opportunities for issue linkage in the course of international negotiations. This allows states to trade off concessions on one particular issue with concessions from their counterparts on a second, separate issue. Had the negotiations been conducted outside an IGO, such linkages would have been far less likely to be made. As a result, neither of the two agreements would have been reached.[4]

In addition to lowering transaction costs and facilitating issue linkage, Keohane (1984) suggests that institutions can facilitate international cooperation by allowing states to establish reputations for compliance. Institutions consist of rules, and states that want to remain involved with institutions need to comply with their rules. In some cases, IGOs have sophisticated monitoring and dispute resolution mechanisms that determine whether or not their member states are complying with the organization's rules. These are especially important in the case of trade agreements, where states continually worry about facing the "sucker's payoff" that would result if their trading partners were to renege on their commitments to undertake what are often politically costly reforms. Given the enormous complexity of trade agreements, the opportunities for states to find ways to cheat are significant. IGOs such as the WTO and the EU therefore devote significant resources to establishing a credible third-party dispute resolution mechanism. In the case of the EU, this takes the form of the extremely powerful European Court of Justice (ECJ)—an institution that now serves as the highest court on questions of EU law for all 28 member states.

By helping states to credibly establish reputations for compliance, IGOs can help states engage in acts of cooperation (e.g., the reciprocal lowering of trade barriers) that might not otherwise have been possible.

But in many cases, however, the ability of IGOs to facilitate cooperation through reputation-building is questionable. Some scholars have argued that this is because states do not pay as much attention to other states' reputations as we think they do, or because reputations are more complex and multi-dimensional than the traditional model suggests.[5] In some cases, though, it is simply because the institutions themselves provide no meaningful way for reputations to form in the first place. This is especially true in the realm of human rights institutions. For example, the UN's Human Rights Council—the body charged with monitoring the human rights performance of all UN member states and the successor to the now-defunct Commission on Human Rights—is rightfully criticized for the fact that it is a committee composed of representatives of its member states, rather than independent human rights experts (Forsythe and Park, 2009). As a result, many of its members are more concerned with shielding themselves and their allies from criticism than from taking meaningful steps to advance human rights.[6]

Another important aspect of the work of IGOs—and one that we shall be examining more closely in Chapter 2—is the dissemination of knowledge. This involves a type of information exchange that is quite different from the monitoring and verification functions provided by trade or arms-control IGOs. In this sense, the information transfer that the IGOs facilitate is not simply intended to solve a cooperation problem, but is instead an effort to identify and promote best practices found among their member states. For example, the OECD currently comprises 34 of the world's most economically developed states. It describes its role as one that "provides a forum in which governments work together to seek solutions to common problems, share experiences and identify best practices" (OECD, 2013: 4). The OECD tries to achieve this by collecting data on its member states' policies in a large number of different issue areas. It then puts together committees consisting of representatives of its member states, independent experts on the issues and representatives of civil society groups. These committees produce reports that identify best practices with respect to a particular policy. These reports tend to be highly respected publications that attract the attention of policymakers throughout the world.

Taken together, these generic functions of IGOs—standard setting, information exchange, lowering of transaction costs, monitoring of compliance, issue-linkage and knowledge transfer—constitute the various aspects of IGO activity that are most familiar to students of international

relations. These represent IGO functions that align with what we generally believe to be the interests of the states that had set up the IGOs in
the first place. This state-centric perspective on IGO activity makes a lot
of sense, but what has attracted less attention in the study of IGOs is the
possibility that the relationship between states' interests and IGO activity
might also operate in reverse—in other words, that membership in IGOs
may serve to reshape the interests of the states that created them. In the
next section we shall consider this idea in more detail.

1.3 IGOs as Norm Transmitters

When IR scholarship began to take a sociological turn in the 1990s,
the emerging school of constructivist research began to ask questions
about how states come to define their basic interests (see Katzenstein,
Keohane, and Krasner, 1998). Constructivists pointed out that many
aspects of state behavior cannot be adequately explained by models that
had traditionally assumed that states are rational, self-interested, and generally security-maximizing actors (e.g., Wendt, 1992; Klotz, 1995; Wendt,
1999). Instead, the constructivists argued that states' basic interests can
often be more usefully thought of as *endogenous* to their behavior. In other
words, how states act depends upon their interests, but, over the long term,
the definitions of these interests will themselves depend upon the sorts
of interactions that the states have with one another. As Wendt argues,
states define their interests differently depending upon the international
"culture of anarchy" they find themselves in. In some cases that culture
will be a Hobbesian world of continuous threats to their very survival,
whereas in others it can be better described as one in which threats to
states' survival are negligible and high levels of cooperation can be more
or less taken for granted (Wendt, 1999: Ch. 5). This insight leads us to
imagine a reciprocal relationship between states' interests and behavior:
interests shape behavior, but that behavior in turn affects how states come
to define their interests.

How exactly might states' behavior on the international stage reshape
their interests? Possible answers to this question fall into two broad
categories, one based on domestic political dynamics and the other on
identity change. The first involves interactions between states having consequences for the composition of state governments—that is, a domestic
politics explanation. Gourevitch (1978) coined the term "the second

image reversed" to describe theories that, rather than explaining international outcomes by reference to domestic politics—what Waltz (1959) refers to as "second image" theories[7]—instead rely on international events to explain domestic political outcomes. For instance, global economic trends—such as the Great Depression of the 1930s—had wide-reaching effects on the domestic political coalitions that formed in many different states, including, of course, the rise of the Nazis in Germany (Gourevitch, 1978: 884). In a similar vein, we can think of many examples of cases where the international security environment has had a profound effect on the domestic politics of states. For instance, in a general election held three days after the Madrid train bombings of March 2004, Spain's ruling Popular Party unexpectedly lost power to the Socialist Party. The new government promptly fulfilled its party's earlier pledge to withdraw Spanish troops from Iraq, leading many observers to believe that the terrorist attacks had caused the Spanish electorate to become much more skeptical of their government's support for the US-led war against Iraq.[8]

The second category of explanations for interest change—and the one that tends to be more closely associated with constructivist scholarship—involves the development of new international norms, or "logics of appropriateness" (March and Olsen, 1998), that affect how states define their identities, and in turn, their interests. Rather than involving changes in domestic political coalitions, this category of explanations involves a more fundamental change in beliefs about legitimate forms of behavior that prevail more broadly within the society. According to the constructivists, once enough states start to behave in a particular way, new international norms develop that act as constraints upon the behavior of other states (Finnemore and Sikkink, 1998). For instance, the sovereignty norm—the general idea that states respect each others' borders—is one that appears to be especially difficult to explain away in terms of the self-interested behavior of states (see Strang, 1991; Wendt, 1999; Hurd, 2003). Similarly, some constructivist scholars have drawn attention to the surprisingly limited use of nuclear and chemical weapons in recent interstate conflicts. They argue that this somewhat puzzling pattern of non-use can be more effectively explained by the development of new international norms than by states acting in their long-term interests (Price, 1995; Tannenwald, 1999).[9]

IGOs have been of particular interest to constructivist scholars because they provide exactly the type of environment in which new ideas concerning legitimate behavior can emerge. As noted in the previous section, much of the day-to-day work of IGOs involves negotiating international agreements and issuing recommendations to their member states. Often these recommendations are legally binding, as in the case of resolutions passed by the UN Security Council or the WTO's dispute resolution panels, but in many cases they are not. The OECD, for instance, is not a law-making body and many of its officials view this as an advantage in that it allows the organization greater flexibility in promoting certain policies. Similarly, the UN General Assembly issues resolutions that are not legally binding on its members but nonetheless contribute to the development of international norms.

A number of scholars have seized on the idea of IGOs as norm-transmitting agents and have attempted to use this insight to explain changes in states' interests. One particularly interesting line of research has focused on the ability of IGOs to "teach" their member states new ideas about how they ought to behave. For instance, Finnemore (1993) shows how UNESCO (the United Nations Educational, Scientific and Cultural Organization) encouraged its member states' governments to play a more active role in directing scientific research. In a study of NATO, Gheciu (2005a) shows how the organization's engagement with prospective member states led to significant changes in the attitudes of elites about appropriate forms of military-state relations. In each case, the IGO played a role in changing the interests of its member states' (or prospective member states') by promoting ideas that lie at the center of the organization's mission.

A second line of research also views IGOs as sites of norm transmission, but adopts a more holistic view of them. Rather than considering the effects that individual IGOs are having on promoting certain practices, it considers the aggregate effects that engagement with large numbers of IGOs is having on state behavior. For instance, in a large-scale statistical study of states' voting behavior at the UN General Assembly, Bearce and Bondanella (2007) provide evidence to suggest that shared membership in IGOs leads to a general convergence among states' interests.[10] Other quantitative studies have used measures of shared IGO memberships to explain more specific outcomes such as interstate conflict (Russett, Oneal, and Davis, 1998; Oneal, Russett, and Berbaum, 2003), democracy (Pevehouse, 2002, 2005; Torfason and Ingram, 2010), international trade (Ingram, Robinson, and Busch, 2005), and domestic economic policy (Cao, 2009, 2010). In these studies, however, the implied mechanisms do not necessarily involve the IGOs reconstituting the interests of their member states—a point we shall return to in Chapter 2.

A parallel line of research in sociology—one that is variously referred to as the "world polity," "world society," or "world culture" school—also adopts a more holistic view of IGOs. World society scholars claim that IGOs (as well as international *non*-governmental organizations, or INGOs) collectively embody a universal set of norms and values concerning how states ought to behave (Finnemore, 1996; Meyer et al., 1997; Boli and Thomas, 1999). This system of values is referred to as "world culture" and emphasizes the rights of the individual over the state, the universality of individual rights, and a commitment to using scientific research to develop solutions to global problems.

According to the world society theorists, the more connected a state is to the institutions of world culture, the more likely it will be to behave in accordance with this set of principles. This insight has been used to explain the surprisingly high degree of similarity found among the ways in which different governments choose to organize themselves (Meyer et al., 1997). Empirical work finds that states that are more tightly connected to the institutions of world society (as measured by the level of the states' engagement with IGOs and INGOs) will more readily adopt models of governance that are consistent with world culture. For instance, Frank, Hironaka, and Schofer (2000) find that states that are more connected to world society adopt a range of environmental policies more quickly than less connected states.

The world society school provides an interesting perspective on IGOs insofar as it encourages us to think about the aggregate effects of membership in large numbers of IGOs. In my view, it represents an important step forward in thinking of how larger communities of IGOs embody certain sets of norms and values. But, unfortunately, its model of norm transmission suffers from two important limitations. First, it pays relatively little attention to variation in the norms embodied in the institutions of world society. All IGOs (and INGOs) of the relevant type are presumed to embody these norms, regardless of the differences that might exist in terms of their membership or their official mandates. As a result, belonging to a human rights IGO like the Council of Europe is considered functionally equivalent to belonging to, say, the Arab Labor Organization. From the perspective of human rights promotion this seems odd given that these two IGOs represent communities of states whose governments hold very different views on state-society relations. From the perspective of world culture, however, both IGOs serve the same role in connecting their member states to a single set of progressive, individualistic values.

World society scholars are interested mainly in the variation that exists in the degree to which different states are connected to the institutions of world society (i.e., whether one state belongs to more IGOs than another), rather than in the potential for variation in the content of the norms that these institutions are believed to embody.

The second, related, problem is that the world society approach only considers the flow of ideas from international organizations to states. In the world society model, ideas flow from IGOs (and INGOs) to states, but the question of how these institutions come to embody these ideas in the first place is not an important part of the research program (Campbell, 2002). Instead, world society scholarship takes for granted the fact that any given international institution will embody the rational, individualistic values associated with world culture. This is perhaps a reflection of the fact that scholars of international organizations—particularly INGOs—have for too long focused their attention on the work of progressive organizations like Amnesty International and Friends of the Earth. Only recently has this begun to change; for instance, Bob (2012) has undertaken a very interesting study of the ability of international networks of right-wing organizations opposed to gay rights and gun control to shape policy outcomes on these issues.

In the next chapter I propose a more flexible model of norm transmission through IGOs that tries to address both of these problems. I draw upon the world society model insofar as I conceive of IGOs as norm-transmitting structures, but rather than thinking of IGOs as embodying a single, global set of values that is then transmitted to the IGOs' member states, I take the view that IGOs embody the norms of their member states, whatever these might happen to be. This model therefore allows two IGOs like the Council of Europe and the Arab Labor Organization to adopt what might be quite different sets of norms due to the fact that they are composed of different sets of states. As a result, for any state, the consequences of belonging to an IGO will differ sharply depending upon *who* the organization's member states happen to be.

1.4 Empirical Strategy (and Plan for the Book)

In the empirical chapters of this book I provide evidence to suggest that, over time, states adopt similar human rights practices to those of the other states with whom they share IGO memberships. In doing so,

I adopt an empirical strategy that involves testing for the existence of a correlation between the human rights practices of a state and those of its fellow IGO members. This is a similar general strategy to that used in other recent studies of policy convergence within IGOs (e.g., Cao, 2009; Bearce and Bondanella, 2007; Torfason and Ingram, 2010), as well as in numerous studies from a broad range of disciplines that have attempted to demonstrate how various forms of social ties induce similarities among behavioral outcomes at the level of individual people.

Conducting this type of analysis at the level of individuals (rather than states) has produced some striking—and sometimes controversial— findings. For instance, in a recent series of widely-cited papers, Nicholas Christakis and James Fowler have used social network analysis to argue that individual health-related outcomes such as obesity, smoking, happiness, and even loneliness are influenced by the extent to which these factors prevail within one's social circle.[11] In other words, the more friends you have who are smokers, the more likely you are to smoke; the more friends you have who are overweight, the more likely you are to be overweight, etc. These studies have forced the medical community to look beyond individual-level factors and pay more attention to the way in which an individual's social context affect his or her health outcomes.

Of course, all of these studies—whether in the field of IGOs or interpersonal networks—make an argument about convergence that relies upon the identification of statistically significant correlations between a network variable (e.g., the number of obese individuals in a person's social circle or the proportion of democracies among a state's fellow IGO members) and an outcome variable at the level of the individual unit (e.g., whether a person becomes obese or whether a state becomes democratic). As is the case with all observational studies, however, these results need to be interpreted with caution; we cannot simply assume that membership in a social network (whether in the form of personal friendships or membership in IGOs) is *causing* the convergence we observe. For example, consider the finding that people are more likely to smoke if their friends are smokers (Christakis and Fowler, 2008). The association that the authors observe could in theory be driven by at least three distinct causal mechanisms.

First, having friends who smoke might make someone more likely to pick up smoking. Perhaps a teenager who spends time with friends who smoke comes under peer pressure to start smoking, or an older person who has smoked in the past finds it more socially acceptable to resume the habit once he finds himself in the company of friends who smoke. Conversely, a smoker might find it easier to quit if she spends time with friends who are also trying to quit. These are all examples of *social influence* effects—that is, cases where one actor's behavior is influenced by the behavior of others.

Second, smokers might prefer the company of other smokers (and vice versa). Perhaps having to take frequent smoking breaks in designated smoking areas causes people to form closer friendships with other smokers. This would give rise to a statistical correlation between a person's smoking status and that of their friends (i.e., smokers are more likely to name other smokers among their closest friends and vice-versa), yet it is not the result of a social influence effect. Instead, the individuals are selecting their friends based upon their prior smoking status. This is what network scientists refer to as a *homophily* effect.

Third, some other factor may be causing a person to smoke and, at the same time, to have many friends who smoke. Perhaps the person lives in a country or region where smoking is especially prevalent. Given that personal friendships still tend to be heavily constrained by geographical proximity, we can expect people who live in societies with high rates of smoking to have many friends who smoke and vice versa. This could occur even in the absence of any social influence or homophily effects; instead, people are simply forming friendships with people who are close to them geographically, and there just so happens to be some important geographical variation in smoking habits. In this example, the smoking rate in the country/region where each individual lives represents a *confounding variable* that needs to be accounted for in the analysis. Had we not accounted for such a variable, we would be guilty of *omitted variable bias*. In other words, we would have inferred a relationship between friendships and smoking when in actual fact none exists.

The exact same logic applies to studies of convergence in IGOs, such as the one undertaken here. Let's suppose—as the results of Chapter 3 will show—that we observe a correlation between a state's level of respect for human rights and the human rights practices of the states with whom it shares IGO memberships. This could be the result of one or more of these same three mechanisms. It could be that belonging to the same IGOs is in fact causing states to influence the human rights practices of their peers (a social influence effect); or that states with similar human rights practices tend to join more of the same IGOs in the first place (a homophily effect);

or that some confounding variable—perhaps economic development—is causing states to develop similar patterns of human rights practices at the same time that they are joining many of the same IGOs.

Any serious analysis of convergence in social networks needs to carefully consider these alternative explanations. Unfortunately there is no statistical silver bullet that allows analysts to clearly distinguish amongst the three. However, various pieces of evidence can be gathered to make a compelling case for why one mechanism is more likely than the others to be responsible for the observed results. In the case of the smoking study, Christakis and Fowler (2008) used longitudinal data to show that people's smoking habits are correlated with those of their peers from an earlier period. This makes homophily less likely to be driving the results, given that individuals in the study are unlikely to be choosing their friends based upon how their smoking habits might change in the future.[12] At the same time, Christakis and Fowler also account for a number of possible confounding variables, such as education level, that are likely to have an effect on both smoking habits and one's choice of friends.

Similar inferential strategies have been used when attempting to explain convergence in IGO networks. All of these studies include control variables that attempt to account for the most plausible confounding factors. Most of these studies rely upon longitudinal data to go some way towards excluding the homophily explanation. Where possible, some also use more sophisticated econometric techniques such as propensity score matching to lend further credibility to the social influence explanation (see, e.g., Cao, 2009; Torfason and Ingram, 2010).

However, as noted above, there is almost never a perfect solution to the problem of causal inference in the social sciences. This is especially true when dealing with observational (as opposed to experimental) data on social networks. Instead, inferring a social influence effect from a large-n analysis of network data relies upon our ability to effectively do all of the following:

1. Demonstrate that a social influence effect is consistent with an understanding at the micro-level of how the units in the system interact with one another.
2. Establish evidence of convergent outcomes that is both statistically significant and substantively important.

3. Show that this effect holds after accounting for plausible confounding variables.

4. Draw upon the results of further statistical analyses and our understanding of micro-level processes to show that the observed convergence effect is unlikely to be driven by a selection effect (homophily).

I shall use this list to set the agenda for the remainder of this book. The discussion of social influence effects within IGOs in the next chapter is intended to address the first item on that list by establishing that IGOs serve as important sites at which states influence the behavior of others. In doing so, I develop a model of norm transmission in which IGOs develop their own cultures of human rights that reflect the norms and ideas that prevail among their member states. As a result of their participation in the IGOs, the member states then begin to adopt human rights practices that look more like those of their fellow IGO members. From this perspective, IGOs can be viewed as clearinghouses for the norms and ideas held by their member states: they bring together diverse groups of states, facilitate interactions among them, and as a result reshape their member states' preferences in a way that leaves them looking more similar to the other members of the organization than they were before.

In Chapter 3 I attempt to address items 2 and 3 on the agenda as I engage in a statistical analysis of the hypothesis that IGOs function as "transmission belts" for human rights norms. I do so using data on one of the most widely studied indicators of human rights practices—the "Physical Integrity Rights Index" developed by David Cingranelli and David Richards. This provides a composite measure of the extent to which states engage in some of the most physically harmful forms of human rights abuse—namely, torture, extrajudicial killings, political imprisonment, and "disappearances." The results of a cross-national time-series analysis strongly suggest that states' human rights practices are closely associated with those of their fellow IGO members. In other words, states' human rights practices become more similar to each other as a result of belonging to the same IGOs. This finding holds even after accounting for a wide range of domestic and international influences on a state's human rights practices.

In the following chapter I pose three questions that are intended to shed light on the causal mechanism(s) underlying the convergence effect noted in Chapter 3—an issue that tends to be given insufficient attention in much of the quantitative literature on diffusion. The first is whether more powerful states are able to exert more influence over the human rights policies of their fellow IGO members. The second is whether IGOs with a human rights mandate are more effective in promoting the diffusion of human rights practices than other, less specialized, IGOs. The third is whether more powerful states are better able to resist IGO-based pressures than weaker states.

Surprisingly, the results of this analysis suggest that (1) material power has only a modest effect on enhancing the influence of states over their IGO partners; (2) having a human rights mandate makes relatively little difference to the ability of IGOs to transmit human rights norms; and (3) the more powerful states are actually *more* receptive to the signals they receive from their fellow IGO members. I conclude Chapter 4 by arguing that these findings are most consistent with a process of norm transmission that relies primarily on states becoming acculturated to the norms that prevail among their fellow IGO members.

Of course, the concept of human rights extends far beyond physical integrity rights. In Chapter 5 I extend the analysis into the fields of women's rights and gay rights. In doing so I take advantage of an interesting difference between these two sets of rights to gain further insight into the mechanisms involved in IGO-based norm transmission. I ask whether human rights norms that are supported by a robust system of international treaties (those that I call "highly legalized") are transmitted more easily through IGO ties than are those that lack a strong foundation in international law. While women's rights have enjoyed a relatively secure status in international law since the adoption in 1979 of the Convention on the Elimination of Discrimination Against Women (CEDAW), the legal protection of LGBT rights rests on a much weaker foundation in the international human rights regime. The theoretical discussion at the beginning of the chapter considers a number of arguments for why, based on existing theories of norm diffusion, highly legalized norms ought to be transmitted more easily through IGOs than other norms. The results of the statistical analysis, however, suggest that both sets of rights can be effectively transmitted through IGOs. The chapter argues that these findings are again consistent with a socialization-based model of norm diffusion in IGOs.

The fourth item on the agenda—the homophily argument—is the focus of Chapter 6. In that chapter I ask whether the convergence among states' human rights practices observed in the preceding chapters is likely to have been caused by their shared membership in IGOs, or whether it is instead simply reflecting a situation in which states with similar practices tend to belong to the same IGOs in the first place. The empirical section of the chapter models the decisions of states to form new IGO ties with one another and tests whether similarity in human rights practices is a predictor of the formation of shared IGO memberships. This analysis uses a particular type of network model that allows us to take account of the dependency that exists among the dyads in the network (Hoff, Raftery, and Handcock, 2002). The results of this exercise reveal that similarity among states' human rights practices has no systematic relationship to the propensity of these states to join the same IGOs as each other. At the same time, the results provide new insights into the broader question of why states choose to cooperate with each other. I find that cultural ties (in the form of shared religion, language, and/or colonial history) play a surprisingly important role in determining with whom states choose to enter into IGO relationships.

Finally, in Chapter 7 I conclude with a discussion of the broader implications of the norm-transmitting potential of the IGO network. I argue that this is something that needs to be taken more seriously by the academic community, which for too long has focused its attention on resolving narrower debates about whether certain IGOs have succeeded in fulfilling their formal mandates. Meanwhile, these findings have important implications for policymakers who continue to debate whether a policy of engagement or a policy of isolation is the better way to deal with human rights-violating states such as North Korea or Iran. The results of this study clearly lend support to the proponents of engagement: allowing a state to remain open to the positive influences of others is, I argue, far better than the alternative of leaving it to languish amidst the influences of other "pariah" states.

Replication Files

Making my case for IGO-based diffusion of human rights depends heavily upon the inferences I draw from statistical analyses of human rights practices. In order to enable interested readers to engage more critically with the statistical analyses presented throughout this book, I have posted a complete replication archive on my page at the Harvard Dataverse

Network.[13] This consists of scripts that will allow readers to reconstruct each part of the analysis from its original sources. It also includes various functions I have written in the R statistical programming language (R Core Team, 2013) that should make it easier to build upon the work presented here and extend it into other substantive areas.

Networks of Influence

This chapter lays out the components of a model of social influence within IGOs. This model encourages us to think about IGOs as social spaces—that is, as venues in which the behavior of one state can start to influence the behavior of the other members of the organization. In doing so, it expands upon theories of IGO-mediated norm diffusion—for example, the idea of IGOs as "teachers of norms" (Finnemore, 1993)—that tend to focus on only one aspect of the diffusion process, namely the transfer of ideas from the IGOs to their member states. The model I propose here suggests that the flow of ideas among states and IGOs occurs in two directions: states influence the norms of the IGOs, and these IGOs in turn influence the norms held by their member states.[1]

This model (illustrated in Figure 2.1) begins with IGOs developing a particular culture vis-à-vis human rights that is largely a product of the human rights norms practiced by their member states. This is what I refer to as the "human rights culture" of the IGO. Importantly, the human rights culture of any given IGO represents the aggregate of the views held by its member states, rather than a set of views expressed by the organization itself.[2] As a result, a human rights culture of some form can be thought to exist in all IGOs, irrespective of whether the organizations themselves are committed to promoting human rights. For example, if a particular IGO consists mostly of states that have abolished the death penalty, that IGO will have a human rights culture that strongly favors abolition. This means that even if the IGO itself takes no position whatsoever on the politics of the death penalty—let's suppose we're dealing with a purely technical IGO like the International Telecommunications Union—the organization can nonetheless develop a culture that favors abolition. (The extent to which the IGOs' own internal bureaucracy is itself is able to

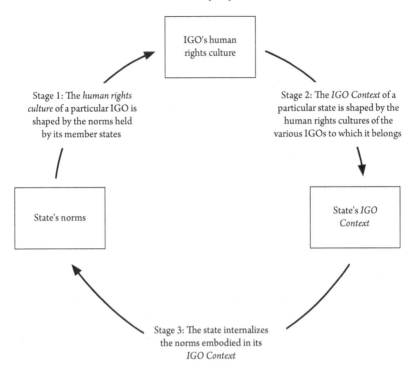

IGO's human
rights culture

Stage 1: The *human rights
culture* of a particular IGO is
shaped by the norms held
by its member states

Stage 2: The *IGO Context* of a
particular state is shaped by the
human rights cultures of the
various IGOs to which it belongs

State's norms

State's *IGO
Context*

Stage 3: The state internalizes
the norms embodied in its
IGO Context

Figure 2.1 The three-stage model of norm transmission.

influence the human rights culture that emerges among its member states
is a question we shall return to later.)

The second stage of the model considers the ways in which states are
influenced by the human rights cultures of the various IGOs to which
they belong. Here I introduce the concept of a state's "IGO Context." The
IGO Context reflects the average of the various human rights cultures to
which the state is exposed as a result of its IGO memberships. Continuing
with the above example, if a particular state that practices the death
penalty belongs to IGOs that, for the most part, have cultures that favor
abolition, that state will operate within an *IGO Context* that generally
favors abolition.[3]

Finally, in the third stage the state internalizes the norms to which
it has been exposed through its *IGO Context*. When successful, this act
of internalization results in changes in the state's practices. But the act
of internalization is by no means automatic. In order for IGO-based
socialization to result in changes to a state's human rights practices, the
objects of socialization—that is, the individuals representing their states

at the IGOs—need to have some influence over the policymaking process in their home states. As I shall discuss later in this chapter, this can occur either as a result of diplomats being able to successfully influence the thinking of policymakers back in their capitals or as a result of policymakers being invited to participate directly in the discussions that take place at the IGOs—something that occurs more frequently in the work of IGOs than most IR scholarship tends to appreciate. In other cases, the connection between IGO-based socialization and policymaking authority can occur when former diplomats acquire policymaking roles at later stages in their careers.

More generally, though, we can expect that some states will be more receptive than others to the influences they receive from their fellow IGO members. This can be thought to occur not only as a result of some states having the capacity to engage more actively than others with IGOs, but also as a result of some states being able to more effectively translate these normative influences into actual human rights practices. Domestic variables that influence the receptiveness of states to IGO-based influences will be explored more fully in Chapter 4.

This model therefore provides a way of thinking about how states can influence each other within IGOs. In the following sections I shall discuss each of the stages of the model in much more detail. But before doing so it is worth pausing to consider one possible concern about the long-term implications of this model: Given that the model posits a reciprocal relationship between each IGO's human rights culture and the practices of its states, does this imply a positive feedback loop among the human rights practices of the various states in the system? In other words, might this model imply that once a state starts to undergo an improvement (or decline) in its human rights practices, its IGO partners will then undergo a similar change, which would then set the states on a path towards ever-improving (or ever-declining) human rights practices? Or—perhaps more realistically—might it imply that all states' human rights practices will, over time, converge to such an extent that we would no longer observe any meaningful differences among states? To put it more starkly, might it suggest that we will eventually witness a Fukuyaman "end of history" with respect to human rights?

The answer is likely to be no, for two main reasons. First, while all diffusion processes imply feedback among the various units of the system, this feedback can be either positive or negative, and the strength of the feedback can be such that it either causes the units to converge towards some sort of average outcome or to undergo some sort of explosive movement towards an extreme outcome. Which of these models best describes the data is ultimately an empirical question. As the results of the statistical analyses presented in the next chapter will show, IGO-based diffusion of human rights practices is best characterized as a process that does indeed involve positive feedback among the IGOs' member states, but a type of positive feedback that results in the gradual convergence of the member states towards the average standards found within each organization.

Second, while I am eager to draw attention to the importance of this IGO-based diffusion effect, I am certainly not suggesting that it is the sole determinant of a state's human rights practices. In other words, the cycle shown in Figure 2.1 should not be thought of as a closed system. The human rights practices that we observe in states are obviously the result of a complex interplay of many influences at both the domestic and the international level. These factors can often push states towards developing human rights practices that are very different from those of their IGO partners, thereby making the overall convergence effect less apparent. (To illustrate this point more clearly, I have provided the results of some simulation exercises in Appendix A.1.) While IGO-based convergence is, in my view, a surprisingly important factor, it is best understood as one of several different forces that shape states' human rights outcomes.

2.1 Stage 1: Establishing the Human Rights Culture of the IGO

The first stage of the model summarized in Figure 2.1 describes how a particular human rights culture develops within each IGO. This can be thought of as an aggregate of the various beliefs held by the organization's member states. Of course, for this to occur we need to accept the view that IGOs, just like universities, corporations, or government bureaucracies, are capable of developing distinct organizational cultures. This is an idea that IR scholars have recently begun to apply in the context of IGOs (see Barnett and Finnemore, 2004; Chwieroth, 2009; Nelson, 2014; Nelson and Weaver, forthcoming). It also requires us to view IGOs as social environments—in other words, as places where the representatives of the various member states can come together and influence the views of others, and, as a result, develop a shared set of norms or "culture."

But what evidence exists to suggest that IGOs develop their own organizational cultures, and that that culture might in turn influence the attitudes and behavior of the individuals who operate within it? When compared to the more intense settings of institutions such as military establishments or boarding schools—the types of institutions that Goffman (1961) referred to as "total institutions"—IGOs obviously have relatively limited scope for developing their own distinct organizational cultures. The individuals who represent states at IGOs spend limited amounts of time there before being transferred elsewhere, and many of the smaller IGOs host delegations from their member states for only a few days or weeks each year. Moreover, as discussed in Section 1.2, IGOs are by definition *inter-governmental* organizations. This means that, with the exception of the individuals employed directly by the secretariat of each organization, the personnel affiliated with IGOs generally serve in their capacity as representatives of their home governments, rather than as employees of the international organization itself.

Yet despite these limitations, IGOs provide spaces in which close relationships can form among the representatives of their member states. After all, one of the primary purposes of IGOs is to provide a physical space in which representatives of their member states can regularly come together to discuss matters of mutual concern. In some cases the interactions that take place between diplomats from different states can be especially intense. For example, a study of decision-making within the EU's Committee of Permanent Representatives conducted by Lewis (2005) finds strong evidence to suggest that state representatives become socialized into group norms of decision-making. Drawing on a series of in-depth interviews with state representatives, Lewis finds that representatives to the organization develop a sense of cohesion and loyalty to fellow members of the group that, in some cases, causes them to place the interests of the group above those of their member states. Lewis suggests that while the degree of internalization was limited in certain important respects, the high degree of socialization into group norms within this particular committee can be attributed to the intensity and duration of interactions between its delegates, and to their relative isolation from the influence of their home governments.

Interviews I conducted with diplomats support the view that service at IGOs cultivates close personal ties that cut across national lines. For example, the committee of the UN General Assembly that deals with human rights issues (the so-called Third Committee) meets for a two-month period every autumn during which a large number of separate resolutions are debated. Representatives from several national delegations described this as a particularly intense period that involves long days of hard-fought negotiations with their counterparts from the other member states. These intense periods of negotiation tend to be followed by a busy schedule of social events to ease the tension and to celebrate the completion of their work. Naturally, this shared experience fosters the formation of strong interpersonal ties that cross national lines. One representative told me that the Third Committee is jokingly referred to as the "party committee" in UN circles, while another spoke of the bonding that takes place among the delegates from different states and described the conclusion of each session as feeling like "having to say goodbye to your friends from summer camp."

The importance of building these informal contacts came up repeatedly in discussions with members of national delegations to IGOs. Diplomats in general place enormous emphasis on cultivating personal relationships at whichever site they are posted, and this seems to be especially true in the case of delegations to IGOs. One UN diplomat I spoke with stressed the importance of the personal relationships he builds through regular informal contacts over coffees and dinners with members of other national delegations; as he put it, "trust is the name of the game." Indeed, most delegations to IGOs provide their delegates with substantial budgets for entertaining their foreign counterparts. Often this is because the large and somewhat formal meetings that take place at the IGOs do not allow delegates to easily explore opportunities to build coalitions with others, so these interactions have to take place elsewhere. Most diplomats consider these informal interactions—which usually take the form of coffee breaks or cocktail parties scheduled around official meetings—to be one of the most useful opportunities to influence others. As a member of another state's mission to the UN put it to me, "If you're not out having coffee or lunch, you're not doing your job!"

The informal interactions that take place among delegates to IGOs obviously serve an important professional function, but they also serve a more personal function. Most diplomats represent their home country at an IGO or an embassy for a defined period of time (usually 3–5 years) before being assigned to another posting, often in an entirely different region of the world. While this lifestyle often appears glamorous to those on the outside, it creates significant difficulties for diplomats and their families as they try to build networks of social support at each new posting. As a result, they tend to form closer ties with others who share similar expatriate experiences, leading to the creation of friendship ties within the diplomatic community that usually reach across national lines. A common example of this is the social networks that form among expatriates who choose to send their children to the same international schools. One European diplomat I interviewed described the formation of what he calls "ersatz families" among the community of diplomats. In his experience, these cross-national friendships among the families of diplomats can be especially intimate, often involving invitations to serve as bridesmaids or groomsmen at each other's weddings or as godparents to each other's children.

The desire to form personal connections with other members of the diplomatic community is fulfilled in different ways, all of which serve to build social capital that bridges national divides. In Paris, for example, the OECD runs an informal group called "OECD Sneakers" that organizes after-work social events aimed at younger members of the OECD secretariat and the permanent delegations, while UNESCO runs a similar group called "Unes Go". (Interestingly, these two groups often organize joint events, thereby providing additional opportunities for IGO-mediated socialization.) Less formally, members of delegations to IGOs often develop their own loosely institutionalized patterns of contact with each other. For example, many of the diplomats I interviewed at the UN described a busy schedule of dinner parties held at each others' homes in New York City. These events provide a more informal opportunity for the diplomats to build relationships with their counterparts from other delegations—a point that all of my interviewees agreed was an essential part of their job.

Interestingly, some of these diplomats described patterns of interaction that span national divides but nonetheless tend to be focused around some other form of identity. For instance, one member of a national delegation to the UN spoke of a group of Catholic ambassadors who regularly attend church services together while serving at the UN headquarters in New York. Another described a regular weekend brunch gathering for some of the female delegates (usually from Western countries) to the UN General Assembly's Third Committee. This brings up the intriguing possibility that more specific human rights subcultures exist within certain parts of each organization and that these subcultures exert socializing effects that are independent of the IGO's more general human rights culture. While accounting for these subcultures could certainly be an interesting project in its own right, for the purposes of the present study I will proceed on the assumption that each IGO can be usefully thought of as having its own distinct human rights culture.

Variation Among IGOs

In proposing the idea that IGOs develop distinct human rights cultures, a question that naturally arises is whether these cultures are directly observable and, perhaps more importantly, whether we can observe differences among the human rights cultures of different IGOs. The answer to these two questions is a qualified yes; while directly observing these differences is theoretically possible, in practice this is very difficult to do. Doing so would involve conducting ethnographic work at multiple IGOs with a view to identifying meaningful differences among them in the ways in which diplomats discuss human rights issues in the course of their off-the-record conversations.

Nonetheless, there are some indirect ways in which we can infer differences among IGOs' human rights cultures. One approach is to look at the extent to which IGOs vary in terms of the (observable) human rights behavior of their member states. As an illustration of this approach, in Table 2.1 I present data on a sample of IGOs that clearly are not concerned with promoting human rights and in which membership is not in any way conditional on human rights performance. The particular sample I have selected consists of eight IGOs whose activities are concerned with promoting exports of particular commodities. For each of these organizations, I have included data on the median human rights scores of its member states (specifically, the Cingranelli-Richards index of physical integrity rights—a measure that will be discussed in much greater detail in Chapter 3), its number of member states in 2005, as well as the name of one member state whose human rights performance in 2005 lies at (or just around) the median of the IGO's member states. Moreover, I have arranged the rows in the table such that the IGOs with the highest median human rights scores are at the top and those with the lowest are at the bottom.

As we can see from the table, the IGO in this group with the highest median human rights score is the Paris-based International Organisation of Vine and Wine (OIV). It is primarily concerned with developing and monitoring international standards concerning the production and marketing of wine. Although it was first constituted in 1924 as an organization consisting mainly of the major European wine and grape producers, it now includes many of the major non-European producers such as Australia, Chile, India, and South Africa. As the data show, the member states of the OIV appear to have reasonably high human rights standards. When we consider the member states' scores on the physical integrity rights index, we find that the median score in 2005 was 7. Given that this scale ranges from 0 to 8 (where higher numbers indicate greater levels of respect for human rights), achieving a score of 7 is reasonably good. Indeed, many of its member states achieved a score of 7 that year, including Switzerland, Australia, Ireland, and Finland, among others. From this we can see that the OIV provides a good example of an IGO that, despite not having any

Table 2.1 **IGOs concerned with commodity exports.**

IGO	Median HR score	Number of members	Representative country
International Organisation of Vine and Wine	7	38	Switzerland
International Olive Council	6.5	24	Italy
International Pepper Community	6	38	United Arab Emirates
International Tropical Timber Organization	5	59	United Kingdom
Association of Natural Rubber Producing Countries	4.5	8	Malaysia
Alliance of Cocoa Producing Countries	4	12	Cameroon
International Rice Commission	4	60	Cameroon
Organization of the Petroleum Exporting Countries	3	11	Libya

Note: The organizations are listed in order of the median human rights scores of their member states in 2005.

substantive connection to human rights issues, nonetheless exposes its members to a culture that generally respects human rights.

As we look further down the rows in Table 2.1 we find export-oriented organizations that consist of member states with less impressive human rights standards. At the bottom of the table is the Organisation of the Petroleum Exporting Countries (OPEC), the cartel of oil-exporting states that, according to its most recent annual report, collectively account for an estimated 80% of the world's proven oil reserves (OPEC, 2013). Its membership consists mainly of authoritarian regimes with poor human rights practices; its median member, Libya, had a score of only 3 points on the physical integrity rights index in 2005. OPEC's regular meetings would therefore appear to provide a setting in which the delegates of its member states are exposed to rather poor models of human rights practices.

Another approach to identifying differences among the human rights cultures of various IGOs is to look at their official positions on human rights issues. Given that only a very small proportion of the world's IGOs deal directly with human rights issues, it is difficult to find much variation in this respect. (For instance, neither the OIV nor OPEC appear to have made mention of countries' human rights standards in any of their official publications.) Nonetheless, there is a growing expectation that the larger IGOs take steps to bring human rights issues on to their agendas. This is especially true in the case of the major regional IGOs. For instance, the mandate of the EU has expanded from its purely economic origins to one that now considers the promotion of human rights to be among its top priorities.[4] This has occurred in spite of the fact that the human rights performance of all 28 EU member states is already subject to careful review by the European Court of Human Rights—an institution established by the Council of Europe, an IGO that is entirely separate from the EU.

But while the EU has moved steadily towards incorporating human rights issues into its agenda, its counterparts among other regional economic IGOs have had a mixed record in this regard. The Organization of American States (OAS) has had some success with its establishment of a relatively powerful inter-American human rights regime (Farer, 1997), whereas the African Union (AU; formerly the Organization of African Unity, OAU) has created what appears to be a legally innovative but largely ineffective human rights regime (Mutua, 2000). What tends to receive more attention from human rights scholars, however, is the reluctance of the Association of South East Asian Nations (ASEAN) to incorporate human rights issues in to its agenda. ASEAN places great emphasis on upholding a norm of non-interference in its members' affairs—a position that, in light of the massive human rights violations carried out by member states such as Burma/Myanmar, has made it the subject of sharp criticism from human rights organizations. One of ASEAN's founding documents, the 1976 Treaty of Amity and Cooperation in Southeast Asia, emphasizes the principle of non-interference in three out of the six fundamental principles that guide the work of ASEAN. The rest of the document makes no mention of the rights of individuals. Only very recently has this begun to change, as the organization has taken some tentative steps towards developing a human rights agenda (see Ciorciari, 2012). From this we can infer that, rather like that of OPEC, ASEAN's human rights culture is one in which states are unlikely to come under social pressure to adopt more progressive human rights practices.

Not All States have Equal Influence

The idea that not all states will make an equal contribution to defining the human rights culture of each individual IGO is important in this model of IGO-based norm transmission. Some member states may, by virtue of their greater influence within a given organization, play a greater role in shaping the culture of that IGO. The extent to which they do so—and the factors that increase or decrease their influence over the IGO's human rights culture—is an empirical question that has significant implications for the inferences we can draw regarding the mechanisms of IGO-based norm transmission. For example, if material inducements play an important role in the transmission of human rights norms,[5] we would expect to find that economically or militarily powerful states play a larger role in shaping the human rights culture of the IGOs to which they belong. This is a proposition I test in Chapter 4 by building models of diffusion that account for variation in measures of state power.

In the case of certain IGOs, internal decision-making procedures have clearly been designed to give some states more influence than others. An obvious example of this is the veto-wielding power of the five permanent members of the UN Security Council. In the case of other IGOs, however, the differences in influence can be more precisely calibrated. For example, in both the International Monetary Fund (IMF) and the World Bank each member state's share of the vote is directly tied to the extent of its financial contribution to the organization. Economically powerful states like the United States can therefore be assumed to exert more influence over the IMF's culture than less powerful states. This suggests that the political and economic conditions attached to IMF loans are more likely to reflect the values held by the United States than those held by a member state that makes only a small financial contribution to the fund—a proposition that is consistent with the findings of recent empirical work on IMF lending (see Nelson, 2014).

Of course, the fact that a powerful state like the United States makes a large contribution to the material resources of particular IGOs such as the IMF or NATO does not mean that US influence is especially high only in these particular organizations. The United States can still exert a disproportionately large influence in shaping the culture of IGOs even where the voting system is based on the principle of "one member, one vote." The key to this is issue-linkage: specifically, the ability of the more powerful state to link issues under consideration in that forum with issues where the difference in material power does in fact make a more significant difference to outcomes (Haas, 1980). Relatively weak states might therefore acquiesce to the demands of more powerful states despite having equal voting rights in a particular forum. As a result, more powerful states can be thought to make a disproportionately large contribution to the culture of IGOs even where formal procedures are designed to ensure that all states have equal representation. For example, in the wake of the 9/11 attacks, the United States allegedly used its influence over its NATO partners to obtain compliance with its policy of extraordinary rendition of terrorism suspects.[6]

A recent example of this type of issue-linkage with respect to human rights is provided by the UN General Assembly, a forum in which each member state has an equal vote. Each year the General Assembly passes a resolution condemning the use of extrajudicial killings. The language of this resolution has traditionally covered a large number of potentially vulnerable groups, and in 1999 it was further expanded to include sexual minorities. In November 2010, however, a group of states led by Benin succeeded by a vote of 79:70 in passing an amendment to the resolution that removed sexual minorities from the list of protected groups. In response, the United States—in conjunction with support from international human rights NGOs—embarked on a vigorous campaign to reverse this amendment and thereby reinstate protections for sexual minorities. The US-led diplomatic effort was ultimately successful, and in December 2010 a resolution was passed by a vote of 93:55 that once again included sexual minorities among the list of protected groups.[7]

The ability of states to shape the human rights culture of the IGOs in which they participate need not be restricted to their economic or military power. Some states may have disproportionately high (or low) levels of influence with respect to particular issue areas owing to their moral standing within the international community, or for other historical reasons. For example, in the realm of human rights we might expect to find that, all else being equal, states that are widely recognized as having consistently high standards of human rights will have a greater ability to disseminate new norms and ideas than states with poorer records. According to this logic, we could expect to find that a state like Norway will have more success in promoting a new human rights treaty than, say, Saudi Arabia. Similarly, states like South Africa (in the post-apartheid era) can be expected to have an especially high level of moral authority with respect to the issue of racial discrimination. Likewise, Japan can be expected to have a similarly high level of moral authority with respect to norms concerning the non-use of nuclear weapons.

An interesting question to consider at this stage is how the practices of the individual member states should be aggregated when defining the human rights culture of the IGO. While the calculation of an average (weighted by some state-level measure of influence such as Gross Domestic Product (GDP)) may seem to be the obvious solution, other possibilities exist. For example, in developing their theory of "norm cascades," Finnemore and Sikkink (1998) suggest that once a certain number of states have adopted a norm, a "tipping point" is reached whereupon states start to adopt the norm out of a desire to imitate the behavior of their peers. If we were to apply the idea of a tipping point to the concept of the IGOs' human rights cultures in this study, we could substitute the calculation of the IGO averages with a dichotomous measure that indicates whether or not a certain critical proportion of states within each IGO have adopted the norm of interest. This is a point we shall return to in Chapter 4.

2.2 Stage 2: Defining the *IGO Context* of the State

In the second stage of the model, individual states can be thought to receive normative influences from the various IGOs to which they belong.

Here I define the concept of *IGO Context* as an average of the human rights cultures of the various IGOs to which it belongs. A state that belongs to IGOs that, for the most part, have cultures that reflect high levels of respect for human rights will therefore have a positive (i.e., human rights-promoting) *IGO Context*. Conversely, states that belong to IGOs whose cultures are generally less concerned with promoting human rights will not come under these positive influences and might even experience a downward drag on their own human rights standards—a view that is consistent with some of the results I shall be presenting in Chapter 3.

Variation in a state's *IGO Context* can be thought to consist of two components. One is the variation that results from changes in the behavior of the states with which it shares IGO memberships. Thus, if a state's fellow IGO members undergo an improvement (or decline) in their human rights practices, the state's *IGO Context* will similarly improve (or decline). The second factor is more structural and results from changes in the IGO ties that connect the the state to others. If the state were to join new IGOs or leave existing IGOs, its *IGO Context* might change if it finds itself being connected to a group of states with a somewhat different human rights profile. Similarly, even if a state were not to undergo any changes in its own pattern of IGO memberships, its *IGO Context* could still change as a result of the IGOs to which it currently belongs admitting new members or expelling existing ones.

A particularly clear example of structural changes in a state's *IGO Context* is provided by the post-Cold War admission of Central and Eastern European states to IGOs that had previously consisted of predominantly Western European states. The maps shown in Figure 2.2 use the case of Hungary to illustrate this point. In these maps, each state is shaded in accordance with its degree of IGO-based influence over Hungary. Darker shades indicate states with which Hungary shares the most common IGO memberships, while lighter shades indicate the states with which it shares the fewest common IGO memberships.[8] These maps reveal the significant change in Hungary's sources of international influence that followed from the end of the Cold War and its eventual accession to various Western-oriented IGOs, including the EU, NATO, and the OECD.

A closer look at the underlying data reveals that in 1985 Hungary's pattern of IGO memberships led to its five most closely-connected IGO partners (in descending order) being Bulgaria, Romania, the Soviet

1985

2005

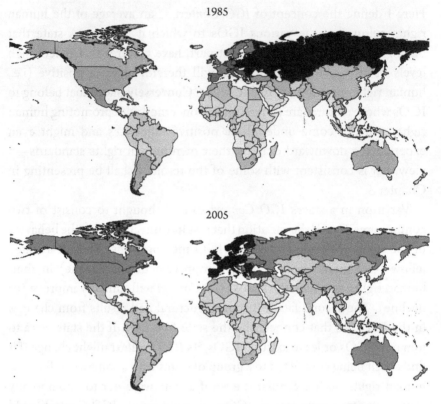

Figure 2.2 Hungary's most closely connected IGO partners in 1985 and 2005.

Union, Poland, and Czechoslovakia. By 2005 (the latest year for which comprehensive IGO membership data is available) this pattern had changed significantly: the composition of its five closest IGO partners had switched to Austria, Italy, Germany, Slovakia and France. Over the same period of time, the influence of Russia over Hungary had fallen from 3rd place to 30th place.

Not All IGOs have Equal Influence

In constructing the influence scores that underlie the Hungary example depicted in Figure 2.2, I had assumed that all IGOs are interchangeable in terms of their ability to act as conduits for the diffusion of human rights norms. The only aspect of the IGOs that I had accounted for was their size; I had assumed that smaller IGOs allow their individual member states to exert greater influence over one another than do larger IGOs. But treating IGOs as interchangeable on all other dimensions is obviously a huge oversimplification. Presumably some IGOs will be far more important than others to the norm diffusion process for a variety of reasons that might include their level of organization, their commitment to human rights issues, and their forms of governance.

To account for these effects, we can construct a measure of *IGO Context* for use in statistical models that takes advantage of data at the IGO level. This will allow us to test hypotheses about the contribution that each IGO makes to the overall *IGO Context* facing individual states. (This is analogous to the way in which I had suggested applying different weights when thinking about the influence that individual states have over the IGOs to which they belong.) For example, we might suppose that the human rights cultures of the more prominent (and usually more heavily institutionalized) IGOs play a larger role in shaping a state's *IGO Context*. For instance, we might expect that, when it comes to the transmission of human rights norms, the human rights culture of the EU matters more to European countries than that of, say, the European Patent Organization.

We can also test whether the human rights cultures of some IGOs are more influential than others due to their specific functions. This question has been explored in some previous studies of the effects of IGO membership. For example, in their study of the relationship between IGO ties and bilateral trade, Ingram, Robinson, and Busch (2005) categorize IGOs into four groups: (1) Economic; (2) Social and Cultural; (3) Military; and (4) General Purpose. They find that both economic and social/cultural IGOs are effective in promoting trade between states. They also follow Boehmer, Gartzke, and Nordstrom (2004) in differentiating IGOs on the basis of their organizational capacity and find that those that are more structured are more likely to promote trade between states.[9] Similarly, in his study of convergence among states' domestic economic policies, Cao (2007: Ch. 5) combines the measures of IGO capacity created by Boehmer, Gartzke, and Nordstrom with the measures of IGO function created by Ingram, Robinson, and Busch. He finds evidence to suggest that convergence among states' economic policies does not arise out of a process of socialization among states, but is more likely to be explained by either the pressure that the more powerful economic IGOs place on their member states or by the learning that takes place within these types of IGOs.

The current study addresses this question by asking whether IGOs that focus on human rights issues are any more likely than other types of IGOs to facilitate the diffusion of human rights norms. One might expect that IGOs with a human rights mandate will be more influential than others, given that these organizations ought to be considered a more authoritative source of information about states' human rights standards. Yet as Chapters 4 and 5 suggest, the mandate of the IGOs appears to make little, if any, difference to the norm-transmitting potential of the IGO network. This is a surprising finding that bolsters the conclusion that IGOs matter not just because of what they claim to do, but rather because of *who* they have among their members. It also suggests that the mechanism that underlies IGO-based convergence of states' practices with respect to human rights is very different from the mechanism driving the economic policy convergence noted by Cao (2009); in the case of human rights, it is more likely that the convergence we observe is due to a process of acculturation than the provision of policy-relevant information.

2.3 Stage 3: Internalizing the Norms

In the third stage of the model, states respond to the influence of their *IGO Context*. In some cases, the states may fully internalize the norms that prevail among their IGO partners and modify their beliefs and behavior accordingly. In other cases, the states might make only limited efforts to behave in conformance with group norms simply to curry favor with their interaction partners. And in some other cases, the states may show no evidence whatsoever of responding to the norms that prevail among their fellow IGO members.

Scholars working on questions of norm diffusion in international politics have come up with many different, yet often overlapping, ways of classifying the mechanisms responsible for the behavioral changes that arise through social influence effects (see, e.g., Checkel, 2005; Johnston, 2008; Simmons, Dobbin, and Garrett, 2008; Goodman and Jinks, 2013; Gilardi, 2014). While each of these classification schemes has its own particular advantages, the approach that I think is most useful to the present discussion is that developed by the international legal scholars Ryan Goodman and Derek Jinks in their work on the human rights-promoting effects of international law (and, by extension, international organizations). Goodman and Jinks (2013) suggest that the various forms of social influence in the international realm can be divided into three distinct

types: material inducement, persuasion, and acculturation. In the sub-
sections that follow, I'll consider each of these mechanisms in
turn.

Material Inducement

Material inducement is perhaps the most straightforward of the three
mechanisms. It involves states changing their behavior to comply with
the demands of their more powerful interaction partners. When this
mechanism operates, states are motivated by the desire to earn rewards
or to avoid having sanctions imposed upon them. Goodman and Jinks
(2013) take care to emphasize that, in order to meet their definition of
material inducement, the rewards and sanctions on offer must be material
in nature (e.g., economic gains or losses), rather than social (e.g., changes
in status vis-à-vis other states). An example of a possible IGO-mediated
behavioral change that results from material inducement would be a state's
compliance with the rules of a multilateral trade organization such as the
WTO. In most cases, the prospect of paying a fine or losing reciprocal
trade benefits presents a clear material incentive for states to modify their
behavior in a way that conforms to the expectations of their fellow IGO
members.

The ability of IGOs to bring about changes in states' human rights
practices through material inducements is, however, somewhat limited.
Theoretically, one way in which this mechanism could operate is through
attaching human rights conditions to membership in IGOs. IGOs can create these material inducements by either (1) granting membership only to
prospective member states whose behavior meets a certain standard—e.g.,
by requiring all new members to have a satisfactory human rights record—
or (2) threatening existing member states with suspension or expulsion if
their behavior falls below a certain threshold. Recent examples of cases in
which IGOs have been able to exert this kind of pressure with regard to the
promotion of democracy and human rights include the EU's relationship
with Serbia (which finally became a candidate for EU accession in 2012),
and the OAS's suspension of Honduras following a military coup in 2009.

In the case of Serbia, the prospect of EU membership has been used
to put pressure on the government to more fully cooperate with the
International Criminal Tribunal for the former Yugoslavia (ICTY) and
to upgrade its relations with Kosovo. After a mixed record of complying
with EU demands over much of the past decade, Serbia turned over

its most wanted fugitive, Ratko Mladić, in 2011 and was rewarded with EU candidacy status the following year. Its status as a candidate state is, however, no guarantee of eventual accession to the organization. This now leaves the EU with a significant degree of leverage over the political reforms taking place in Serbia.

In the case of Honduras, a military coup in 2009 against then-president Manuel Zelaya led the OAS to suspend Honduras in protest at the new government's violation of democratic principles. Its suspension was lifted two years later following the signing of an agreement that allowed Mr. Zelaya to return from exile and continue to participate in Honduran politics. But whether the actions on the part of the OAS had any independent effect on ending the political crisis in Honduras is difficult to say; the suspension from the OAS coincided with pressure from other major international actors including the United States, the EU, and the World Bank. Moreover, when compared to the pressure that the EU can exert over European states, the pressure that the OAS can apply to states in the Americas is much lower due to its relatively smaller role in the political and economic affairs of its region.

Yet despite possible exceptions such as these, IGOs in general have only limited opportunities to influence the behavior of their member states through either the promise of accession or the threat of expulsion. (And even in these cases, it is difficult to clearly distinguish the material aspects of the reward of IGO membership from the social ones.) The success of the EU in this regard can be attributed to its ability—somewhat unique among IGOs—to effectively link accession negotiations to human rights standards. But even there the EU has arguably compromised its standards in order to bring relatively unstable regimes under the umbrella of the organization (Stahl, 2013). Excluding a state from an IGO depends upon securing the consent of its existing member states, many of which will be reluctant to forgo potential gains from cooperation by deciding to adopt a more restrictive membership policy. (In other words, they lack what Gruber (2000) describes as the "go-it-alone power" necessary to credibly threaten to exclude many other states.) At the same time, the state that is being considered for potential accession or expulsion must value participation in the IGO highly enough to enact what are often very costly political reforms. At present, very few IGOs are similar to the EU in terms of their ability to offer prospective member states a high enough level of benefits to compel them to make politically costly reforms.

Indeed, in a wide-ranging study of attempts to link human rights and democracy conditions to membership in IGOs, Duxbury (2011) finds surprisingly few cases where the threat of exclusion has been meaningfully applied. For instance, despite near-universal condemnation of its policy of apartheid, various attempts at excluding South Africa from the UN ended in failure. This was not merely the result of the permanent members of the Security Council exercising their veto; the supporters of a proposal to expel South Africa even failed to secure the support of a majority of states in the General Assembly where the veto is not in play (Duxbury, 2011: Ch. 2). Instead, the opposition to excluding South Africa stemmed from the strong desire of most UN members to maintain the universality of the organization, and a belief on the part of some members that reform in South Africa could be more effectively achieved by keeping open channels of international influence.

Another way of thinking about how material inducement might operate (albeit not in the way that Goodman and Jinks had in mind) involves shifting our focus to actors at the sub-state level of analysis. Theories of sub-state actors explain how policy changes can occur as a result of membership in IGOs changing the balance of power among domestic political groups or enabling domestic political actors to more credibly signal their intentions to other domestic actors.

One of the most widely-cited examples of this logic is Andrew Moravcsik's theory of democratic "lock-in." Moravcsik (2000) tries to explain why some European states were much more willing than others to bind themselves to the European Convention on Human Rights (ECHR) in the aftermath of World War II. Unlike most human rights treaties, the ECHR is one with real enforcement powers. It is supported by the European Court of Human Rights (ECtHR), a strongly independent court whose judgments against its member states have been met with a much higher level of compliance than most other human rights courts (see Farer, 1997; Hawkins and Jacoby, 2010).[10] What explains why some states were so willing to bind themselves to the convention? Moravcsik (2000) points out that most of the states that ratified the ECHR were Europe's newly-established democracies, and argues that their governments—unlike those of the more secure democracies—had a special interest in ensuring that the recent democratic transitions would be protected. Membership in international organizations that helped to promote democracy and human rights was seen as an effective way to do so, even if this came at the cost of a significant loss of state sovereignty.

More recently, Simmons and Danner (2010) extended this logic to explain why some states were more willing than others to commit to the International Criminal Court (ICC)—another international court with relatively strong enforcement powers. They found that states that (1) have relatively weak democratic institutions and that (2) have recently experienced a civil war were more likely to join the ICC than those that do not meet both of these conditions. They argue that the leaders of these states rely upon the prospect of a future ICC indictment to send a credible signal to their political opponents that they are serious about pursuing non-violent resolutions to their domestic conflicts. In other words, opponents of the government are more likely to take the risk of pursuing a strategy of non-violent opposition because they are secure in the knowledge that a violent crackdown by government forces will be met with international criminal proceedings against the leaders of the state. When we return to the inter-state level of analysis, we can once again see that an international organization (the ICC) is reshaping the interests, and subsequent behavior, of its member states.

The logic of credible commitments also plays an important role in Pevehouse's account of democratic diffusion within IGOs. In an article titled "Democracy from the Outside-In," Pevehouse (2002) finds that authoritarian states are more likely to undergo a transition to democracy if they belong to IGOs with many democratic members. By doing so he challenges a literature that has tended to focus on the role that domestic, rather than international, factors play in democratic transitions.[11] One of the causal mechanisms Pevehouse identifies involves domestic political actors in authoritarian states—such as business elites—not necessarily being resistant to democratization per se, but nonetheless being concerned with how their business interests will be affected under the new regime. For instance, they might fear a scenario in which a populist government comes to power and engages in an aggressive program of nationalization of privately-held assets. Pevehouse argues that, in some cases, belonging to IGOs can mitigate these fears. States that have joined IGOs that promote market-oriented reforms will face higher costs for taking such actions and, as a result, will be able to assure business elites that the transition to democracy need not pose such a serious threat to their interests. Taken together, arguments like these make the claim that international institutions can not only help states to send credible signals to other states (as institutionalists such as Keohane (1984) have long argued) but to domestic political audiences as well.

Persuasion

The second mechanism in the three-part typology proposed by Goodman and Jinks (2013) is persuasion. As its name suggests, this involves actors undergoing a genuine change in their beliefs as a result of their interactions with others. This mechanism is also referred to as "learning" in other theoretical discussions of social influence (see Simmons, Dobbin, and Garrett, 2008; Cao, 2009; Gilardi, 2010), thereby implying a higher level of agency on the part of the actor whose beliefs are changing.[12] But as I shall be discussing later, whereas the stated objectives of many IGOs include the dissemination of best practices, very few appear to make a formal commitment to promoting human rights practices.

Of the IGOs that are concerned with achieving behavioral change through what we might call learning or persuasion, perhaps the best example is the OECD. In many respects, the OECD serves as an intergovernmental think tank on a wide range of issues that include economic development, energy policy, the environment, and education. Its Paris-based headquarters consists of a secretariat employing around 2,500 staff, many of whom conduct research in each of the specific policy areas that the OECD covers. Located in the immediate vicinity of the OECD secretariat is a cluster of permanent delegations from all 34 of its member states. Each of these delegations consists of an ambassador and a small permanent diplomatic staff.

What is central to the OECD's role in disseminating knowledge, however, is that these delegations serve as a host to the continual traffic of home-country experts who visit Paris to participate in specialized OECD meetings. The British delegation, for example, hosts around 700 visiting officials from the UK government every year.[13] These visiting officials meet with their counterparts from the other member states and participate in the drafting of OECD publications that document best practice in a particular field. As a result of these interactions, the OECD issues specific policy recommendations to their member states and generates a wealth of publicly available research reports.

Other prominent IGOs also play an important role in promoting the transfer of knowledge. For example, one of the less well-understood aspects of the World Bank is the role it plays in disseminating knowledge about successful development strategies among its member states. As one of its senior economists explained to me in an interview, an important part of what the bank does is simply "exposing a country to different ways of doing something." To that end, the bank sponsors so-called study tours in which officials from different governments are brought together to study a recent policy innovation that is likely to be of interest to them. For example, following India's successful implementation of a smart card-based health insurance program for the poor (*Rashtriya Swasthya Bima Yojana*), Indian government officials have held meetings with their counterparts from Bangladesh, Ghana, the Maldives, Nepal, and Pakistan, among others, to share the lessons learned from its experience with the program.

NATO also transmits knowledge in important ways. In addition to its traditional role as a military alliance, NATO's mission in the post-Cold War era has become increasingly concerned with promoting democracy in its wider region. This was especially important during the period in which NATO had been preparing former Soviet bloc states for admission to the organization. In doing so, NATO created a formal program, the Membership Action Plan, in which candidate states are required to submit annual reports detailing their progress on a number of different security and political indicators.[14]

At the same time, NATO has been making extensive efforts to educate military and political elites as well as the general public about Western norms of military-state relations. In an analysis of NATO's efforts in this regard, Gheciu (2005*a*) argues that the hundreds of workshops and seminars organized by NATO and its partners led to a real change in the attitudes of elites in the Czech Republic and Romania. These attitudinal changes led to the passage of legislation that consolidated these reforms. Most important for her argument, however, is that Gheciu is able to show that (at least in the case of the Czech Republic) this program of reforms continued apace even after the state had become a full member of NATO and no longer had an obvious instrumental motive for continuing it.

Acculturation

The third and final mechanism in Goodman and Jinks (2013) typology of social influence is acculturation, often referred to as socialization in the literature on social influence.[15] It refers to the way in which an actor changes his or her beliefs and behaviors in order to conform to the norms of a new social environment. As noted earlier, acculturation differs from the first mechanism—material inducement—insofar as the change in attitudes and behaviors that takes place is the result of social, rather than material, forces. Individuals (or even states) are therefore driven to behave in ways that are similar to their peers not because of the economic benefits on offer, but rather because of a desire to maximize their status within the group or perhaps simply because they want to "fit in."

Acculturation also differs from the second mechanism—persuasion—insofar as the actors involved do not rely upon a process of thoughtful deliberation in order to form a particular opinion or to start behaving in a certain way. Instead they do so simply because it feels like "the right thing to do." In many of the cases of interest to scholars of policy diffusion, there is simply not enough information available to allow the actor to reach a clear conclusion as to whether one particular policy would work better for them than another. Often without even realizing it, actors in these situations tend to reduce their risk by simply adopting policies that match those of their peers. For instance, Simmons and Elkins (2004) found that, in the absence of clear evidence for or against specific policy choices, states were often more likely to adopt economic liberalization programs if culturally similar states had already done so.

In distinguishing acculturation from persuasion, Goodman and Jinks (2013: Ch. 2) note that acculturation often—but not always—involves what they call "incomplete internalization." This means that actors adopt a certain set of behaviors as a result of social pressure to conform to group norms, even though they may not necessarily believe in these principles themselves. As an example of this, they cite the fact that many illiberal states have been willing to ratify human rights treaties with which they appear to have no intention to comply—a phenomenon referred to as "decoupling" in the sociology literature (see Hathaway, 2002; Hafner-Burton and Tsutsui, 2005). However, Goodman and Jinks (2013) take care to point out that what begins as incomplete internalization—or what can also be thought of as "public conformity without private acceptance" (see Johnston, 2001: 499)—does not necessarily stay that way: the gap between the principles embodied in these commitments and the private beliefs of the governing elite often begins to narrow over time once these principles become more deeply embedded in the practices of the state (Goodman and Jinks, 2013: Ch. 8).

The concept of acculturation can be applied at many different levels of analysis. Perhaps one of the simplest and clearest demonstrations of acculturation comes from a study by Sacerdote (2001) of freshmen at Dartmouth College. Sacerdote was able to take advantage of the fact that Dartmouth was for a period of time randomly assigning roommates to its incoming freshmen. This allowed him to conduct a relatively "clean" test of whether students' academic performance is influenced by that of their roommates. He found that the freshman-year GPAs of the students in his sample were indeed positively correlated with those of their roommates. The effect was modest, but the findings were highly statistically significant and the random assignment allowed him to exclude self-selection as an alternative explanation. Moreover, given what we know about the nature of relationships among college roommates, it seems much more likely that a mechanism of acculturation—rather than, say, material inducements or persuasion—was responsible for the convergence he observed among the roommates' academic performance.

The study of college roommates presents a relatively "easy" test of the acculturation hypothesis for various reasons: in most cases, the students will have been living away from home for the first time; living at such close quarters provides ample opportunity for interaction; and college students tend to be at a stage in their personal development that leaves them especially open to outside influences. IGOs obviously present a harder case than this, but for the various reasons discussed in Section 2.1 of this chapter, IGOs nonetheless provide opportunities for meaningful social ties to form among the diplomats who work there. By helping to build a sense of community among the representatives of their various member states, IGOs create conditions in which these individuals are more likely to exert influence over one another. Experimental work in social psychology lends strong support to the idea that inducing a sense of shared group identity allows individuals to more effectively influence the attitudes of others (Abrams et al., 1990). Most IR scholars would agree that states attach a high value to perceptions of status and prestige (see Paul, Larson, and Wohlforth, 2014), and IGOs provide a social environment in which concerns over these issues are made especially salient (Johnston, 2001).

In the course of the interviews I conducted with representatives to major IGOs, it became clear that most diplomats care deeply about how the state they represent is perceived in the eyes of their foreign counterparts. Most are very eager to ensure that their state is not cast as an outlier on any given issue and that its behavior is generally consistent with what would be expected of a modern, human rights-respecting state. This is perhaps unsurprising given that it is the diplomats posted to IGOs—rather than their colleagues serving back home—who have to bear the immediate social costs of whatever international disapproval their states' behavior might generate. Nonetheless, this desire to present a favorable image to the international community can have real consequences for how a state behaves. For instance, a diplomat from Kazakhstan explained to me how the country embraced the opportunity to serve as chair of the Organization for Security Cooperation in Europe (OSCE) in 2010 when it was presented with an opportunity to do so. Despite being a largely ceremonial role, the diplomat explained that the chairmanship was especially important because it provided an opportunity for Kazakhstan, as the first Central Asian state to hold the OSCE chair, to show the world that it had finally attained the status of a mature member of the international community. However, in order to secure the support of the Western members of the OSCE, Kazakhstan had to make significant concessions with respect to reforming its national legislation (including its criminal code) and cooperating with international election observers. In the opinion of my interviewee, it was the promise of OSCE chairmanship that was critical to overcoming resistance from certain parts of the government that were quite reluctant to undertake these reforms.

In a more general sense, diplomats serving at IGOs appear to have a very strong desire to demonstrate consistency in their states' behavior. This idea of consistency applies both in terms of consistency with previous statements made by the government, and consistency with the state's international legal obligations. Many of the diplomats I interviewed discussed how they are able to exploit this desire for consistency in order to extract concessions from other states over various issues. Yet from a purely rationalist perspective, this desire to maintain consistency is often difficult to explain. For instance, diplomats at the UN invest enormous efforts in negotiating the text of UN General Assembly resolutions which—unlike Security Council resolutions—are not legally binding and in all but a few cases generate no significant media coverage. Why would states spend so much effort on agreements that seem so inconsequential? It seems that states do this because, no matter how inconsequential these agreements might be in practice, they provide an important opportunity for states to manage their image in the eyes of the international community. The diplomats negotiating these agreements become personally invested in how their states (and, by extension, themselves) might be perceived by others. They therefore go to great lengths to ensure that they are presenting their states as reliable, law-abiding, and generally cooperative members of the international community. As a result of this, it would appear that participation in IGOs provides greater opportunities for states to influence the human rights practices of others than rationalist theories suggest.

From the Diplomats to the Policymakers

So far we have discussed the various ways in which delegates to an IGO are able to influence, and be influenced by, the members of other national delegations. But the discussion has until now focused on the professional diplomats who staff the permanent missions to the larger IGOs, and not on the policymakers back home whose job it is to implement government policy. How, then, can the attempts that one state makes to influence the members of another state's delegation to the IGO be relied upon to bring about the required changes in policy?

The answer will depend upon the type of influence involved. In the case of attempts at material inducement, this step is relatively straightforward: the main task of the diplomats is to effectively communicate to their home governments the details of whatever proposal is on the table. This might involve the diplomat relaying a message along the lines of, "The representatives of countries A, B, and C have informed us that our chances of being elected to committee X will be greatly enhanced if we adopt policy Y." The policymakers back at the home government would then decide whether the expected economic benefits of X can justify the costs of Y and instruct their delegates accordingly. (Having said that, the communication between the diplomats and their home governments is never a purely mechanical task; the more experienced diplomats will be more attuned to the ways in which the proposal could be made to look more or less attractive to their colleagues back at the home country.)

In the case of influence that relies upon mechanisms of either persuasion or acculturation, the separation that exists between the diplomats and the policymakers can create more difficulties. For successful internalization to take place, one of two things must happen: either the diplomats must influence the policymakers in a way that leads them to adopt beliefs that are similar to those of the diplomats, or the diplomats must somehow acquire policymaking authority. The success of either of these mechanisms, however, cannot be taken for granted.

The first mechanism is easier to imagine in the case of persuasion, although it can be applied in cases of acculturation too. The simplest case would involve a two-step process in which the diplomat is first persuaded by her fellow IGO members of the merits of a particular policy, and she then goes on to successfully present the same argument to her colleagues in the relevant government ministry. To use same-sex marriage as an example, the experience of serving alongside more progressive states at an IGO may convince a previously skeptical diplomat of the need for her own country to adopt legislation permitting same-sex marriages. In the course of her subsequent conversations with other government officials, she would then present them with arguments that are similar to the ones that had originally convinced her.

Of course, for this to work effectively, the act of persuasion would need to be successful in convincing both the diplomat and the various government officials with whom she subsequently interacts. Were the diplomat to be unable to convince the relevant policymakers for whatever reason—whether due to domestic political obstacles that make it difficult for the policymakers to contemplate proposing new policies, or barriers to communication between the foreign ministry and other government departments that would deny the diplomat the opportunity to even attempt to persuade the policymakers to change their course—the chain of influence that began with one state trying to influence another at the IGO would be broken.

The second mechanism involves the diplomat actually becoming a policymaker herself. One way that this might occur is if the diplomat's career trajectory causes her to move from the foreign service into a more political role, or into another government department that gives her more policymaking power. For instance, many US ambassadors to the UN have gone on to occupy other very senior positions in the US government. Some examples include Madeleine Albright (Secretary of State), George H. W. Bush (President), Daniel Patrick Moynihan (US Senator), John Negroponte (Director of National Intelligence), Susan Rice (National Security Advisor), and Bill Richardson (Governor of New Mexico).

The movement of people among government departments is an idea that plays an important role in Alistair Iain Johnston's study of China's participation in international institutions (Johnston, 2008). He studies how beliefs in the benefits of collective security developed as a consequence of China's increased level of participation in international institutions over the 1980s and 1990s. One specific example he gives is of China's participation in the UN Conference on Disarmament. He argues that China had originally joined this organization in 1980 mainly because of its desire to maintain a higher profile on the international stage. Once inside, however, it needed to build up some expertise in the field of arms control, which led to its Ministry of Foreign Affairs establishing a team of arms control experts (Johnston, 2008: 52–53). Johnston finds that many different ministers from the Ministry of Foreign Affairs were rotated through this particular unit, which led to a wider diffusion of ideas about the value of disarmament through the government. He also shows how this arms control bureaucracy, once established, started to expand and form more linkages to other government agencies, thereby further cementing its role in the Chinese foreign policy establishment.

Another way we can think about the second mechanism operating—that is, the merging of the roles of the diplomat and the policymaker—is if the policymaker is given the opportunity to participate directly in the meetings of the IGO. This has the effect of exposing the policymaker directly to the same persuasive or acculturating influences to which the diplomat would usually be exposed. As mentioned earlier, national delegations to the OECD are constantly hosting representatives from various government departments (e.g., treasury, environment, education) that have an interest in participating in meetings of any of the OECD's approximately 200 different policy committees. For many of these policymakers, attendance at an OECD policy committee represents a rare opportunity to gain an international perspective on what otherwise tend to be very domestic-focussed policy debates. Interestingly, one of the diplomats I interviewed at a national delegation to the OECD remarked on how he finds it so much easier to persuade policymakers from his home government to adopt particular positions once they have had a chance to experience firsthand the discussions that take place at the relevant OECD committees.

While the OECD provides what is perhaps the clearest example of policymakers playing a direct role in the discussions that take place at IGOs, most other IGOs hold regular meetings that are attended by the relevant policymakers themselves, rather than only by representatives from the government's ministry of foreign affairs. For example, NATO holds meetings for its member states' ministers of defense as well as occasional summits for their heads of state; the WTO holds biennial meetings for trade ministers; and the international police organization INTERPOL often holds meetings for ministers of justice or home affairs at the start of its annual General Assembly.

But in addition to these high-profile organizations, the work of the less prominent IGOs also depends upon directly engaging policymakers from the relevant government ministries of each of their member states. For instance, the International Bureau of Weights and Measures (BIPM) is a technical IGO based in Paris whose goal is to coordinate and verify the systems of measurement employed by its 56 member states. Each year it has a general meeting that lasts for about three days and is attended by delegations from each member state that usually consist of representatives from the state's embassy in Paris, its government agency responsible for measurement standards, as well as whichever government department has responsibility for this agency.[16]

What this all suggests is that the social influence that takes place at IGOs need not be restricted only to the members of each state's permanent delegation. These organizations provide venues in which not only diplomats but also representatives from many different government agencies are given the opportunity to come into contact with their foreign counterparts. As a result, IGOs provide a mechanism through which international norms and ideas can, in certain cases, penetrate deeply into the bureaucracies of their member states.

Moderating Variables

At this stage of the model we can again take advantage of state-level variation to test hypotheses about how states vary in their ability to internalize international norms. One of the ideas I explore in Chapters 4 and 5 is whether more materially powerful states are any more receptive to the influences of their IGO partners than less powerful states. As one might expect, compelling arguments can be made in both directions. On the one hand, the more powerful states might be better positioned to ignore the influence of other states. For example, consider the recent case of Russia's refusal to yield to international pressures on its gay rights policies, a position that generated significant international criticism in the lead-up to the 2014 Winter Olympics. In cases like that, we might expect to find that it is the less materially powerful states—for example, developing states that are eager to curry favor with their more powerful counterparts—that are the most receptive to IGO-based influences.

On the other hand, one could argue—and the results of Chapter 4 lend support to this view—that more materially powerful states ought to be *more* receptive to IGO-based influences because they have greater capacity to receive and to respond to these influences. The more powerful states not only field much larger delegations to IGOs in the first place (thereby making them more exposed to international influences), but they also have greater capacity to effectively implement the ideas that they receive from their fellow IGO members. This means that weaker states might not be able to respond to IGO-based influences on their human rights practices even when representatives of their governments wish they could. For instance, the governments of very poor states may simply lack the resources to increase the capacity of their criminal justice system and thereby remain unable to bring their civil rights practices in line with those of their fellow IGO members.

At the same time, we can test the hypothesis that democracies, and states with more active civil societies, are more receptive to IGO influences. Governments of states with stronger civil societies ought to be held more accountable to their citizens for their behavior with respect to prevailing international norms. For example, the citizens of a state with very active human rights NGOs should be in a better position to hold their government accountable for any failures to fulfill its obligations under international human rights treaties (see Murdie and Davis, 2012). Indeed, Neumayer (2005) finds that ratification of international human rights treaties is associated with improvements in human rights performance only when the ratifying state has a sufficiently high presence of international NGOs. We can therefore expect to find that states that are more democratic and/or have more active civil societies will be more likely to adopt human rights practices that follow those of their peers.

The Temporal Dimension

How quickly might we expect these IGO-based diffusion effects to result in observable changes to a state's human rights practices? The foregoing discussion of the various mechanisms of norm internalization suggests that the type of mechanism involved is likely to have interesting implications for the timescale over which these effects become apparent. When material inducement is involved, we might expect changes in human rights standards to occur to relatively quickly. As noted above, all that is needed for this to occur is for information regarding the potential costs and benefits of a particular course of action to be communicated from the delegates at the IGO back to their counterparts at the capital.

In the case of either persuasion or acculturation, however, we can expect the diffusion to occur somewhat more slowly. In the context of human rights standards, knowledge is rarely transmitted from one state to another in the form of a neatly packaged bundle of prescriptions for how a state ought to behave. This knowledge is instead far more likely to be transmitted in the form of a gradual accumulation of ideas and principles that emerge in the course of an ongoing conversation among the representatives of different states. A similar logic applies to processes of acculturation. To the extent that acculturation is in play, we should expect to see changes occurring over an extended time period as the individuals concerned begin to conform to the norms of the group. Indeed, this is the logic that Bearce and Bondanella (2007: 724) applied in their study of interest convergence within IGOs: they reported a convergence effect that was most pronounced after a four-year lag, and inferred from this that a process of socialization, rather than information exchange, is likely to be responsible for the convergence among states' interests.

However, applying this logic to the IGO-based diffusion of human rights practices becomes somewhat more complicated. This is because in the present study I am concerned with indicators of human rights practices, rather than indicators of states' *interests* with respect to human rights standards. The governments of some states might have a strong interest in promoting human rights at home, but owing to capacity constraints or domestic opposition, they may take a very long time—or perhaps remain permanently unable—to effectively translate these changed interests into concrete changes in behavior. This could lead some cases of social influence to remain unobserved or only be observed long after the social influence actually occurred.

Another complication arises from the fact that some states start to make changes to their human rights practices in anticipation of joining an IGO. As discussed earlier, organizations such as the EU and NATO have engaged prospective member states in lengthy pre-accession talks, during which time the states begin the often-difficult process of bringing their human rights practices in line with the norms of the organization—a process that is likely to be driven by a combination of material inducements, persuasion, and acculturation. As a result, these pre-accession changes could lead us to underestimate the time involved in the IGO-based diffusion of human rights practices given that states are not formally members of the organizations during this period. (Interestingly, this logic directly parallels the criticism that Goldstein, Rivers, and Tomz (2007) leveled against Rose (2004) in challenging his claim that membership in the WTO does little to increase trade among its member states.)

Overall, then, the relationship between the mechanisms of IGO-based diffusion and the timing of changes in human rights practices is likely to be a complex one. Regardless of the precise mechanism(s) involved, what we can say with some confidence is that the IGO-based diffusion of human rights is likely to involve a multi-year process. In Chapter 3 I shall look more closely at the dynamics of IGO-based diffusion and present evidence to suggest that it consists of a mix of both short- and long-term effects.

2.4 Next Steps: Collecting Evidence of Diffusion

This chapter has proposed a three-stage model of norm diffusion in which individual IGOs can be thought of as developing human rights cultures that reflect the norms and practices held by their member states. This culture can then start to influence the subsequent behavior of the IGO's member states. As I shall show in the chapters that follow, this model is consistent with my findings that over time states' human rights practices converge with those of their fellow IGO members.

To demonstrate this convergence effect, I adopt a statistical approach that tests whether various indicators of states' human rights practices become more similar to those of their fellow IGO members, even after controlling for a number of other domestic and international factors that might influence a state's human rights performance. I also test whether this diffusion effect is apparent for both "good" and "bad" patterns of human rights performance, and whether characteristics of the states and the IGOs themselves affect the ability of human rights norms to diffuse within the IGO network. As these results will show, shared membership in many different types of IGO facilitates the diffusion of human rights practices, whether for better or worse.

As with most studies of diffusion, most of the evidence that I'll be presenting lies at the macro level of analysis—in other words, it depends upon inferring convergence using a statistical analysis of data on a very large sample of countries. Observing evidence of diffusion at the micro level, however, is much more difficult. This is because most—but certainly not all—diffusion processes arise through the accretion of many very small instances of social influence that are often very difficult to identify.

To illustrate why this is so, let's consider again the frequently cited study of smoking cessation that I discussed in the context of causal inference in previous chapter. Christakis and Fowler (2008) found that, after controlling for various possible confounding variables, the probability that an individual will stop smoking is strongly associated with the number of his or her close friends and family members who had stopped smoking. The idea that an individual's smoking habits are subject to social influence makes intuitive sense and Christakis and Fowler base their argument on a robust statistical finding, but it is worth taking a slight detour at this stage to consider what type of evidence a researcher might be able to find to support this at the micro level. In doing so, I shall apply Goodman and Jinks' three-part typology of social influence discussed in the previous section.

One possibility is that some individuals who had stopped smoking did so because they had come under direct pressure from their friends and family. It seems plausible that, if asked by a researcher, some of the individuals would be able to recount examples of times when a spouse or friend pleaded with them to stop smoking—perhaps even to the point of threatening to terminate their relationship. (Interestingly, having family members provide these types of ultimatums is actually a tactic often used in a clinical setting when dealing with more dangerous types of addiction, although it is interesting to note that the evidence available to support the efficacy of these types of interventions is somewhat limited (see Wild, 2006).)

A second possibility is that individuals respond to persuasive messages from their peers. A large body of evidence exists to suggest that smokers are significantly more likely to quit following a conversation with their doctor about the importance of doing so (Aveyard et al., 2012), and a growing body of research suggests that peer-to-peer education campaigns can be effective at reducing smoking among adolescents (see Steglich et al., 2012; Campbell et al., 2008). As with the more coercive approach discussed above, it seems plausible that the individuals concerned would be able to identify acts of persuasion by their peers as pivotal moments in their decision to stop smoking.

The third possibility is that individuals respond to broader contextual signals about the appropriateness of smoking. As they notice that fewer of their friends and colleagues are smoking and that smoking is banned from more and more public spaces, their perception of the social desirability of smoking will start to change. As a result, many smokers will presumably become more motivated to quit. However, identifying any specific event that leads an individual smoker to quit is much more difficult than it is in the case of the other mechanisms of social influence discussed above. The desire to quit is likely to have arisen through an accumulation of many factors, each of which contribute in a small way towards making smoking generally less socially desirable and less convenient for the individual concerned. For example, a smoker's decision to quit could have been the result of a combination of his best friend deciding to quit, his workplace no longer permitting smoking anywhere inside the building, and perhaps the fact that he no longer feels comfortable smoking in the presence of his children. In a situation like that, the smoker will no doubt have come under strong social pressure to change his behavior, yet if interviewed by a researcher he would find it difficult to identify any single factor that drove his decision.

To a large extent, the same logic applies to the diffusion of human rights norms within IGOs. In cases where states use material inducements or persuasion in an attempt to change the human rights practices of their IGO partners, there ought to be a reasonably accessible trail of evidence to link the act of social influence to the state's change in behavior. For instance, it should be reasonably straightforward to trace Serbia's more recent cooperation with the ICTY back to its desire to join the EU. Similarly, in cases where learning or persuasion are at work—for example, in Gheciu's study of NATO discussed on page 44—it is possible to draw fairly clear causal connections between NATO's educational efforts and the domestic reforms that subsequently took hold in some of the states of Central and Eastern Europe.

But in cases where the behavioral change is driven by acculturation—e.g., in cases where states improve their human rights practices because they want to be taken more seriously in their interactions with other states—demonstrating the causal connections is much more difficult; not only is it difficult to identify a single cause of the change (as in the example of the smoker above), but diplomats and policymakers seem generally reluctant to admit to themselves that the domestic political changes in their own states are often the result of international influences. Indeed, one thing that struck me when interviewing diplomats is that while most of them seem to confidently believe in their ability to influence the policies of other states, they are very reluctant to acknowledge cases where their own beliefs might have been shaped by the influences of others. To do so would mean accepting they have to some extent succumbed to the danger all overseas diplomats face of "going native" and thereby compromising their obligations to their home governments.

Yet while it can be very difficult to find evidence at the micro level of acculturation that leads to improved human rights practices, it is equally—if not more—difficult to trace the process through which states allow their human rights standards to *decline* in response to weak or declining standards of their peers. In cases of downward influence, the most plausible explanation is likely to be one of acculturation: it is difficult to think of many cases where states were put under pressure by others to adopt worse human rights practices or where they were persuaded by others of the benefits of relaxing their standards.[17]

Instead, what is more likely to have happened in these cases is that the states simply fail to maintain or improve their human rights standards because they are no longer under any social pressure to do so. In a sense, then, this can be thought of as an international analogue of the "broken windows" theory of crime control (Wilson and Kelling, 1982; Kelling and Coles, 1996): once states observe—whether consciously or subconsciously—that human rights standards are no longer being upheld in their IGO "neighborhoods," they feel at greater liberty to let their own standards decline.

Given the difficulties involved in collecting clear evidence of diffusion at the micro level, the strategy I adopt in the next part of this book is as follows. I use the first half of the next chapter (Chapter 3) to provide initial evidence of convergence among IGO members' human rights practices in a large-n framework. In a series of robustness tests, I then show that this finding is unlikely to be the result of many possible confounding variables and/or alternative channels of diffusion. I also use the example of one particular country, Bahrain, to shed more light on how its human rights practices have tracked those of its fellow IGO members. In Chapter 4 I adopt a more nuanced model of IGO-based diffusion that allows us to study the effects of the various state- and IGO-level variables

that the theoretical discussion in this chapter suggests are important in
distinguishing among alternative causal mechanisms. In doing so, I will
show that the convergence effect documented in Chapter 3 is generally
more likely to be the result of acculturation than material inducements or
persuasion.

3

Demonstrating Diffusion

3.1 Introduction

This chapter introduces the modeling strategy used throughout the remainder of the book and presents a proof of concept for the IGO diffusion hypothesis.[1] In doing so, it uses widely studied data on one of the most basic categories of human rights—the so-called physical integrity rights that refer to the right of people to be free from acts of torture, political imprisonment, extra-judicial killings and "disappearances."

The results will show that even after accounting for many other important domestic and international influences, states' human rights practices tend to become more similar over time to those of their fellow IGO members. At the same time, the results suggest that this diffusion effect operates symmetrically: IGOs appear to provide a forum in which states are influenced not only by the states with better human rights practices than their own, but also by states with worse human rights practices.

This chapter proceeds as follows. The first section describes the data used in conducting the statistical analysis—specifically, the data on IGO memberships, the data on physical integrity rights, as well as details of the construction of the network variable that I use to capture the concept of IGO Context described in the previous chapter. Section 3.3 presents the results of this model, followed by a series of a robustness checks that test various alternative explanations for the outcomes we observe. In Section 3.4, I then engage in a more detailed examination of one particular country-case, Bahrain, to further elucidate the relationship between its human rights practices and those of its fellow IGO members.

3.2 The Data

IGO Memberships

Throughout this book I use data on states' patterns of membership in IGOs obtained from the Correlates of War 2 International Governmental Organizations Data Set, version 2.3 (Pevehouse, Nordstrom, and Warnke, 2004). This dataset provides information on states' membership in a total of 495 IGOs, spanning the period from 1815 to 2005. Pevehouse, Nordstrom, and Warnke (2004) use the following criteria to define an organization as an IGO:

- Its members must be sovereign states (as opposed to individuals or non-governmental organizations);
- It must consist of at least three member states;
- Its founding document is a treaty that has been signed by its member states. (This differentiates formal IGOs from organizations that are essentially subcommittees—albeit in some cases very important ones—of existing IGOs.);[2] and
- It is not simply a legal entity, but is instead an active organization that has a permanent secretariat and holds meetings at least once every 10 years.

Recall that Figure 1.1 from Chapter 1 showed what appears to have been an explosive growth in IGOs over the period covered by the data, especially in the post-WWII period.[3] As one might expect, IGOs vary significantly in terms of their numbers of member states, while the states themselves vary significantly in terms of the numbers of IGOs to which they belong. To give a sense of how these quantities are distributed in 2005 (the latest year for which we have systematic data), Figure 3.1 provides a pair of histograms showing the variation among IGOs in terms of their numbers of member states (in the left-hand panel) and variation among states in terms of their total number of IGO memberships (in the right-hand panel).

These histograms show that while some IGOs are almost universal in terms of their membership (e.g., the United Nations with its current total of 193 member states),[4] a very large proportion (58%) of IGOs have fewer than 20 members. The vast majority (84%) of these small IGOs tend to be regional IGOs—for example, the 6-member Gulf Cooperation Council (GCC), or the 15-member West African Health Organization. As we shall

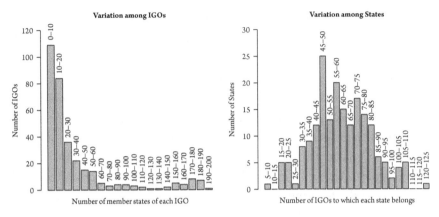

Figure 3.1 Patterns of IGO membership in 2005.

see in Chapter 4, the IGO-based diffusion effect turns out to be more pronounced among these small regional IGOs than it is amongst the full group of IGOs.

At the same time, states vary significantly in terms of the number of IGOs to which they belong.[5] The states that belong to the smallest number of IGOs tend to be very poor states or microstates whose governments are too small to create a demand for participation in many of the more specialized IGOs (e.g., East Timor, Palau, or Liechtenstein).[6] At the other extreme, the richest states tend to be among the states with the greatest number of IGO memberships. Interestingly, the states with the most IGO memberships are almost always European states, presumably reflecting the greater degree of international institution-building in that region.[7]

Dependent Variable: *PIR Score*

The measure of human rights performance used in this chapter is the Physical Integrity Rights (PIR) index from the Cingranelli-Richards Human Rights Dataset. This index measures the extent of human rights violations involving a direct threat to the physical safety of the individual (Cingranelli and Richards, 2004) and is one of the most widely used cross-national measures of human rights performance. Importantly, the PIR score reflects the actual behavior of each state with respect to certain types of human rights violations and takes no account of whether each state may or may not have passed legislation in an effort to protect these rights. The PIR index should therefore be thought of as an indicator of a country's compliance with established human rights norms, rather than merely a reflection of its expressed commitment to upholding these norms.

The PIR index is created by combining information on the following four types of human rights violations for each country-year: 1) torture; 2) political imprisonment; 3) extrajudicial killings; and 4) disappearances. Cingranelli and Richards compiled information on the frequency of these violations by carrying out a detailed content analysis of both the US State Department and Amnesty International's annual Country Reports.[8] For each of the four types of rights violations, Cingranelli and Richards assigned a score of 0, 1, or 2 to each country-year depending on whether the abuses were carried out frequently (50 or more reported incidences), occasionally (fewer than 50 incidences), or not at all. The scores for each of the four categories were added together to produce an aggregate PIR score for each country-year.[9] This cumulative score ranges from 0 to 8, with higher numbers indicating higher levels of respect for physical integrity rights.

Figure 3.2 provides an illustration of the spatial and temporal variation that exists among states' scores on the PIR index. The map at the top of the figure provides a snapshot of the level of respect for physical integrity rights in 2006, the latest year in the data used in this analysis. Darker shades on this map indicate higher PIR scores, and hence higher levels of respect for physical rights.[10] As one might expect, the richer, more democratic countries tend to have better human rights performances, although of course some important exceptions stand out: the United States, for instance, had only a middling performance on the PIR index in the mid-2000s in large part due to human rights violations carried out during the War on Terror.

On the bottom left-hand side of the figure is a graph that shows the temporal variation in PIR scores over the period under examination. In this graph the black line represents the global mean PIR scores, while the grey bands represent the interquartile range at each point in time. As this graph shows, there is wide variation in PIR scores at the global level *within* each year, but relatively little variation in the global mean when we look *across* years. At the global level, then, levels of respect for human rights—at least as they are reflected in the PIR index—appear to be somewhat stagnant.[11] At first glance this seems surprising given the extent to which democracy has spread around the world (see Gleditsch and Ward, 2006), but it is important to keep in mind that the PIR scale reflects

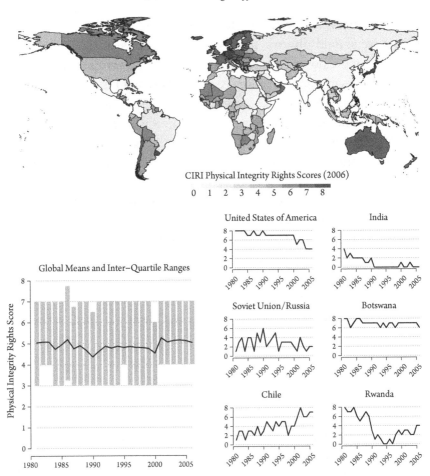

Figure 3.2 Spatial and temporal trends in the Physical Integrity Rights Index.

categories of human rights violation that are often perpetrated even in reasonably well-established democracies.[12] Of course, this stability in physical integrity rights at the global level masks some interesting trends at the national level. For instance, human rights standards in Latin America have improved significantly in recent decades while those of many Asian and African states have remained poor, or have even worsened (Hafner-Burton and Ron, 2009). To give a more concrete sense of how individual states have fared in terms of their respect for physical integrity rights over the 1981–2006 period, the six graphs at the lower right-hand side of Figure 3.2 show the trajectory of PIR scores for a sample of six illustrative cases: the United States, Russia, Chile, India, Botswana, and Rwanda.

An interesting implication of the diffusion model developed in Chapter 2 is that we should observe the average PIR scores of individual IGOs becoming more homogenous over time.[13] In other words, as states influence the human rights practices of their fellow IGO members, the variation found among the PIR scores of each IGO's member states should start to decline. Although the accession of new member states to existing IGOs often works against this trend, I do find some evidence to suggest a decline in variation within individual IGOs. When I calculate the standard deviation of the PIR scores for each IGO in each year, I find that the average of these IGO-level standard deviations has indeed declined over the time period: the average standard deviation of the IGOs in 2005 was 19% lower than it was in 1981. I also find that this difference is significantly larger among the regional IGOs (a decline of 22%) and even more so among the IGOs with 10 or fewer members (a decline of 28%).[14] The stronger norm-transmitting effect of the smaller organizations is a point we shall return to in our examination of IGO-level variation in the next chapter.

Key Explanatory Variable: *IGO Context*

In most studies of social influence effects, the analyst tries to construct an explanatory variable that reflects the extent to which each individual in the network comes under the influence of others. So in the case of, say, a study of how an individual's smoking habits are influenced by the habits of his or her close friends (the example we discussed in Chapter 2), we would want to construct a variable that indicates the proportion of smokers found among each person's friends. Obviously this will depend upon knowing about the structure of the friendship network that exists among the people in the study (i.e., who is friends with whom), as well as data on each individual's smoking status at various points in time. We would then want to test whether a correlation exists between this variable—the proportion of smokers found among each person's closest friends—and the outcome variable, which in this case will be each individual's smoking status. (If we find evidence for such a correlation, we would then want to think carefully about the issues of causal inference we discussed in Section 1.4.)

In this chapter I test the IGO-mediated diffusion hypothesis practices by following a very similar logic. Here I construct a network variable that reflects the average human rights standards found among each state's

IGO partners. This variable—which I shall refer to as *IGO Context*—can most simply be thought of as an indicator of whether the IGOs to which each state belongs provide an opportunity for the state to interact with other states that have "good" human rights practices or with states that have "bad" human rights practices. (We can think of this as being directly analogous to a measure of the extent to which each individual in a friendship network surrounds himself with smokers or non-smokers.) In this case, *IGO Context* can be thought of as simply an average of the human rights scores (specifically, the PIR scores) of a state's fellow IGO members. *IGO Context* is therefore directly analogous to the spatial lags that are commonly used in spatial econometrics, but where the concept of geographical proximity is replaced by the concept of shared membership in an IGO.[15]

Although the basic intuition behind the construction of *IGO Context* is straightforward, the question of how to model the IGO network is actually quite complex. This has implications for the sort of weighted average we use when trying to assess the influence of a state's fellow IGO members. The most straightforward conceptualization of an IGO network consists of states being bound to other states such that the thickness of the ties (or "edges" as they tend to be called in the networks literature) between each pair of states reflects the number of shared IGO memberships.[16] In the language of social network analysis, this type of network is said to be "unipartite"—that is, it has only one type of node (the state)—and has "valued" edges, meaning that the strength of the ties between nodes are not equal but instead take on a value proportional to the number of shared IGO memberships.[17]

A simple example of this type of network conceptualization is shown in Figure 3.3. In this case Country A belongs to four of the same IGOs as Country B, but only two of the same IGOs as Country C. This particular network model assumes that because of the greater number of IGO ties, the behavior of Country A is influenced more strongly (specifically, twice as strongly) by the behavior of Country B than by the behavior of Country C. When it comes to calculating the *IGO Context* variable for this type of network conceptualization, the influence of, say, the human rights performance of countries B and C on that of Country A in this very simple network would be equal to $\frac{4}{4+2} \times B + \frac{2}{4+2} \times C$. This is simply the average of the behavior of countries B and C, weighted by the strength of the ties to each of these nodes. (Going back to the smoking example, this would be akin to saying that A is a much closer friend of B than she is of C, so B's

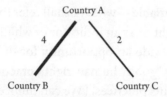

Figure 3.3 Network of states with valued edges.

smoking status carries more weight than that of C in determining whether A ultimately decides to stop smoking.)

However, an important drawback of the conventional model of IGO ties is that it only considers IGOs as a series of direct channels connecting one state to another. In other words, IGO ties are treated as if they are similar in structure to trade ties or telecommunication ties between states. In this conceptualization, the influence that Country B or Country C has on Country A depends only upon the number of IGOs in which each pair of states share common membership and takes no account of the differing degrees of influence that some states have over others as a result of differences in the structure of the interconnecting IGO ties. Thus, the conventional model assumes that Country B's influence over Country A is the same irrespective of whether the four IGOs connecting these countries are small IGOs like the North American Free Trade Agreement (NAFTA) in which Country B can exercise significant influence over its partners, or whether they are large IGOs like the UN where Country B's influence over its fellow member states is likely to be significantly diluted.

In order to provide a more flexible model of the way in which IGOs can act as transmission belts for the diffusion of norms among states, I conceive of the IGO network as a bipartite network.[18] This is one in which there are two types of nodes (in this case states and IGOs), and edges only exist between nodes of different types. In other words, no direct state-state or IGO-IGO connections exist. An important feature of this type of network model is that it can account for the different ways in which IGOs can mediate the ties between Country A and countries B and C. To help understand how this is possible, consider the two network diagrams shown in Figure 3.4. In both of these graphs Country A shares four IGO connections with Country B and two with Country C. In that respect the strength of the A-B and A-C ties are consistent with how they were represented in Figure 3.3. However, in the upper graph of Figure 3.4 the two ties that Country A shares with Country C involve two of the set of four IGOs that connect A to B, whereas in the lower graph the IGOs

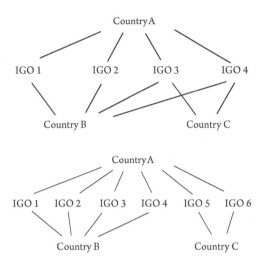

Figure 3.4 Bipartite network involving states and IGOs.

Note: In both graphs Country A shares four ties with Country B and two with Country C.

that connect A to B are entirely independent of the IGOs that connect A to C.

This can have important implications for the way in which diffusion effects are conceptualized. In the upper graph, Country A comes under the influence of four IGOs. IGOs 1 and 2 each have an average human rights score that, for the purposes of this simple example, reflect the human rights performance of Country B alone. IGOs 3 and 4, on the other hand, each have an average human rights score that is equal to $\frac{1}{2}B + \frac{1}{2}C$. So Country A's *IGO Context* is therefore equal to $\frac{1}{4}(B+B+\frac{1}{2}B+\frac{1}{2}C+\frac{1}{2}B+\frac{1}{2}C)$ or simply $\frac{3}{4}B + \frac{1}{4}C$. Note that this is quite different from Country A's *IGO Context* $\frac{2}{3}B + \frac{1}{3}C$ implied by the network in Figure 3.3.

In the lower graph, however, each of the IGOs that A belongs to has only a single connection to countries B and C, so Country A's *IGO Context* is given by $\frac{1}{6}(B+B+B+B+C+C)$ or simply $\frac{2}{3}B + \frac{1}{3}C$. This time the result is the same as that obtained for the simple network shown in Figure 3.3.

This example is desgined to show that applying the concept of a bipartite network to model the norm-diffusing effects of IGOs provides a more nuanced account of the relationship between states and IGOs than is obtained using the more conventional unipartite model. On a practical level, it is can account for the fact that the IGO ties that connect pairs of states are not necessarily equivalent. Some IGOs provide for a more direct channel of communication between pairs of states than others. For example, IGOs 5 and 6 in the lower graph in Figure 3.4 connect Country C to A more directly than do IGOs 3 and 4 in the graph above. Using a bipartite network therefore allows us to account for the fact that the influence of certain states is reduced when the bulk of the connections they have with other states are mediated by large IGOs.

Another advantage of using the bipartite model is that it allows us to examine variations in the relationships between states and IGOs at two different points. Not only can we account for the fact that some IGOs may play a more important role in norm-diffusion than others, but we can also take account of the fact that some states play a more important role than others *within* the IGOs to which they belong. To put it another way, rather than simply calculating the average human rights performance of IGOs 1–6 by taking the mean of the human rights scores of their member states, we could instead weight these state-level scores by some state-level measure of theoretical interest, for example, economic and/or military power. In that case we could test the hypothesis that some states are more influential transmitters of norms than others, even when the structure of the IGO network is held constant. In addition, we can test the hypothesis that some IGOs are more influential over their member states than others. We can also interact the *IGO Context* variable with theoretically interesting state-level attributes to test conditional hypotheses about the receptivity of states to particular types of international norms. These are all possibilities that we'll consider in Chapter 4; for the rest of this chapter, I'll set aside these considerations and focus on the structural effects of the IGO network.

From a practical point of view, constructing the *IGO Context* variable using the bipartite framework takes place in two stages. In the first stage, I take each state in turn and calculate an average PIR score for each of the different IGOs to which the country belonged in that year. (This captures the concept of the human rights culture of the IGO that I discussed in Section 2.1.) I do this by taking the mean of all the PIR scores of its fellow members in each particular IGO while leaving out the PIR score of the focal state to prevent its score from appearing on both sides of the regression equation.[19] For example, the United States' score for its membership in NAFTA in the year 2000 is simply the mean of the PIR scores of Canada and Mexico for that year.[20] In the second stage, I calculate each state's *IGO Context* by taking the mean of the IGO scores for all of the different IGOs to which the state belongs. (In the case of the United States, this would be the average of the

IGO-means for the 93 different IGOs to which the United States belonged in 2000.)

As noted above, as a first cut I shall construct the *IGO Context* variable in a way that assumes that all states have equal influence over the human rights culture of the IGOs to which they belong and that each state is equally influenced by the cultures of all of the IGOs to which it belongs. These simplifying assumptions provide a relatively hard test of the IGO diffusion hypothesis, and will be relaxed when we investigate the effects of sender, receiver, and IGO effects in Chapter 4.

Figure 3.5 provides a series of box plots that show how the distribution of *IGO Context* varies over time. In this figure, the solid black line represents the median values of the variable, the grey boxes the inter quartile range, and the whiskers the minimum and maximum values. A couple of points are worth noting when considering this graph. First, as one would expect, the global median of *IGO Context* is very similar to the global median of physical integrity rights. (Keep in mind that *IGO Context* is, after all, simply a weighted average of other states' physical integrity rights scores.) As a result, the average level of *IGO Context* remains fairly static over the time period used in this study. Second, there is much less inter-country variation in *IGO Context* than there is in the underlying physical integrity rights scores (compare with the lower left-hand panel of Figure 3.2). This again reflects the fact that *IGO Context* is an average of many other states' physical integrity rights scores. Having said that, it is important to note that the *IGO Context* variable does not simply

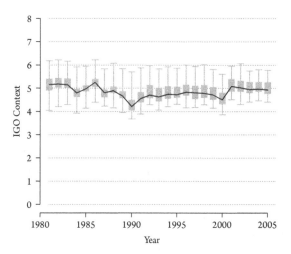

Figure 3.5 Variation over time in the global mean of *IGO Context*.

reflect trends in the global average level of respect for human rights; in the regression analyses that follow, I'll be able to show that *IGO Context* has a statistically significant relationship to physical integrity rights even after controlling for year-specific effects.

The Models

As noted in the introductory section, the goal of this chapter is to establish whether a statistically significant correlation exists between the human rights practices of a state's IGO partners and that of its own human rights practices in subsequent periods. In all of the analyses that follow, I'll therefore be regressing the physical integrity rights index (*PIR Score*) on *IGO Context* while controlling for a number of other variables that are likely to influence states' human rights practices. (In these models, all of the covariates will be lagged by one year.) The unit of analysis is therefore the country-year, but to mitigate the problem of serial correlation I'll be including a lagged dependent variable (i.e., a measure of each state's prior year *PIR Score*) in all models. In estimating these models, I'll begin with a simple ordinary least squares (OLS) framework before moving on to using more complex models.

In testing for a relationship between *IGO Context* and *PIR Scores*, we need to think carefully about potentially important omitted variables—that is, variables that we believe to be determinants of a state's human rights practices but at the same time are also likely to be correlated with its level of *IGO Context*. Broadly speaking, these variables can be divided into domestic and external influences on a state's human rights practices.

On the domestic front, two of the strongest predictors of a state's human rights performance are its level of economic development and the strength of its democratic institutions. The model includes a measure of GDP per capita (expressed in constant 2000 US dollars) obtained from the World Bank's *World Development Indicators* online database. Following standard practice I take the natural log of this measure to reduce the skewness of its distribution. To account for each state's level of democracy, the Polity 2 score was obtained from the *Polity IV* database (Marshall and Jaggers, 2009). This scores each state according to a number of criteria such as the strength of the constraints placed on the power of the executive, the competitiveness of elections, and the ability of its citizens to participate in the political process. Its values range from -10 (representing the most autocratic states) to $+10$ (representing the most democratic states). One would expect both *GDP per capita* and *Democracy* to show a strong positive relationship to the states' *PIR scores*.

Other domestic-level variables that have been found to show a strong relationship to human rights performance include regime durability and population density (Hafner-Burton, 2005*b*). The argument for including regime durability as a separate variable is that more stable regimes tend to engage in fewer human rights violations, irrespective of their democracy scores. One would expect to find that even relatively authoritarian regimes engage in fewer violations of basic human rights if the regime is able to maintain a secure grip on power.[21] The measure of regime durability used in this model was obtained from the *Polity IV* database. This indicates the number of years that have elapsed since a significant change occurred in a country's Polity 2 score.[22] The measure of population density (in people per square kilometer) was obtained from the *World Development Indicators* online database. This variable has previously been found to show a statistically significant negative relationship to physical integrity rights; one possible explanation for this is that increased competition for resources tends to be associated with domestic unrest, which in turn triggers a harsh government response (Hafner-Burton, 2005*b*: 617).

One would also expect states to be more likely to abuse their citizens' physical integrity rights when the ruling regime faces a major security threat. Previous quantitative studies have reported a strong correlation between the presence of civil or international war and the frequency of human rights abuse. A dichotomous indicator for the presence of an armed conflict (defined as a conflict involving the government of the state that results in at least 25 battle-related deaths) was obtained from the UCDP/PRIO Armed Conflict Dataset (Gleditsch et al., 2002).

I also consider two other variables that relate to the relationship between economic globalization and human rights. Here, however, our theoretical expectations often point in opposing directions. For example, one might argue that higher levels of trade or foreign investment can be detrimental to efforts to safeguard human rights because the wealth they generate can help the leaders of oppressive regimes to maintain their grip on power (Meyer, 1996). One could also argue that countries that are more dependent on access to foreign markets and/or capital will have an incentive not to take steps towards improving human rights if doing so makes their exports more expensive to produce. For example, it might be the case that in some countries labor costs are kept low as a result of the government employing coercive tactics to prevent labor mobilization.

On the other hand, one could argue that increased levels of trade and foreign investment lead to an improvement in states' human rights performance. In this case the theoretical argument would be that higher levels of trade and/or foreign investment help to make the country richer, which in turn creates a larger middle class that agitates for better protections of civil and political rights. So far a number of quantitative studies have found aggregate levels of trade and/or foreign direct investment (FDI) to be positively related to high levels of respect for physical integrity rights (Apodaca, 2001; Hafner-Burton, 2005*b*; Hafner-Burton and Tsutsui, 2007), although for a discussion of how different operationalizations of these variables might suggest otherwise see Hafner-Burton (2005*a*); Richards, Gelleny, and Sacko (2001). I take account of the effects of trade and FDI using data on trade as a percentage of GDP and net FDI inflows as a percentage of GDP obtained from the *World Development Indicators* online database.

3.3 Results

A Simple Model

The estimates obtained from the regression analyses are shown in Table 3.1. In presenting these results I depart from the conventional approach to presenting regression output by dispensing with standard errors and significance stars and instead presenting a (two-tailed) p-value in parentheses below each coefficient estimate. This has the advantage of helping the reader gain a more complete picture of the statistical significance of each variable without being unduly influenced by whether its p-value falls slightly to one side or the other of the $p = 0.05$ threshold.[23]

The first column in the table shows the results of a simple linear model of IGO-based diffusion that will serve as our baseline for further comparisons. In this model (Model 1), the *IGO Context* variable is included alongside many of the standard control variables used in models of physical integrity rights, in addition to a lagged dependent variable. This model includes data covering 154 countries over the period 1982–2006. Here we find a positive and highly statistically significant effect of *IGO Context*. Not only is its p-value very low, but its effect size is substantively important: given that Model 1 is a simple linear model, the coefficient of 0.22 suggests that for every one-point increase in the average *PIR Score* of a

Table 3.1 **Models of physical integrity rights.**

	Model 1	*Model 2*	*Model 3*	*Model 4*
IGO Context	0.22	0.31	0.52	0.28
	(0.00)	(0.00)	(0.00)	(0.00)
GDP per capita (logged)	0.09	0.17	0.14	0.09
	(0.00)	(0.00)	(0.00)	(0.00)
Regime Durability	0.00	−0.00	0.00	0.00
	(0.06)	(0.94)	(0.64)	(0.00)
Population Density	−0.00	−0.00	−0.00	−0.00
	(0.02)	(0.13)	(0.18)	(0.02)
Democracy	0.02	0.02	0.03	0.02
	(0.00)	(0.00)	(0.00)	(0.00)
Trade Dependence	0.00	0.00	0.00	0.00
	(0.00)	(0.00)	(0.00)	(0.00)
FDI Dependence	0.00	0.00	0.00	0.00
	(0.95)	(0.98)	(0.32)	(0.76)
Conflict	−0.67	−0.65	−0.68	−0.47
	(0.00)	(0.00)	(0.00)	(0.00)
Lagged DV	0.67	0.51	0.49	0.56
	(0.00)	(0.00)	(0.00)	(0.00)
N	3063	3063	3063	3063
AIC	9773.47	9767.1	9694.33	9224.6

Note: Model 1 is a simple OLS model; Model 2 includes country random effects; Model 3 includes both country and year random effects; and Model 4 is an ordered probit model. P-values are shown in parentheses below each coefficient estimate.

state's fellow IGO members, its own *PIR Score* can be expected to increase by 0.22 units in the following year.

While this might not sound particularly impressive, this does actually turn out to be a significant effect when compared to that of the other variables included in the model. In Figure 3.6 I provide an illustration of these effects by plotting a series of "first differences." These represent the expected change in the outcome variable, *PIR Scores*, that results from varying each of the explanatory variables over its interquartile range while holding all of the other variables in the model constant at their median levels. Of course, because there is some uncertainty associated with each of the coefficients estimated in the model, we have to account for the

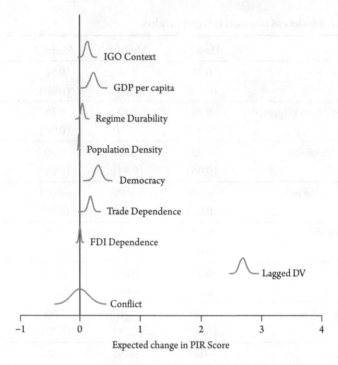

Figure 3.6 First differences plot for the variables included in Model 1.

uncertainty that this introduces to our estimates of the first differences. In the figure I have tried to convey this uncertainty in the form of a probability distribution; the center of the distribution represents the expected values while the length of the tails gives a sense of uncertainty associated with these estimates. From these plots we can see that varying the *IGO Context* variable over its interquartile range has an impact on a state's physical integrity rights that remains substantial when viewed in comparison to *GDP per capita* and *Democracy*—two of the most well-studied predictors of human rights outcomes.

As the results shown in both Table 3.1 and Figure 3.6 suggest, the control variables included in Model 1 behave largely as expected. As noted above, I find a positive and statistically significant effect of both *GDP per capita* and *Democracy*. I also find that *Regime Durability* and *Trade Dependence* have positive relationships to physical integrity rights, while the coefficients for *Population Density* and *Conflict* indicate negative relationships to physical integrity rights. Meanwhile, *FDI Dependence* shows no evidence of a statistically significant relationship to physical integrity rights.

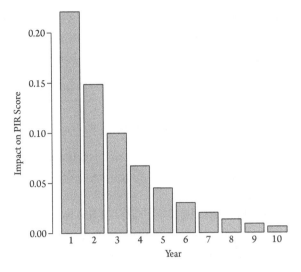

Figure 3.7 Lag distribution of *IGO Context* in Model 1.

In addition to estimating the effects that a change in *IGO Context* has on a state's human rights practices in the following year, we can also take advantage of the dynamic structure of the model to estimate its longer-term effects (De Boef and Keele, 2008). (Keep in mind that all the models include a lagged dependent variable, thereby allowing for changes in the levels of covariates to have effects that propagate through the subsequent periods.) Figure 3.7 shows the estimated impact that a one-unit increase in *IGO Context* will have on the state's *PIR Score* over the next 10 years. As the graph shows, the effect after one year is the increase of 0.22 units in the *PIR Score* that the coefficient for *IGO Context* in Model 1 had indicated. In the second year this drops to 0.15, and in the third year to 0.10. Extending this series indefinitely leads to a cumulative effect (what is referred to in the time series literature as the "long range multiplier") of 0.67 units. In other words, the results of Model 1 suggest the short-term impact of *IGO Context*—that is, the observable impact after one year—accounts for only about one-third of its total long-term impact.

In the remaining columns of Table 3.1, I test whether the effect of *IGO Context* holds up under alternative specifications of the model. Model 2 shows the results of the same model estimated using country-specific random effects. Here I also find a positive and highly statistically significant relationship between *IGO Context* and physical integrity rights, while the estimated effects of the other variables (with the exception of

Regime Durability) remain fairly similar. In Model 3 I include both country and year-specific random effects, and again find similar results. Finally, in Model 4 I re-estimate Model 1 using an ordered probit model and find very similar results.

Upward or Downward Pressures?

The positive coefficient for *IGO Context* suggests that states are becoming more similar to their fellow IGO members. Like all spatially lagged variables, a positive coefficient indicates convergence between the value of the variable (in this case the *PIR Score*) of the focal state and those of the other states to whom it is most closely connected.[24] What it does not tell us, however, is whether this convergence comes about as a result of upward pressures (a so-called race to the top), downward pressures (a race to the bottom), or perhaps some combination of the two.

Theoretically, the convergence we observe among states' human rights practices could be the result of either process. While it's easy to imagine states with poor human rights practices coming under pressure from their IGO partners to improve their practices (whether as a result of coercion or a desire to conform to group norms), it is also possible to imagine situations where these influences lead to downward trends in human rights practices. For instance, states with reasonably good human rights standards might begin to attach lower priority to human rights programs once they realize that some of their more important peers are taking human rights issues less seriously. Indeed, many commentators would argue that the United States' use of torture and detention without trial in the years following the 9/11 attacks has created an environment in which other states feel at license to commit similar violations.[25]

To assess whether the IGO-mediated convergence in human rights practices is the result of either upward or downward pressures, I employ a method that is very similar to that used by Konisky (2007) in his study of the adoption of state-level environmental regulations within the United States. This involves dividing the data into two subsets—one in which the observations are thought to be exposed only to upward pressures and another in which they are thought to be exposed only to downward pressures—and then asking whether we find a statistically significant coefficient for *IGO Context* in the models estimated using the data from each of these subsets. If we find evidence of a convergence effect only among the observations exposed to upward pressure, then we can infer that the convergence we had originally observed using the full data set was primarily the result of a race to the top dynamic. If, on the other hand, we find evidence of convergence only among the observations exposed to downward pressure, then we can explain the original results in terms of a race to the bottom dynamic.

Konisky (2007) suggests operationalizing this in two different ways. One approach is to distinguish between observations (country-years in this case) whose levels of the dependent variable (*PIR Score*) are higher than the spatially lagged variable (*IGO Context*) and those whose levels of the dependent variable are lower than the spatially lagged variable. This separates the states whose own human rights performance is superior to their peers from those whose human rights performance is inferior to their peers. Presumably, a positive and statistically significant effect of *IGO Context* in the first group would suggest that states are responding to downward pressures on their subsequent human rights performance, whereas a positive and significant effect of *IGO Context* in the second group would suggest that states are responding to upward pressures.

The second approach Konisky proposes is designed to capture more subtle signals from a state's peers. Rather than asking whether a state's own human rights practices are higher or lower than those of its IGO partners at any single point in time, we would instead ask whether the human rights practices of the state's peers are rising or falling. The logic here assumes that even if a state already has superior human rights practices to its IGO partners, it might nonetheless continue trying to improve them in response to an upward trend in its peers' human rights record. Operationalizing this involves simply distinguishing between country-year cases whose levels of *IGO Context* are either higher or lower than the previous year.

The results of rerunning the analysis using these two approaches are shown in Table 1 of the online appendix.[26] These results suggest a firm conclusion: no matter how we slice the data, it appears that *both* upward and downward pressures are at play. In other words, shared membership in IGOs is associated with both a race to the top dynamic among the states subject to the influence of others with better (or improving) human rights practices *and* a race to the bottom dynamic among states that are exposed to others with worse (or declining) human rights practices. IGOs would therefore appear to play a role in facilitating convergence among their member states' human rights practices, whether for better or worse.

Alternative Diffusion Pathways?

The results of Model 1 provide some fairly compelling initial evidence to suggest a correlation between a state's physical integrity rights score and those of its fellow IGO members one year earlier. But while these results are consistent with the sort of IGO-based diffusion process that I outlined in Chapter 2, they might also be consistent with some other (non-IGO) diffusion processes. For instance, we know that states often adopt policies that are similar to those of their close neighbors. This has been well-studied in the US context where a rich literature exists on policy diffusion among the 50 states. When considering whether to adopt a new policy, it is likely that state legislators will give more serious consideration to the policy choices of their neighboring states. This could be the result of having more information available as a result of common news sources and greater interaction among the citizens of the two states, or because legislators in one state are more likely to look to their neighboring states when looking for models of successful policies. For example, it is probably no coincidence that in 2008 the state of Washington became only the second state in the United States to adopt a physician-assisted suicide law after Oregon—the state immediately to its south—had pioneered this type of legislation in 1994.

In the field of IR, geographical diffusion has been particularly well-studied in the context of democratization and the spread of liberal economic policies (see O'Loughlin et al., 1998; Kopstein and Reilly, 2000; Gleditsch and Ward, 2006). Studies such as these challenge the conventional wisdom that democratization is primarily driven by domestic, rather than external, influences and thereby serve as an important corrective to first-generation quantitative analyses that have tended to pay insufficient attention to states' geographical and historical contexts. But recently some quantitative IR scholars have gone even further towards paying attention to contextual factors by arguing that "space is more than geography" (Beck, Gleditsch, and Beardsley, 2006)—in other words, that the external sources of influence on a state's policies and practices extend far beyond those of their geographical neighbors and also include culturally similar states, economic partners, and, of course, IGO partners.

This insight has led to some interesting results. For instance, in a widely-cited study of economic liberalization, Simmons and Elkins (2004) find that states are more likely to embark on liberalization programs when states with which they share a common religious identity have already done so. This seems especially surprising given that the major religions have little if anything to say about questions of macroeconomic policy. What Simmons and Elkins (2004) suggest is that it is not the religion per se that has anything to do with these policy choices, but rather that states are more likely to adopt the policies of culturally similar others when dealing with high levels of uncertainty. Religion, in this case, just happens to be a particularly salient marker of cultural similarity.

To account for the possibility that states' human rights policies might be influenced by those of their geographical or cultural neighbors, I create two additional spatially lagged variables that try to account for these alternatives channels of diffusion. Given that IGOs often form among states that are either geographically proximate or that are culturally similar—a point we shall explore in more depth in Chapter 6—including these control variables allows us to more confidently infer that the IGOs themselves are having an effect on human rights outcomes.

First, I try to capture geographical diffusion by creating a variable that I refer to as *Neighborhood Effect*. This provides a simple mean of the *PIR score* found among each state's 10 closest neighbors based upon the distance between their capital cities.[27]

Using a similar logic, I then create a second spatially lagged variable to control for the correlation between states' human rights practices that might result from states adopting policies that emulate those of culturally similar others. I refer to this variable as *Cultural Similarity*. This variable captures the average *PIR score* found among states that are similar to the focal state on three different cultural indicators: a common official language, a common colonial history, or a common religion.[28] In constructing this variable, I first create a weights matrix where each cell takes on a value of either 0, 1, 2, or 3 to reflect the total number of types of cultural tie (i.e., language, religion, and/or colonial history) that it shares with the focal state. I then multiply the weights matrix by a vector where each element represents the corresponding state's *PIR Score* for that year. The result is a variable that reflects the average *PIR Score* found among each state's culturally similar neighbors, where the influence of each other state on the focal state is weighted by the number of different cultural ties they share with it.

While it may be tempting to include all three of these spatially-lagged variables (*IGO Context, Neighborhood Effect,* and *Cultural Similarity*) in a single model, the downside of this approach is that interpreting the coefficients can become difficult owing to the high degree of overlap that exists among the various networks. It is relatively easy to think of examples of regions—for example, Latin America—where any given state's closest geographical neighbors coincide to a large degree with the group of states with which they share the closest linguistic, religious, colonial, and/or IGO ties. This can pose a problem akin to the familiar multicollinearity problem in multivariate regression analysis. An alternative approach, recently proposed by Zhukov and Stewart (2013), is to deal with this problem by estimating a series of models in which only one spatially lagged variable is included at a time, and then assessing which of these models best reflects the underlying structure of the data based upon measures of model fit and/or out-of-sample predictive power. Using this approach, I find that the model with the *IGO Context* variable performs consistently better in a series of cross-validation trials than the alternative models in which *IGO Context* is replaced with either *Neighborhood Effect* or *Cultural Similarity*. Specifically, I find that the model with *IGO Context* has greater out-of-sample predictive power than the model with the *Neighborhood Effect* variable in 74 out of 100 cross-validation trials and also outperforms the model with *Cultural Similarity* in all 100 trials. (I provide a detailed explanation of my cross-validation protocol in Section A.2 of the Appendix.)

Yet using the simpler approach—that is, including *IGO Context* alongside *Neighborhood Effect* and *Cultural Similarity* in a single model, I am also able to show that the *IGO Context* variable remains positive and statistically significant when included in a single model alongside both the *Neighborhood Effect* and *Cultural Similarity* variables (see Table 2 of the online appendix). Taken together, the results of this exercise lend support to my claim that shared membership in IGOs, rather than the cultural and geographic ties that are often correlated with shared IGO membership, are having an independent effect in promoting convergence among states' physical integrity rights scores.

Additional Robustness Checks

Given that the we are dealing with time-series cross-sectional data, a possible concern is that the statistically significant effect of *IGO Context* is being influenced by larger, systemic changes occurring over the 1982–2006 period. For instance, during this period the world witnessed the end of the Cold War as well as the beginning of the US-led War on Terror, both of which presumably have had significant consequences for states' human rights practices.

In a series of robustness tests (full details of which are available in the replication archive), I show that the key finding of this chapter—the positive and statistically significant coefficient of *IGO Context*—still holds in each of the following alternative specifications of the model:

- Including a dummy variable for the end of the Cold War (post-1990);
- Including a dummy variable for the War on Terror (post-2001);
- Including an annual global mean of the *PIR Score*;
- Including year fixed effects; and
- Including a cubic time trend (see Carter and Signorino, 2010).

Interestingly, the results of these models suggest that, conditional on the other covariates included in the model, states' physical integrity rights have been undergoing a slight decrease over the period covered by the study. In an important recent article, Fariss (2014) argues that global levels of respect for physical integrity rights have actually improved over time, but increasingly rigorous measurement standards have created the appearance of human rights practices staying constant or becoming worse in many states. To deal with this problem, Fariss proposes a measurement method that relies entirely on continually updated event-based data. While the new measure that Fariss develops focuses more on political killings than on the other violations physical integrity rights studied here, I find an effect of *IGO Context* that is positive and somewhat statistically significant ($p = 0.10$) when I rerun the analysis using this measure.[29] In other words, the IGO-based convergence effect that I report in this chapter is unlikely to be an artifact of the CIRI index's changing measurement standards over time.

Another consideration is whether the results are being driven by trends within certain states, or groups of states. As a general (but somewhat blunt) test of this, I re-estimated Model 1 while including country fixed effects and found that the *IGO Context* coefficient remains positive and highly statistically significant ($p<0.005$). I also tested whether these results are being driven mainly by the effects of membership in the EU—the IGO which perhaps provides the most likely case for the IGO-mediated diffusion of human rights practices. However, I again found that the effect of *IGO Context* was positive and statistically significant (p <0.05) and that this held regardless of whether I included an EU membership dummy variable or restricted the sample to only non-members of the EU.

Finally, another concern might be that the states with the higher levels of *IGO Context* also happen to be connected to a greater number of IGOs and/or international *non*-governmental organizations (INGOs). To account for this possibility I included as additional control variables the total number of IGOs to which each state belongs, as well as the total number of INGOs with a focus on human rights that that are active in each state. Data on human rights INGOs were obtained from Smith and Wiest (2012).[30] Yet when I included these variables either separately or together, I again found that the effect of *IGO Context* remains positive and statistically significant. (In Chapter 4 I will however show that, as one might expect, the IGO-based diffusion effect is felt more strongly by states that belong to a greater number of these organizations).

3.4 A Detailed Drill-Down

Having presented what I hope is fairly convincing evidence of a relationship between *IGO Context* and *PIR Score* in a large-n setting, it is useful to consider how this relationship manifests itself at the micro level. One way of approaching this is to search for a country whose *PIR Score* appears to have tracked its changing level of *IGO Context* over the period under examination, but where relatively few potential confounding factors exist. One country that meets these criteria is the Kingdom of Bahrain.

Bahrain is a tiny but strategically important island state in the Persian Gulf that has been under the tight control of the al-Khalifa monarchy since British rule ended in 1974 (Owen, 2012). A pro-democracy uprising that began during the 1990s was violently repressed by the ruling regime. This uprising finally came to an end shortly after the new king, Hamad bin Isa al-Khlalifa, came to power in 1999 promising various political reforms (Hanieh, 2013). Despite having made some significant progress towards these reforms, including the dismantling of some of the more repressive parts of the state's security apparatus, King Hamad ended up reneging on his promise to create an independent legislature with real powers (Hanieh, 2013). In 2011, at the beginning of the Arab Spring, growing frustration with the slow pace of reform and high levels of income inequality resulted in large-scale protests in the capital Manama. These protests were brutally put down by the state in conjunction with forces from other members of the GCC.

Turning to the data, we can see that Bahrain's scores on the physical integrity rights index broadly reflect this recent history. After having had a fairly stable *PIR Score* of around 5 or 6 during the 1980s and early 1990s, this value dropped significantly during the late 1990s in response to the government's efforts to put down the popular uprising. It then began to improve significantly in the years following King Hamad's ascension to the throne. Its scores remained reasonably stable at either 6 or 7 during the 2000s before undergoing an even more dramatic decline in 2011 following the regime's brutal crackdown of protestors during the Arab Spring.

Interestingly, these fluctuations in Bahrain's *PIR Score* appear to closely track the changes in its *IGO Context*. To illustrate this association more clearly, Figure 3.8 provides a series of plots showing how Bahrain's *PIR Score*, as well as its levels of *IGO Context* and all of the control variables

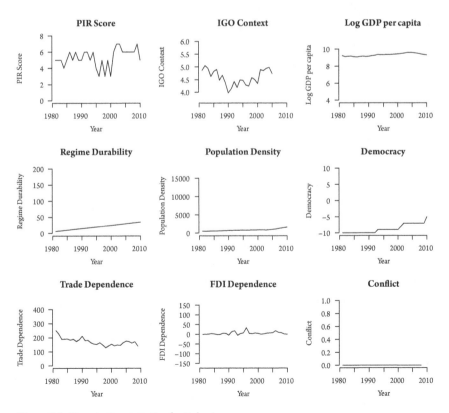

Figure 3.8 Descriptive statistics for Bahrain.

included in the basic model, have varied over the period. To make it easier
to consider Bahrain's performance in a global context, I have scaled the
y-axis of each of these graphs to cover the full range of values found in the
cross-national data.

As the first two panels in the figure show, Bahrain's *PIR Score* appears to
closely track changes in its levels of *IGO Context*. The decline in Bahrain's
PIR Score in the mid-1990s follows in the wake of a steady decline in its
IGO Context throughout the 1980s. Similarly, its improvement in respect
for physical integrity rights in the early 2000s appears to follow a gradual
improvement in its levels of *IGO Context* throughout the 1990s.

Figure 3.8 also shows that throughout this entire period, the levels
of the covariates included in the model have undergone relatively little
change. Bahrain's level of economic development stayed almost perfectly
flat and its level of democracy/autocracy (as reflected in its Polity 2 score)
underwent only a very modest improvement over this period. It seems
that in this particular case, the changes in the levels of *IGO Context* provide
the most obvious explanation for the variation in Bahrain's performance.
But what explains the variation in Bahrain's levels of *IGO Context* in the
first place? Was the state undergoing a dramatic change in its pattern of
IGO memberships during this period, or can this variation be explained
in terms of changes in the human rights behavior of its fellow member
states?

An examination of the IGO membership data reveals that Bahrain
did indeed undergo a significant net increase in its total number of IGO
memberships. As Figure 3.9 shows, its total number of IGO memberships
rose from a total of 29 in 1981 to 50 in 2005. To break this down further,
Figure 3.10 shows how the composition of its IGO memberships changed
over this period. As this figure shows, some of the more notable new
organizations that it joined during this period included the GATT/WTO,
the Arab Labour Organization, and the World Customs Organization.

Yet it appears that the changing structure of its IGO memberships
accounts for only a small portion of the variation we observe in Bahrain's
IGO Context. If we were to recalculate *IGO Context* by assuming that no
changes occurred in its pattern of IGO memberships (i.e., by freezing its
memberships at their 1981 configuration), we end up with a trend in *IGO
Context* that for the most part looks very similar to the trend in its actual
levels. The differences between these expected values of *IGO Context* and
its actual values is apparent from the gap between the lines plotted in
Figure 3.11. As these lines show, the only notable difference between these

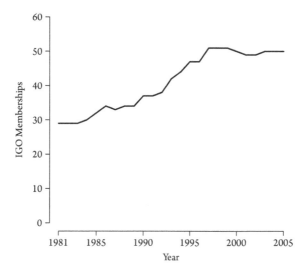

Figure 3.9 Bahrain's total IGO memberships, 1981–2005.

two trajectories comes after the mid-1990s, by which time we start to see Bahrain's changing pattern of IGO memberships leading to values of *IGO Context* that are somewhat higher than would be expected were it to have retained its 1981 configuration of IGO memberships. This suggests that influences from the newly-acquired IGO memberships can account for only a small part of the post-2000 improvement in the state's human rights practices.

Interestingly, of the 26 new IGOs that Bahrain joined during this period, only 7 were restricted to Arab or Persian Gulf states, whereas the other 19 were more global in nature. This is consistent with a story in which Bahrain's improvement in human rights practices (at least in the period before the Arab Spring) was to some extent the result of its becoming more exposed to influences from outside of its region.

Yet while the shifting patterns of IGO memberships can account for a portion of the variation in Bahrain's *IGO Context*, Figure 3.11 reveals that the main source of variation actually lies in the changing human rights performance of its existing IGO partners. Even if Bahrain had not undergone any changes in its configuration of IGO memberships over the period, the trend in its *PIR Score* still appears to follow the general U-shaped trend in its levels of *IGO Context*. This suggests that we need to understand this trend primarily in terms of the changing behavior of the states with which Bahrain is most closely connected through its IGO ties.

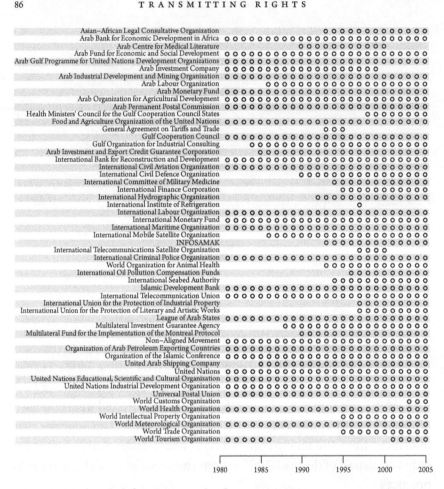

Figure 3.10 Bahrain's shifting IGO memberships, 1981–2005.

Indeed, this turns out to be representative of a more general phenomenon within the data. By re-estimating Model 1 (i.e., for *all* countries)
while using values of *IGO Context* that are based upon membership
patterns that are frozen at 1981 levels, I also find that the overall effect of
IGO Context is very similar to that estimated using the actual (dynamic)
IGO membership data.[31] This suggests that, as the case of Bahrain illustrates, the changing human rights behavior of states' fellow IGO members
is generally more important than changes in its IGO memberships in
accounting for the IGO-based diffusion effect.

Returning again to the case of Bahrain, Figure 3.12 identifies the states
that are "closest" to Bahrain in terms of their relative positions in the
IGO network. The measure of closeness that I construct is essentially
an indicator of the proportion of Bahrain's overall *IGO Context* that is

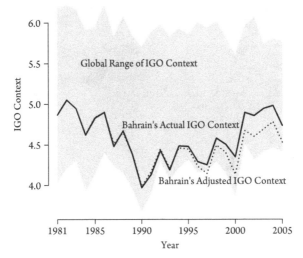

Figure 3.11 Bahrain's *IGO Context* calculated with and without post-1981 changes in IGO membership.

Note: The shaded area represents the cross-national range of *IGO Context* values found within the data at each point in time.

accounted for by each other state. In doing so, it takes account of both the number of shared IGO memberships and the size of the IGOs concerned (given that smaller IGOs presumably allow individual states to exert greater influence over their fellow IGO members).[32]

The map in the upper panel of Figure 3.12 shows how states vary in terms of their influence over Bahrain. Darker shades indicate greater levels of influence. As the map shows, Saudi Arabia and a number of the Gulf states have the greatest influence over Bahrain's *IGO Context*, followed by a large swath of North African states. Interestingly, while it is clear from the shading on the map that geographical proximity correlates positively with the strength of these IGO ties, on closer examination we can see that the relationship is about more than just geography. For instance, despite being located only about 100 miles across the Persian Gulf from the coast of Iran, it appears that Bahrain is influenced to a significantly greater extent by states like Morocco or Mauritania on the opposite side of Africa. In addition, the states of central Asia have much less influence than one would expect on the basis of their proximity to Bahrain. So while Bahrain's nearest neighbors in the IGO network correspond fairly closely to its nearest neighbors in the geographical sense, there is still a notable difference between the two—a point that is consistent with the finding from the cross-national analysis that the statistically significant effect of

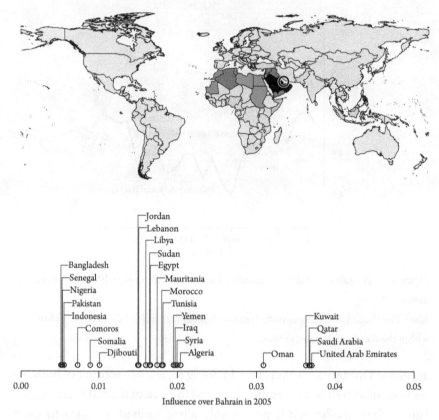

Figure 3.12 Relative influence of Bahrain's influential IGO partners.
Note: In the upper panel, the countries in the map are shaded in accordance with their
relative degree of influence over Bahrain. In the lower panel, the positions of the circles
plotted along the x-axis provides a more detailed view of how Bahrain's 25 most
influential IGO partners compare in terms of their ability to influence its *IGO Context*.

IGO Context is robust to the inclusion of a spatially-lagged variable (see
Section 3.3).

To enable us to view the potential for IGO-based influence with more
precision, the graph in the lower panel of Figure 3.12 plots the influence
scores of Bahrain's 25 closest IGO partners along a number line. This
reveals a tight cluster of four states—the United Arab Emirates, Saudi
Arabia, Qatar and Kuwait—whose members have an especially high level
of influence over Bahrain. Following a little further behind is Oman. Taken
together, these five Gulf states—which happen to comprise Bahrain's
fellow members of the GCC—collectively account for almost 18% of the
variation in Bahrain's levels of *IGO Context*.

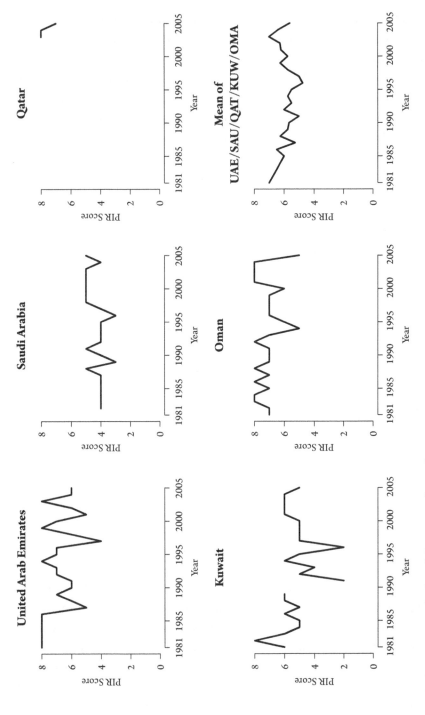

Figure 3.13 PIR Scores of Bahrain's five most influential IGO partners.

Finally, Figure 3.13 plots the trends in the *PIR Scores* (where available) for each of the five most influential states as well as the average of all of their annual scores. As the figure shows, the mean level of PIR score among these states appears to track the U-shaped trend in Bahrain's *IGO Context*, and by extension, its scores on the PIR index.

To sum up, then, the main takeaways from this drill-down exercise are as follows. First, the case of Bahrain allows us to see evidence at the level of an individual state that corroborates the IGO-mediated diffusion effect inferred from the results of the large-n analysis in the previous section. Second, this investigation reveals that variation in a state's *IGO Context* is primarily the result of changes in the human rights practices of its IGO partners, as opposed to changes in a state's pattern of IGO memberships. This finding is consistent with the fact that, in general, human rights practices tend to be much more variable than states' patterns of association through IGOs. Third, the diffusion effect that we observe cannot be explained away merely in terms of geographical proximity. While a state's most influential IGO partners are often found among its closer neighbors due to the large number of region-specific IGOs, the type of influence maps shown in Figure 3.12 reveal that geographical proximity is not the whole story. IGO-based diffusion is therefore not the same as the policy diffusion that is thought to occur as a result of contact between neighboring societies—a point that also emerged from the results of the statistical analysis using alternative diffusion variables on page 80.

Although I have only presented results for the case of Bahrain here, interested readers can easily rerun this entire exercise for any state of their choice using an R script that I have included for this purpose in the replication archive.

3.5 Taking Stock

The statistical analysis I've presented in this chapter has used a relatively simple model of IGO-based diffusion to establish the following. First, states' levels of respect for physical integrity rights—arguably the most fundamental category of human rights—are indeed positively correlated with those of their fellow IGO members. Second, this convergence effect occurs in both directions: states' human rights practices can be subject to either upward or downward pressures in response to their IGO context. Third, this relationship is not only statistically significant but it is also practically important: as the results of Figure 3.6 have shown, the variation in the human rights performance of a state's IGO partners turns out to be almost as important a predictor of a state's subsequent human rights performance as GDP per capita or democracy. Fourth, this diffusion effect is unlikely to be driven by other (non-IGO) channels of diffusion between states; the results presented in Section 3.3 suggest that it is diffusion through the IGO network, rather than through networks based on physical proximity or cultural similarity, that can best account for the observed convergence in human rights practices.

Taken together, these results present a strong initial case for an IGO-based diffusion process. In the next chapter I shall begin to unpack this process by examining the extent to which it is driven by the actions of the more powerful states, or by the IGOs that focus on human rights issues.

4

State and IGO Characteristics

This chapter examines the role that state power and IGO mandates play in the IGO-based transmission of human rights. Recall that in the previous chapter I had adopted a fairly restrictive set of assumptions about the way in which states influence one another through their IGO ties. Specifically, when I constructed the *IGO Context* variable for the regression models I had assumed that:

1. All states make an equal contribution to establishing the human rights culture of each IGO;
2. States are influenced to the same degree by the signals they receive from all of the various IGOs to which they belong; and
3. All states are equally receptive to the signals received from their IGO partners.

Obviously these are not realistic assumptions, and as discussed in Chapter 2, we have strong theoretical reasons for believing that variation at each stage of the three-stage model of norm transmission can significantly affect the overall outcome. In this chapter I shall relax each of the above assumptions in turn in order to test hypotheses concerning the process through which states are influenced by their IGO partners. I shall begin by relaxing the first assumption—that all member states play an equally important role in shaping the human rights culture of the IGOs to which they belong—in order to test whether more materially powerful states, or those with more "soft power," are any better than others at influencing the human rights practices of their fellow IGO members.

4.1 Shaping the Human Rights Culture

Material Power

In the same way that not all employees can be expected to make an equal contribution to shaping the organizational culture of their firms, it seems reasonable to assume that not all states will make an equal contribution to establishing the human rights culture of the IGOs to which they belong. For starters, one might expect that states that are economically powerful will have greater opportunities to influence the behavior of their fellow IGO members. This might be due to their greater opportunities to coerce weaker states—perhaps by linking improvements in human rights to the economic or political issues being negotiated at the IGOs—or simply due to the fact that the richer states are more likely to be perceived as role models by states eager to emulate them.

To test whether richer states have more influence, I can recalculate the *IGO Context* variable used in the models in Chapter 3 in a way that assigns greater weight to the richer states. Recall that I had calculated *IGO Context* in two stages. In the first stage I calculated an estimate of the human rights culture for each IGO in each year by simply taking the mean of the PIR scores for each member state (while excluding that of the focal state so that its score does not appear on both sides of the regression equation). In the second stage I calculated the mean of the human rights cultures of all the IGOs to which each state belongs. This generated the original *IGO Context* variable. Thus, in order to take account of state-level differences in influences, I can replace the simple mean of the states' physical integrity rights scores at the first stage with a weighted mean that assigns greater weight to the richer members of each IGO.

An important theoretical concern is how to operationalize the concept of richer states when thinking about their relative influence within IGOs. To the extent that material inducements play a role in IGO-based diffusion, we would expect that the economically powerful states would be more able to convincingly tie economic benefits to improvements in their partners' human rights practices. This could best be operationalized by measures of total national wealth such as GDP that would rank states like the United States, Japan, Germany, and China among the most influential. If, on the other hand, a process of acculturation is driving the IGO-based diffusion, we would expect the more developed states (but not necessarily those with the largest economies) to serve as more effective role models.

In this case using *per capita* GDP would be more appropriate. It would assign greater emphasis to the role that small states like Norway or Sweden can play in influencing the human rights practices of others.

A second, more practical, question to consider is whether to use the measure of GDP in its raw form or whether to adopt the more commonly used logarithmic transformation. If we were to weight states' influence at IGOs on the basis of their raw levels of GDP, we would, for instance, assign the United States a level of influence that is fully nine times greater than that of Mexico.[1] Perhaps this differential is unrealistically large; yet if we were to instead apply the (natural) log transformation, the relative influence of the United States would be only about 8% greater than that of Mexico.

In light of the fact that reasonable arguments could be made in both directions, I recalculated *IGO Context* using all four permutations of the weighting scheme—that is, using GDP, GDP per capita, logged GDP, and logged GDP per capita. I then re-estimated Model 1 (the simple linear model of IGO-based diffusion used in Chapter 3) while replacing the original *IGO Context* variable with each of these GDP-weighted variants.[2] The effect that this has on the estimated size of the *IGO Context* variable is shown in Figure 4.1. This figure is essentially a first difference plot that shows the estimated change in the level of the dependent variable (the nine-point physical integrity rights index, *PIR Score*) that results from a change over the full range of observed values of *IGO Context* in each of the models under consideration. To better understand how this works, consider first the top row of the figure. This shows the result for the unweighted model—that is, the model that assumes that all states make an equal contribution to the human rights cultures of the IGOs to which they belong. (This represents Model 1 from Chapter 3.) The position of the black dot along the x-axis suggests that were we to vary *IGO Context* over its full range of observed values (while holding constant all other covariates), we would expect the state's *PIR Score* to increase by approximately 0.6 points, with a 95% confidence interval that ranges from about 0.3–0.9.

The second row of the figure shows the equivalent result for a model where *IGO Context* is calculated while weighting each state's influence by its level of GDP. In this case the estimated effect of *IGO Context* is stronger: its mean is about 0.95 and its 95% confidence interval ranges from about 0.6 to 1.3 on the physical integrity rights scale. The remaining rows in the figure suggest that the alternative GDP-based weighted

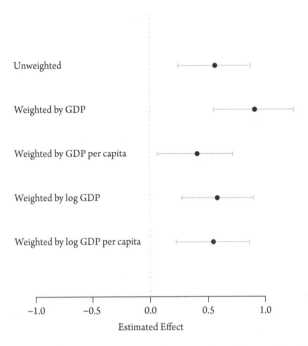

Figure 4.1 Accounting for GDP in setting the human rights cultures of the IGOs.

schemes produce results that are generally very similar to the unweighted form of *IGO Context*.

In order to ensure that these findings did not result from simply "over-fitting" a model to the data, I conducted another series of cross-validation trials using the protocol described in Appendix A.2. The results very clearly indicate that weighting by either raw GDP or logged GDP results in a significant increase in the models' out-of-sample predictive power: these variants of the model outperformed the baseline unweighted model in all 100 of the cross-validation trials. Of these two models, the raw GDP model also outperformed the logged GDP model in all 100 trials. The alternatives based upon *per capita* GDP (in either its raw or logged forms) failed to outperform the baseline model in any of the trials.

So do these results suggest that accounting for the wealth of the state more accurately captures the underlying diffusion process? The answer is a qualified yes: there is some evidence of a larger effect for GDP, but the effect size is modest. At the same time, we see no improvement when weighting by GDP per capita. Taken together, these results suggest that states with larger economies, but not necessarily those that are more economically developed, have somewhat greater influence over the human rights practices of their interaction partners.

Soft Power

So far we have found some evidence to suggest that materially powerful states exert greater influence over the human rights practices of their IGO partners. But what about states that are not particularly powerful in a material sense, but are nonetheless more influential than others due to their greater levels of moral authority, or what we might call their "soft power"?[3] To the extent that states might be genuinely persuaded by the arguments of others (rather than simply coerced by them), we might expect that, when it comes to discussions of human rights issues, a state like Norway is likely to have greater influence than a state like China.

To test this hypothesis, I begin by asking whether only democracies have an influence over the diffusion of human rights norms within IGO networks. States that are not democratic generally have great difficulty speaking authoritatively about the types of individual human rights captured by the PIR index. Instead they prefer to restrict their discussions of human rights to issues such as self-determination, the right to development, respect for religious differences, as well as the obligations to one's community that these rights imply. To the extent that a process of persuasion or acculturation operates, we would therefore expect democracies to be more influential in the diffusion of physical integrity rights than non-democracies.

I create two different weighting schemes to capture differences between democracies and non-democracies. The first involves creating a dichotomous measure of democracy that indicates whether each state has a Polity 2 score of six or higher and weighting the influence of each state in the IGO by that dichotomous indicator. This has the effect of creating a model in which only the established democracies have a voice on human rights issues at IGOs. The second involves a continuous weighting scheme where the influence of each state is weighted by its 21-point Polity 2 score.[4]

I then consider whether a state's influence is moderated by a more direct measure of its human rights performance. As noted in Chapter 3, the relationship between democracy and human rights is not necessarily as straightforward as many observers assume. Some states can score reasonably well on institutional measures of democracy but still perform poorly in terms of preventing human rights abuses. To account for this

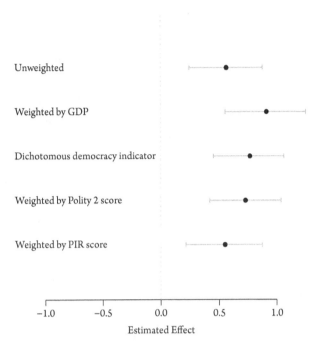

Figure 4.2 Accounting for GDP in estimating the human rights cultures of the IGOs.

possibility, I create an alternative weighting scheme where each state's influence over its IGO partners is weighted by its *PIR Score* (i.e., the same variable that happens to serve as the dependent variable in these analyses[5]).

As before, I use these weighting schemes to recalculate *IGO Context* and then re-estimate the basic model of physical integrity rights (Model 1 from Chapter 3). I then consider the effect that this has on the estimated impact of the *IGO Context* variable, in addition to the out-of-sample predictive power of the model as a whole. The results of these analyses are shown in Figure 4.2. Here we see that weighting states' influence by either the dichotomous or the continuous indicators of democracy results in a modest increase in the impact of *IGO Context* relative to the unweighted baseline model. Its effect is, however, not as large as the effect of the GDP weighting scheme discussed earlier.

When I assess the predictive power of these weighted models in a series of cross-validation trials, it appears that both of the democracy-weighted models produce a robust increase in predictive power relative to the baseline model.[6] This suggests that more democratic states are significantly more influential over their peers in terms of the transmission of human rights norms, suggesting that a persuasion or acculturation mechanism operates at least to some extent. However, weighting states' influence by their existing levels of respect for physical integrity rights results in a model that fails to improve upon the predictive power of the original (unweighted) model.[7]

How do the results for the democracy-weighted models compare with those of the GDP-weighted models discussed earlier? In the majority of cross-validation trials (76 out of 100), the GDP-weighted models do a better job of predicting outcomes than the democracy-weighted models. However, it should be noted that the margin of victory tends to be very small; in most cases the democracy-weighted models do almost as well as the GDP-weighted models, and they certainly do much better than the unweighted baseline model.

Taken together, these results suggest that states that are richer (in terms of their total, rather than per capita, wealth) and more democratic tend to have greater influence over human rights issues in the IGO setting. These results therefore lend support to the view that multiple mechanisms of diffusion are contributing towards the convergence in human rights practices that we observe.

Is There A Tipping Point?

One of the assumptions implicit in the way I have calculated *IGO Context* is that a linear relationship exists among the human rights performance of an IGO's member states and the resulting human rights culture of that IGO. But what if this relationship is non-linear—in other words, what if an IGO develops a human rights-promoting (or inhibiting) culture only if a critical mass of its member states have adopted good (or bad) human rights standards?

In a highly influential article on norm diffusion in the international system, Finnemore and Sikkink (1998) suggest that once a critical number of states have adopted a new norm, a tipping point is reached that causes the remaining states in the system to become far more likely to do so. An interesting contemporary example of this is legislation permitting same sex marriages, which was considered a fairly radical innovation only a decade ago but has since been adopted in some form by a majority of developed countries. Indeed, if we were to examine the adoption of almost any new innovation that spreads through a social system, we would usually find that the pattern of adoption follows an S-shaped curve: the number of adopters rises slowly at first, rapidly increases once the innovation becomes more mainstream, and then begins to level off once most of the population has adopted the technology (Rogers, 2003: Ch. 7).

The logic behind this S-shaped adoption pattern is two-fold. On the one hand, the members of any social system (individuals, firms, states, etc.) are likely to vary naturally in their willingness to embrace new ideas. Usually this characteristic tends to be more or less normally distributed with a small number of early and late adopters on either tail of the distribution and a large majority in the middle (Rogers, 2003: Ch. 7). This suggests that even if all members of the system are exposed to an idea at the same point in time, we should expect to find that the overall rate of adoption rises rapidly once we head towards the middle of that distribution.

The non-linearity of this adoption pattern, however, is exacerbated by the fact that in most cases the members of the system are *not* exposed to the idea or innovation at the same point in time. Instead they are exposed to the idea by coming into contact with other individuals or states who have already adopted the idea. This creates opportunities for a chain reaction or snowball effect whereby one individual who is exposed to the idea can in turn expose many others to the idea, who themselves can expose an even larger number of others, etc. This suggests that the rate of adoption will rapidly accelerate.

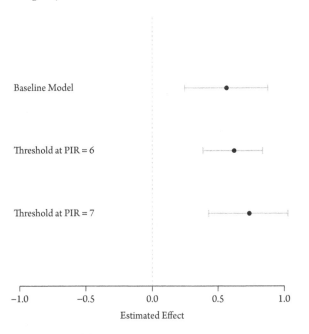

Figure 4.3 Tipping point models.

Is this tipping-point dynamic likely to be relevant to the study of diffusion in IGOs? There are several ways in which we can think of tipping points operating in the context of the IGO-based diffusion model described in Chapter 2, but the one that is most relevant to the present discussion involves the process through which the human rights culture of each IGO is established. So far I have calculated the human rights culture for each IGO by either taking a simple mean of the human rights scores of each member state (as in Chapter 3), or—as in this chapter—by calculating a weighted mean based upon characteristics of the member states. A third option would be to posit that the human rights culture of the IGO is instead determined by some non-linear function of the average human rights practices of its member states. We could therefore test the hypothesis that, once a certain critical mass of states within an IGO has adopted a norm, it switches from being an organization that has little effect in promoting the norm to one that plays a much more significant role in encouraging its member states to change their behavior.

To operationalize this idea, I calculated the *IGO Context* variable according to a different logic. Instead of calculating an average of the PIR scores of each IGO's member states, I assigned each IGO (in each year) a score of either 1 or 0 depending on whether the average *PIR Score* of its members was above or below a given threshold. This aims to capture the idea that membership in a certain IGO will only make a difference to the subsequent human rights standards of its member states if its human rights culture is especially progressive (or regressive). I then calculated an *IGO Context* for each state that was simply the mean of the all of the 0/1 scores of the various IGOs to which it belonged in that year. I repeated this exercise over a wide range of possible thresholds in order to determine whether any evidence exists in support of a tipping point effect.

I evaluated the results of this analysis in the same way as before: I used the cross-validation protocol described in the Appendix to determine which, if any, of these alternative constructions of *IGO Context* improved the models' out-of-sample predictive power relative to the baseline model. I then examined the substantive impact of the *IGO Context* coefficient in each model to determine whether these alternative specifications revealed a stronger or weaker diffusion effect.

The results of this analysis suggest that a tipping-point model does indeed represent an improvement upon the baseline model, albeit by a small margin. I found that when I applied a threshold at a *PIR Score* of either 6 or 7 on the 0–8 scale, the tipping point model outperformed the baseline in all 100 cross-validation trials. However, the substantive significance of the diffusion effect that we can infer from these models is not significantly different from the baseline model. As the results shown in Figure 4.3 indicate, varying the level of *IGO Context* over its observed range of values results in an expected change in the dependent variable that is only slightly larger than in the baseline model. Overall this provides relatively weak empirical support for a tipping point process, at least insofar as the establishment of the IGOs' human rights culture is concerned.

4.2 IGO Characteristics

So far we have considered how characteristics of states affect their ability to shape the human rights cultures of the IGOs to which they belong. Now we'll turn to the second stage of the three-stage model of norm transmission described in Chapter 2 and ask whether differences in the IGOs themselves affect their ability to influence their member states' human rights practices.

As noted in that discussion, one of the most interesting questions to consider is whether IGOs with a human rights mandate (e.g., the UN or the Council of Europe) play a greater role than other IGOs in transmitting human rights norms among their member states. Given that human rights issues comprise most of the formal discussion that takes place at these IGOs, one might think that these are the types of organizations that provide a "most likely" case for the diffusion of human rights practices.

I tested this hypothesis using the following general approach. First, I recalculated the *IGO Context* variable using a weighting scheme that places greater emphasis on the IGOs whose mandate focuses on human rights. Second, I re-estimated the basic model (Model 1 from Chapter 3) using the modified version of *IGO Context* in place of the old. Finally, I considered how the estimated effect of *IGO Context* differs from that of the original model and how the model as a whole differs from the original in terms of its out-of-sample predictive power.

In practice, distinguishing IGOs that are concerned with human rights from those that are not turns out to be rather difficult. While some IGOs—for example, the ICC or the Council of Europe—have an unambiguous human rights mandate, other IGOs—such as NATO—are primarily concerned with a very different set of issues, but nonetheless have incorporated the promotion of human rights into their mandate. In other cases—for example, the World Bank—the IGOs concerned are only just beginning to take the human rights implications of their work more seriously and have not yet made the promotion of human rights a core function of their organization.[8]

In light of these difficulties, I have adopted a number of different approaches to identifying the IGOs that are concerned with promoting human rights, each of which has its own advantages and disadvantages. First, I relied upon the description of the organization's aims that each IGO self-reports to the Union of International Associations' *Yearbook of International Organizations*. (Recall that the *Yearbook* is the source of the IGO membership data used in this project.) I coded an IGO as having a human rights mandate only if the actual terms "human right" or "human rights" appears in its description of its aims. In cases where the IGO had not reported details of its aims to the Union of International Associations, I extracted the relevant description from the organizations' websites (where available). The result is a set of IGO weights that consists of a dichotomous indicator of whether each IGO considers the promotion of human rights to be among its core objectives.

One obvious downside of this approach is that identifying human rights IGOs based only on their self-reported aims casts a fairly wide net with respect to the organizations' interests in human rights: some of these organizations will obviously have a much deeper commitment to the promotion of human rights than others. Nonetheless, this search produced a select group of 18 IGOs that includes the most likely candidates (e.g., the UN, the Council of Europe, and the OSCE) as well as some others whose association with human rights is perhaps less obvious (e.g., NATO, the World Tourism Organization, and the Andean Community).[9] It does not, however, include organizations such as the World Bank that have not yet identified human rights promotion as an official part of their mandate.

Rather than relying only on each IGO's self-reported mandate, a second approach aims to create what we might consider to be a *de facto* indicator of the extent to which each IGO is concerned with human rights issues. To do this, I used Lexis-Nexis searches to score each IGO based on its number of appearances in newspaper articles that mentioned human rights.[10] As one might expect, IGOs such as the UN, the Council of Europe, the EU, the ICC, and the International Labour Organization (ILO) are among the highest-scoring IGOs by this measure. By producing a continuous measure of human rights attention, this approach obviously allows for a more nuanced picture of the extent to which each IGO is involved with human rights. An obvious downside, however, is that the connection between each IGO and human rights issues is not necessarily positive; some IGOs such as the World Bank or IMF score relatively high on this measure because they are often mentioned in the context of the negative human rights consequences of their work.

A third approach relies upon data on human rights IGOs that was recently published in an article by Hafner-Burton, Mansfield, and Pevehouse (2013). In keeping with the predictions of a credible-commitment model, Hafner-Burton et al argue that states undergoing a democratic transition are more likely than others to join human rights IGOs, but only if these organizations impose high "sovereignty costs" on their members. The authors apply their own protocol for identifying the human rights IGOs used to test their argument. Their protocol relies upon identifying human rights mandates based upon information that the IGOs self-report to the *Yearbook of International Organizations*, but it does so using a larger pool of IGOs than I used above. Specifically, it includes the so-called emanations—the more task-specific outgrowths of existing IGOs—that were deliberately excluded from the IGO dataset upon which this study is based (see Section 3.2). The result is a list of 57 IGOs with a human rights mandate, 31 of which are emanations. The authors then code each of these IGOs on a 10-point scale of sovereignty-costs that takes account of factors such as the extent to which the organization focuses on human rights, whether it reports on its member states' human rights practices, and whether it has any enforcement powers. In simple terms, then, the sovereignty cost measure can be thought of as an indicator of how serious each IGO actually is about promoting human rights.

For the purposes of the current investigation, I use the Hafner-Burton et al data to create two different sets of IGO-specific weights for calculating *IGO Context*. First, I create a simple dichotomous indicator of whether each IGO (including the 31 emanations) have been classified by Hafner-Burton et al as human rights IGOs. Second, I weight each of the 57 human rights IGOs (including the emanations) by their sovereignty costs, while assigning a score of zero to all the IGOs that are not classified as human rights organizations. I then test whether the *IGO Context* variable constructed using each of these weighting schemes suggests a stronger diffusion effect than it did in the original model.

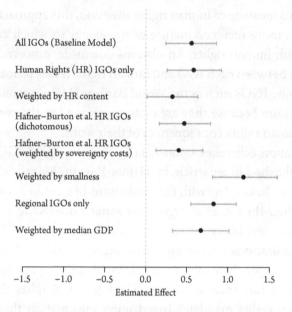

Figure 4.4 Varying the types of IGOs included in the analysis.

Interestingly the results, shown in Figure 4.4, suggest that the IGO-based diffusion effect is not significantly stronger among the organizations that have a human rights mandate than it is in the original model that assigns equal weight to all IGOs. The coefficient for *IGO Context* is positive and statistically significant at the 0.05 level using each of the different weighting schemes described above, but in no case is the coefficient significantly larger than that of the baseline model in which all IGOs are assigned equal weight. (In the case of the model produced using the continuous measure of human rights content, the size of the *IGO Context* coefficient is notably smaller than that of the baseline model.) Moreover, none of these human rights-weighted models succeed in consistently outperforming the baseline model in terms of their out-of-sample predictive power.[11]

This suggests that the ability of IGOs to transmit human rights norms is not restricted only to the IGOs with a substantive commitment to human rights. Instead it implies that the diffusion effect is the result of a more general ability of IGOs to bring states into contact with one another and to provide venues in which representatives of states can come under pressure to conform to group norms—in other words, an acculturation effect.

Further support for this view comes from examining the effect of the smaller IGOs. Presumably, the more intimate settings that the smaller IGOs provide increases the extent to which the representatives of each states come under pressure to conform to the norms of the group. To test this hypothesis, I weighted the influence of each IGO by what I call its smallness—specifically, $\frac{1}{N_y}$, where N is the number of member states of the organization in year y. As the results in the bottom line in Figure 4.4 show, by assigning greater weight to the influence of the IGOs with fewer members, I find that the overall diffusion effect appears to be significantly larger than in the baseline model. Moreover, the model produced using this weighting scheme also outperforms the baseline model in all 100 cross-validation trials. (I also find evidence to suggest a larger-than-baseline diffusion effect when I restrict the sample only to the regional IGOs, most of which tend to have fewer members in the first place.)

Finally, I can revisit the question from Section 4.1 of whether the richer states are better able to influence their fellow IGO members by using a different approach. In addition to assigning greater weight at Stage 1 of the three-stage model to the richer states as I had done in Section 4.1, I can now separately test the effect of attaching greater weight at Stage 2 to the IGOs that are composed of the richer states.[12] Put simply, this hypothesis tests whether states are influenced to a greater extent by the human rights cultures of IGOs like the OECD that are composed of many powerful states than they are by IGOs like the African Union that consist mostly of very poor states.

To do this, I weighted each IGO by the median GDP of its member states and recalculated *IGO Context* accordingly. The result, however, suggests only a modest increase in the size of the diffusion effect relative to the baseline model. A possible interpretation of this result is that material power matters most when states can apply it directly to the other states with whom they share membership in an IGO (as we had found in Section 4.1), rather than through a process of acculturation in which some IGOs start to be perceived as more prestigious (and therefore more influential) by virtue of having richer states among their members.

4.3 Receiver Effects

We can now turn to the third stage of the three-stage model of norm transmission and ask how various characteristics of states affect their receptiveness to the signals they receive from their IGO partners. The analysis in this section can be thought of as the mirror image of Section 4.1: rather than asking whether more powerful states exert greater influence over their IGO partners, I am now asking whether more powerful states are any more or less receptive to the signals they receive from their IGO partners. In the analysis that follows, I test this by interacting the *IGO Context* variable with a number of variables that one might expect to affect a state's openness to external pressure on its human rights performance.

Material Power

Should we expect richer, more powerful, states to be more or less receptive to IGO-based signals than their less powerful counterparts? Theoretical arguments can be made in both directions. From a rationalist perspective—in which behavioral change is always thought to occur as a result of material inducements—more powerful states ought to be better placed to resist international pressure to improve their human rights practices. For instance, one might expect a powerful state like Russia to more easily resist IGO-based pressures on human rights standards than a less powerful state like Ukraine. In the field of gay rights, for example, Russia has conspicuously brushed off efforts by the international community to liberalize its policies and—possibly in response to these pressures from Western states—has adopted even more conservative policies than before.

From a more sociological perspective, however, richer states may be more likely both to receive IGO-based signals and to act on these signals once they are received. Richer states usually field much larger delegations to IGOs than poorer states are able to afford. World polity theorists argue that richer states are generally more "plugged in" to the world polity for this reason (see Beckfield, 2010). For instance, in 2013 Russia's permanent mission to the UN headquarters in New York consisted of 80 accredited diplomats, whereas that of Ukraine consisted of only 13.[13] All else being equal, we might therefore expect a country like Russia to have more opportunities than a country like Ukraine to be exposed to the norms and ideas held by other UN member states.[14]

A related issue is that of implementation. All else being equal, we would expect states that are richer to have greater capacity to implement political reforms in response to external pressures. This is because protecting even the most basic civil and political rights costs money; among other things, it depends upon having a professional, well-paid police force and a reliable criminal justice system—conditions that tend not to be met by many of the poorer states in the international system. This suggests that even if the government of a state adopts an approach to a human rights issue that mirrors that of its IGO partners, it may be unable (at least in the short term) to take meaningful steps towards implementing the necessary changes.

To test whether richer states are, on average, more or less receptive to these signals, I re-estimate the basic model (Model 1 from Chapter 3) in the presence of an interaction term between *IGO Context* and logged GDP. In the first panel of Figure 4.5 I show the results of that model using the graphical method suggested by Brambor, Clark, and Golder (2006). Each point on the graph shows the effect that a unit increase in the key independent variable (*IGO Context*) can be expected to have on the dependent variable (*PIR Score*) at each possible level of the interaction variable (logged GDP). (To help with the interpretation, I've added a histogram below the graph that shows how the values of GDP are distributed.)

The upward slope of this graph shows that as the GDP of the state increases, the effect of a unit increase in its value of *IGO Context* becomes significantly larger. In other words, at higher levels of GDP a state becomes more responsive to changes in the human rights practices of its IGO partners. To make this more concrete, consider the difference between a state like Estonia with a GDP close to the global median (US$8 billion in 2005, or 22.8 on the logarithmic scale) and a state like Canada with a relatively high GDP (US$820 billion in 2005, or 27.4 on the logarithmic scale). Our model predicts that, all else being equal, a unit increase in *IGO Context* can be expected to translate into an increase of 0.17 units on the *PIR Score* of the middle-income state, and an increase of 0.77 units for the rich state—an effect that is more than four times larger.[15] It is important to note that at these high levels of GDP, the effect of *IGO Context* is much larger than its effect size of 0.22 estimated by the simpler, unconditional model developed in Chapter 3.

Similar results are obtained when I estimate an interaction model using logged GDP per capita instead of logged GDP (results not shown). Again it seems that the richer states are more receptive to IGO-based pressures than the poorer states. In both of these models, including the interaction term resulted in an overwhelming improvement in terms of

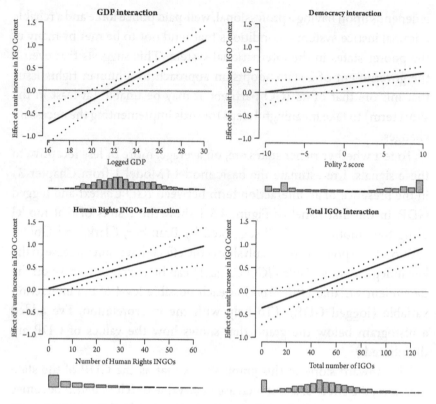

Figure 4.5 Interaction with various characteristics of the receiver states.

their out-of-sample predictive power relative to the models that lacked the interaction terms.

Democracy and Other Factors

In Section 4.1 we found that democracies have greater influence over their IGO partners than non-democracies. But are democracies also any more receptive to the influences of others? In addition to having generally better human rights practices than non-democracies (a point we discussed in Chapter 3), we should also expect them to be generally more receptive to external influences on their human rights practices. This is likely to result from the fact that citizens of democracies tend to know more about what goes on in other societies and have greater ability to hold their leaders accountable if they deviate too far from prevailing international norms.

To test this hypothesis, I performed a similar analysis to that of the GDP interaction discussed above, but in this case I interacted *IGO Context* with the states' Polity 2 score. The results are shown in the second panel of Figure 4.5. As expected, we see evidence of a positive relationship between the level of democracy and the marginal effect of *IGO Context*. For strongly authoritarian states there seems to be no statistically significant effect of *IGO Context*, but once the Polity 2 value exceeds -3 (on the -10 to $+10$ scale) the marginal effect starts to become positive and statistically significant at the 0.05 level. For well-established democracies with a Polity 2 score of 10—for example, Australia, Denmark, Japan, among many others—the estimated effect of *IGO Context* is 0.45. This is more than twice as large as the marginal effect estimated in the unconditional model (Model 1 of Chapter 3).

A related hypothesis concerns the strength of international non-governmental organizations (INGOs) in the "receiver" state. In their seminal work on transnational advocacy networks, Keck and Sikkink (1998) show how citizens are able to bring international pressure to bear on their home governments when they enjoy close linkages to INGOs. One implication of this is that governments of states with stronger connections to networks of human rights INGOs will be more receptive to the IGO-based diffusion effect discussed here. Presumably the governments of these states will be more easily held accountable to their citizens for their human rights practices and therefore more responsive to international pressures.

I tested this hypothesis by interacting *IGO Context* with a count of the number of human rights INGOs active in each state for each of the years in the sample. Data on human rights INGOs were obtained from Smith and Wiest (2012).[16] As the third panel in Figure 4.5 shows, I again find strong evidence of a moderating effect; states with a greater presence of human rights INGOs appear to be significantly more sensitive to IGO-based pressures.[17]

Finally, the IGO-based diffusion effect is also likely to be moderated by the extent to which the state engages with IGOs in the first place. All else being equal, a state that is a member of 100 different IGOs is likely to be more strongly influenced by the behavior of its IGO partners than a state that belongs to only 10 IGOs. As before, I can test this hypothesis by interacting the *IGO Context* with the total number of IGOs to which each state belongs each year. The results are shown in the fourth panel of Figure 4.5. As the upward slope of this graph suggests, the marginal effect of *IGO Context* becomes significantly stronger once states belong to a larger number of IGOs.

Comparing the Receiver Effects

In this section I have been able to show that states that are richer, more democratic, and have more numerous connections to both INGOs and IGOs are more susceptible to IGO-based influences. The marginal effect plots in Figure 4.5 suggest that, over the entire range of observed values of each of these conditioning variables, GDP has the strongest effect. However, this is somewhat misleading given how right-skewed the distribution of GDP data is. To allow us to get a sense of the relative strength of these conditioning effects at more realistic levels of each variable, Figure 4.6 shows the estimates of the marginal effect of a unit increase in *IGO Context* when the relevant conditioning variable is held at its 75th percentile value. For comparison, the estimated effect of *IGO Context* in the simple, unconditional model (Model 1 from Chapter 3) is provided at the top of the figure.

As these results show, all of the interaction models suggest that the effect of *IGO Context* becomes significantly stronger than the baseline model suggests when the relevant conditioning variable is high. However,

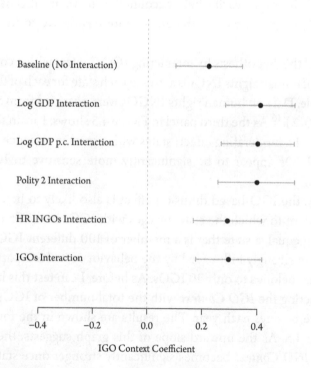

Figure 4.6 Comparing across the conditioning variables.

Table 4.1 **Correlations among the conditioning variables.**

	Log GDP	*Log GDP p.c.*	*Polity 2*	*IGOs*	*INGOs*
Log GDP	1.00	0.48	0.37	0.70	0.69
Log GDP p.c.	0.48	1.00	0.45	0.25	0.33
Polity 2	0.37	0.45	1.00	0.46	0.55
IGOs	0.70	0.25	0.46	1.00	0.80
INGOs	0.69	0.33	0.55	0.80	1.00

what is also apparent from the figure is that the choice of conditioning variable makes relatively little difference: whether we consider GDP, democracy, the number of INGOs or IGOs, etc., the conditioning effect remains similarly strong. This is actually more surprising than it first appears given that the correlations among these conditioning variables—while always positive—are not always as strong as one might expect (see Table 4.1).

Taken together, these result suggest that states that are richer, more democratic and/or are more connected to networks of international organizations are more likely to internalize the human rights norms that prevail among their IGO partners.[18]

4.4 Discussion

It is now useful to take stock of the empirical findings and consider to what extent they lend support to each of these norm-transmission mechanisms. Recall that in Chapter 2 I discussed three possible mechanisms that might account for the observed diffusion effect. Following Goodman and Jinks (2013), I refer to these mechanisms as (1) material inducement, (2) persuasion/learning, and (3) acculturation.

To help organize the discussion in this section, I provide a summary of this analysis in the form of the scorecard presented in Table 4.4. The rows in the table represent each of the main findings from this chapter, while the columns indicate the implications that these have for each of the three mechanisms. Cells marked with a check indicate cases where the empirical finding is consistent with one of the mechanisms, whereas cells marked with an x indicate findings that are inconsistent with the relevant mechanism. (Cells that are left blank indicate findings that do not provide especially compelling evidence in either direction.)

Table 4.2 **Evidence that is consistent with (✓) or that challenges (✗) each of the causal mechanisms discussed in Chapter 2.**

Finding	Material Ind.	Persuasion	Acculturation
1. Richer states have greater influence over the IGOs' human rights cultures	✓		
2. Democracies have greater influence over the IGOs' human rights cultures			✓
3. Insensitivity to whether the IGOs have a human rights (or other) mandate		✗	
4. Richer states are more receptive to IGO-based influences	✗	✓	✓
5. More democratic states, or those with stronger connections to international human rights NGOs, are more receptive to IGO-based influences		✓	✓

In using the data in Table 4.2 to weigh the evidence for and against each of these mechanisms, we need to remain mindful of two important points. The first is that, in some cases, a single finding could be consistent with more than one mechanism. While I have placed a ✓ or ✗ mark in the cells where the evidence seems to most firmly lend or deny support to a particular mechanism, this does not rule out the possibility that the same piece of evidence might also have some implications—albeit less significant ones—for the other mechanisms under consideration. For instance, a powerful state may be more influential both because of its capacity for coercing other states (the material inducement mechanism) and because of its tendency to make other states want to imitate it (the acculturation mechanism).

The second point is that, even if a test were to exist that is capable of perfectly distinguishing one mechanism from another, it is still possible that more than one mechanism can be operating at the same time. For instance, a state's efforts to improve its human rights practices might be motivated both by a desire to maintain favorable terms with its trading partners (see Hafner-Burton, 2009) and by a desire to be perceived by the international community as a more modern state.

With these caveats in mind, we can proceed to evaluating the extent to which the available evidence supports these proposed causal mechanisms. As I shall argue below, the evidence seems to suggest a clear ordering of the various mechanisms in which acculturation is the most important, persuasion is in second place and material inducement is in third.

Let's begin by considering the case for the material inducement mechanism. Perhaps the best case that can be made for material inducement would involve combining the first finding in Table 4.2—the finding that weighting the influence of each state by its total GDP results in a stronger diffusion effect—with the finding from Chapter 3 that a sizable proportion (about one-third) of the total diffusion effect is apparent after only a one-year time lag (recall Figure 3.7 from page 75). At first glance this would appear to provide evidence in favor of material inducement: if states are able to influence the human rights practices of others by linking human rights changes to trade or aid privileges (or to the threat of sanctions), we would expect to find that the more materially powerful states can exert greater influence and that this should result in a relatively quick change in human rights practices.

Yet as noted above, these same findings could also be construed as lending some support to the other mechanisms. For instance, one might argue that more materially powerful states are more likely to become a target for emulation by other states. (In other words, the hard power associated with economic size carries with it a certain level of status that, like the measures of soft power considered earlier in the chapter, could be thought to invite imitation by others.) One might also argue that, by virtue of having a larger and more professionalized diplomatic corps, the more powerful states are better placed to influence others through persuasion. And, as far as the timescale of the diffusion is concerned, one might also note that the bulk of the diffusion appears to take place over a longer time horizon—a result that would be more consistent with either a persuasion or an acculturation mechanism.

What is especially problematic for the material inducement mechanism, however, are the findings of the third stage of the model—what I call the receiver effects (see Section 4.3). Recall from that discussion that if states are influencing the human rights practices of others through a combination of carrots and sticks, we would expect the weaker states in the system to be most vulnerable to this kind of pressure. But as it turns out the results suggest the opposite: the more powerful states are actually *more* receptive to the signals they receive from their IGO partners than are the weaker states. This is a finding that is clearly at odds with the material inducement mechanism. It instead lends support to the view that something other than coercion is going on—something that renders the more powerful states more willing and able to respond to IGO-based influences.

Both the persuasion and the acculturation mechanisms would appear to be consistent with this finding. This is consistent with the view that the richer states maintain greater levels of representation at IGOs and are therefore better positioned to both learn from and effectively implement policies that are similar to those of their fellow IGO members. At the same time, the finding that states that are more democratic and/or more connected to networks of human rights INGOs are more receptive to IGO-based influences is also consistent with the persuasion and acculturation models. It suggests that governments that are more open to ideas emerging from both inside and outside of the state are more likely to adopt policies that are similar to those of their IGO partners.

But how might we distinguish between the persuasion and acculturation mechanisms? Trying to cleanly separate the two mechanisms is difficult, but there are some pieces of evidence that tend to favor acculturation over persuasion. Recall from Chapter 2 that persuasion involves actors deciding to adopt a policy after having consciously evaluated the arguments for and against, whereas acculturation involves actors doing so out of a desire to fit in to a given social environment. With that in mind, the results of the tests of IGO characteristics from Section 4.2 are potentially helpful. If IGOs provide venues in which states can convince other states of the benefits of adopting different policies vis-à-vis human rights—or where they can share some of the technical knowledge required to implement these changes—we would expect to find that the diffusion effect is most pronounced within the IGOs where human rights issues are at the top of the agenda. Yet this is clearly not the case; none of the various attempts in Section 4.2 to weight the influence of IGOs by their human rights content showed evidence of a stronger diffusion effect relative to the baseline model.

However, these results need to be interpreted with care. While this approach provides some evidence to help distinguish between the two mechanisms, there are some important limitations to this approach. For instance, while human rights IGOs certainly generate much discussion of policies aimed at promoting human rights, one could argue they also create an environment in which the human rights practices of their member states become more salient. So a state that is eager to look more like its fellow IGO members might therefore pay more attention to their human rights practices (as opposed to their other characteristics) when it belongs to a human rights IGO than when it belongs to another type of IGO. Another limitation stems from the fact that the networks of IGOs concerning human rights and those concerning other issues are closely correlated with each other. This means that it's not always easy to cleanly separate the effects of human rights IGOs from non-human rights IGOs using observational data.

In my view, the case for acculturation becomes more compelling once we consider two other factors. The first is the finding from Section 4.1 that more democratic states have greater influence over setting the human rights culture of IGOs than do the less democratic states.[19] Presumably the more democratic states are more likely to serve as legitimate role models for other states (consistent with an acculturation mechanism), but are not necessarily more effective at persuading states of the merits of adopting particular human rights policies.

The second, and perhaps more fundamental, piece of evidence stems from the nature of changes in the types of human rights practices of concern to us here. Given that I have been concerned until now with physical integrity rights—that is, the right of the individual to be protected against acts of torture or extrajudicial killing, among others—one would not expect a lack of information to be responsible for the fact that many states continue to violate these rights. In that respect human rights is very different from other policy areas—such as economic development, health, or education—where the work of IGOs such as the World Bank or World Health Organization in facilitating the transmission of technical knowledge can play a critical role in overcoming obstacles to reform. While it is true that the tendency of some states to engage in abuses of physical integrity rights could be reduced to some extent through the provision of technical know-how—for example, by sharing successful models for training police officers—the ongoing repression of citizens in many states is more commonly understood as a choice that their leaders make in an attempt to maintain their grip on power (see Davenport, 2007; Valentino, 2014).

Taken together, the main findings of this chapter are two-fold. The first relates to the question I posed at the beginning of this chapter, namely whether the power of states matters to IGO-based norm transmission. Interestingly, the results of this analysis suggest that it does, but not in the way that is consistent with a typically rationalist understanding of norm diffusion that depends upon material inducements. Instead, these results suggest that power matters in a very different way: it matters insofar as it allows states to make their presence more strongly felt at IGOs and to more effectively receive and implement the signals transmitted from their peers.

The second concerns the role of the IGOs themselves. In finding that the mandate of the organization makes little difference to its ability to transmit human rights norms, these results suggest that participation in IGOs can have far-reaching unintended effects. It suggests, among other things, that human rights scholars and advocates ought to consider not only the implications that states' membership in prominent human rights IGOs such as the Council of Europe have for the development of their human rights standards, but also how these standards could be affected by membership in other, seemingly irrelevant, IGOs.

‖ 5 ‖

Gay Rights and Women's Rights

5.1 Variation Among Rights

So far I have presented evidence to make the case that the global network of IGOs serves as a transmission belt for the diffusion of human rights norms. Yet all of the evidence presented thus far deals with only one category of human rights, namely physical integrity rights. While focusing on physical integrity rights has certain advantages—it is after all the category of rights that people most often invoke when they hear the term human rights—physical integrity rights nonetheless constitute only one part of a larger human rights rubric. This chapter will turn to the question of whether we find evidence of norm transmission consistent with an IGO-based socialization mechanism when we look at other categories of rights.

In doing so I would like to focus on variation along one dimension that I think is particularly relevant to a discussion of the norm-transmitting effects of IGOs. That source of variation concerns the extent to which rights are embodied in international law. This chapter therefore tests the hypothesis that human rights that have a well-established basis in international law tend to diffuse more easily through IGO networks than those that do not. It does so using time-series data on two types of human rights norms that share certain similarities but differ markedly in terms of their codification in international treaties, namely gay rights and women's rights.

Each of these categories of rights involves the protection of previously marginalized groups, but whereas the international human rights regime has taken bold steps towards recognizing the political and social rights of women—including, most notably, the passage of the 1979 Convention on the Elimination of All Forms of Discrimination Against Women

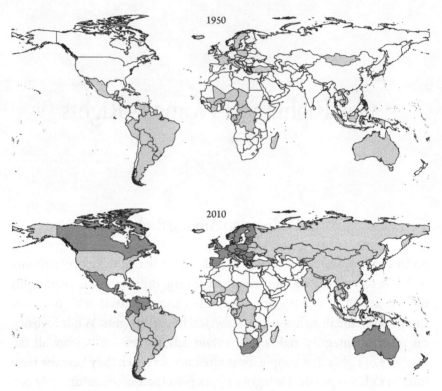

Figure 5.1 Policies towards homosexuality in 1950 and 2010.

Note: States where homosexual acts are legal are colored light grey. States that have taken the further step of passing legislation to prohibit employment discrimination on the basis of sexual orientation are colored dark grey. Data were obtained from Bruce-Jones and Paoli Itaborahy (2011).

(CEDAW)—no similar degree of international legal recognition has been granted to the rights of gays, lesbians, and other sexual minorities.[1] Yet despite its lack of codification in international law—as well as some retrograde steps taken very recently by Russia and Uganda, among others—a large number of states have nonetheless made significant progress towards protecting the rights of sexual minorities (see Figure 5.1). At the same time, social scientists have started to become more interested in explaining cross-national variation in LGBT rights (see Kollman, 2007; Asal, Sommer, and Harwood, 2013; Ayoub, 2014, forthcoming). In this chapter I shall ask whether the difference between the international legal status of these two sets of rights has had a significant effect on the role that IGO networks have played in promoting their diffusion.

Why Might Legalization Matter?

One might expect that once a norm is codified in an international treaty, it acquires a certain legitimacy that facilitates its more widespread adoption. No longer does the norm simply describe the peculiar habits or practices of a particular group of states, but it becomes part of the "logic of appropriateness" that describes the way in which modern states ought to behave (March and Olsen, 1998; Sikkink, 1998; Hurd, 2003). According to the world society scholars discussed in Chapter 2, international organizations embody prevailing ideas of legitimacy and, following this logic, membership in IGOs ought to promote the dissemination of the ideas that are deemed to be more legitimate.

Women's rights represent one such category of rights that, despite significant problems with its implementation, enjoys widespread legitimacy as a theoretical concept. For example, it is fairly clear that CEDAW, as one of the core UN human rights treaties that has now been ratified by 185 states, establishes the general legitimacy of the idea that men and women should enjoy equal rights. Even Saudi Arabia—which continues to place severe restrictions on the ability of women to participate equally in many different aspects of political and cultural life—ratified CEDAW in 2000, albeit subject to the reservation that Islamic law will prevail in the case of any conflict between it and the state's obligations under CEDAW. Although this might suggest that Saudi Arabia is a party to CEDAW "in name only" (Keller, 2004: 39–40), the mere act of ratification has nonetheless signaled the state's acquiescence to the more general principle of non-discrimination against women.[2] Even if intended as nothing more than "cheap talk," this could nonetheless begin a process in which states are increasingly held to account for their behavior by their own citizens and the wider international community (see Thomas, 2001; Baldez, 2014).

Another possible argument for the greater transmissibility of highly legalized norms is more instrumental in nature. It is based on the assumption that complying with highly legalized norms provides greater opportunities for states to develop a reputation for complying with international law.[3] If having a reputation for compliance makes it easier for states to achieve certain foreign policy goals (see Guzman, 2008: 35),[4] we should expect to find that compliance with more legalized norms provides greater opportunities for states to develop their reputations in this regard. Thus, in the cases of women's rights and gay rights, a state that values its reputation for compliance with international human rights law has more to gain by making reforms to its laws and practices that concern women's rights than to those that concern gay rights. In other words, highly legalized norms provide more tangible rewards to states that are eager to signal to their fellow IGO members that they are committed to their international obligations.

Finally, a less instrumental, but perhaps more important, reason why legalization might have a positive effect on a norm's transmissibility is that the process of legalization serves to highlight the importance of a particular norm and to more clearly specify what the states' obligations should be (Finnemore and Sikkink, 1998: 900). In other words, norms that are highly legalized tend to create expectations about appropriate forms of behavior that are less ambiguous and easier for states to follow, which in turn causes the norms to diffuse through the international system more easily. Proponents of the "transnational legal process" view of compliance argue that codification in international law enables a process of identification and management of the causes of non-compliance, which gradually narrows the gap between rules and behavior (Chayes and Chayes, 1993; Koh, 1997). In this sense, states may be equally willing to comply with norms of varying degrees of legalization but in practice will end up being more successful at adopting the norms that are highly legalized.

The International Legal Regime

The difference in the degree of legalization of women's rights and gay rights norms at the international level is striking. While the 1966 International Covenant on Civil and Political Rights (ICCPR) makes relatively little direct reference to women's rights, Article 3 makes clear that all of the rights enumerated in the covenant should apply equally to both women and men. In addition, Article 23 deals directly with women's social rights, stating that no-one shall be forced into a marriage without her full consent and that men and women shall enjoy equal rights during a marriage and following the dissolution of a marriage. Nevertheless, many commentators have pointed out that many of the acts of oppression carried out against women cannot be subsumed within the category of general violations of civil and political rights and require special attention in international human rights instruments (see Bunch, 1990).

In response to this criticism, the international human rights move-ment began to embrace the issue of women's human rights during the 1970s. The UN declared the period 1976–1985 the "Decade for Women," and in 1979 the UN General Assembly adopted CEDAW, which now ranks as one of the most widely ratified human rights instruments. The adoption of CEDAW has also involved the establishment of an indepen-dent committee of experts that monitors states' compliance with their obligations under the convention, and in doing so contributes towards a continually-evolving body of law on women's rights (Baldez, 2014). In addition, the UN has also devoted significant efforts to ensuring that women's rights remain a significant part of its agenda through the spon-sorship of a series of major international conferences that have helped to extract commitments from national governments to better protect women's rights (True and Mintrom, 2001; Gray, Kittilson, and Sandholtz, 2006).

However, at present the rights of gays and lesbians enjoy no such recognition in international law, nor in the work of most IGOs that are concerned with human rights issues. The major human rights instruments have been silent on the issue of the rights of sexual minorities and may in fact have inadvertently provided legal cover to states that continue to outlaw homosexual acts. For example, Article 12 of the ICCPR allows the civil and political rights enumerated in the covenant to be waived when necessary to protect "public order, public health or morals" (Fellmeth, 2008: 806).[5] At present, the only international legal instrument of any sort that deals directly with the rights of sexual minorities is the 2007 Yogyakarta Principles on the Application of Human Rights Law in Rela-tion to Sexual Orientation and Gender Identity. This is not a treaty or convention that is open to ratification by states, but is merely a statement prepared by international legal scholars that aims to clarify the rights of sexual minorities under existing human rights laws (O'Flaherty and Fisher, 2008).

5.2 Data and Methods

This chapter's examination of the diffusion of gay rights and women's rights uses the same general strategy that I had used for physical integrity rights in the previous chapters—that is, regressing an indicator of human rights performance on the relevant measure of each state's *IGO*

Context. Before presenting the results, however, it is worth pausing to consider some of the issues specific to gay rights and women's rights that will affect how I construct these models and how we ought to interpret their results.

Gay Rights

The variable I use as an indicator of respect for gay rights is a simple dichotomous indicator of whether or not male homosexuality constitutes a criminal offense in each country-year observation. The variable is coded as 1 in the cases where male homosexuality has been legalized (or had never been a criminal offense in the past) and 0 otherwise. I constructed this variable using data from a worldwide survey of laws concerning the rights of sexual minorities that was prepared by Bruce-Jones and Paoli Itaborahy (2011) for the International Lesbian, Gay, Bisexual, Trans and Intersex Association (ILGA), a Brussels-based international federation of NGOs that campaign for equal rights for sexual minorities.[6]

Identifying which countries have or have not legalized homosexuality is surprisingly complex. In preparing the ILGA report, Bruce-Jones and Paoli Itaborahy (2011) apply a rule whereby the legalization of homosexuality is recognized in cases where the state does not have formal legislation prohibiting homosexual acts that take place in private places between consenting adults who are above the legal age of consent. This means that country-years will still be coded as having legalized homosexuality if laws remain in place that have higher ages of consent for homosexual sex than for heterosexual sex. This was the case in the United Kingdom which had legalized homosexuality in 1967 but did not equalize the age of consent until the year 2000, following a successful anti-discrimination case brought against the UK government in the ECtHR.

Another difficulty concerns the distinction between homosexual acts involving men and those involving women. Many states that criminalize homosexuality have laws that expressly prohibit homosexual acts among men but either fail to recognize female homosexuality or have less precise laws concerning these acts. For example, in the case of the United Kingdom, female homosexual acts had never been illegal, and when male homosexual acts were legalized in 1967 with an age of consent set at 21, no corresponding age of consent was established for female homosexual acts (Waites, 2002). Because laws with respect to female homosexual acts cannot therefore be used as a reliable indicator of states' policies towards homosexuality, I have coded the *Legalization* variable by reference only to the status of male homosexual acts as reported by Bruce-Jones and Paoli Itaborahy (2011).

A greater difficulty, however, concerns the often large gulf that exists between a state's laws with respect to homosexuality and its treatment of gays and lesbians in practice. For example, in many states in Asia and Africa, homosexual acts are not illegal as such but would nonetheless result in prosecution for other types of public order offenses (Fellmeth, 2008: 815). On the other hand, despite being relatively progressive in terms of its public attitudes towards homosexuality, the United States only officially legalized homosexuality at the federal level following the 2003 Supreme Court decision in *Lawrence v. Texas* that struck down the rarely enforced anti-sodomy laws that still remained on the books in 13 states. However, given the absence of reliable data on states' *de facto* regulation of homosexual acts, I have coded the gay rights legalization variable to reflect states' *de jure* regulation of homosexuality only.[7]

Women's Rights

I construct a composite measures of women's rights by combining three separate variables from the CIRI dataset. Cingranelli and Richards (2004) have constructed measures of women's political social, and economic rights based upon a content analysis of the US State Department's Country Reports on Human Rights Practices. These variables are designed to capture both the extent to which each country has legislation in place to safeguard women's rights and the extent to which these laws are actually enforced. Each of these variables is coded on a four-point (0–3) scale where 0 represents the lowest and 3 the highest level of respect for women's rights in that particular category.[8]

The *Women's Political Rights* variable captures the extent to which women are allowed to participate in the political process, as well as the extent to which women are represented in the national legislature and/or high-ranking political positions.[9] Countries that have no laws granting political rights to women are given a score of zero (e.g., Saudi Arabia, or Afghanistan under the Taliban regime). Countries that grant women the legal right to participate in the political process, but where only a small proportion of political positions are held by women, are assigned scores of 1 or 2 (depending on whether women constitute less than 5% or less than 30% of political positions, respectively). A score of 3 is awarded to any country in which more than 30% of political positions are held by women. Importantly, the CIRI dataset treats women's political rights as independent of democracy. Some non-democracies like Cuba still attain the highest possible score in this category provided that there are no laws that treat women differently from men with respect to political participation, and that women constitute at least 30% of seats in the national legislature (Cingranelli and Richards, 2008: 72).[10]

The *Women's Social Rights* variable concerns the ability of women to enjoy the same rights as men in the realms of education, family life (e.g., with respect to divorce and inheritance), and property ownership. This category also includes the right to be protected from violent cultural practices such as forced circumcision, honor killings, and bride burnings, but does not extend to women's rights to be protected against individual acts of sexual or physical violence (Cingranelli and Richards, 2008: 85). As with the *Political Rights* variable, *Social Rights* is coded as zero in country-year cases where no legal protections exist but is otherwise given a score ranging from 1 to 3 depending on the scope of these legal rights and the extent to which the government enforces them in practice.

Finally, the *Economic Rights* variable concerns women's rights in the workplace. This includes, for example, the right to equal pay and to non-discrimination in hiring decisions. It too is coded on the 0–3 scale in a way that reflects both the extent of the laws on the books to guard against discrimination and the extent to which these laws are actually enforced.

For the purposes of the analysis in this chapter, I add these three measures of women's rights together to create a 10-point composite measure that I refer to as simply *Women's Rights*. Although this variable ranges in value from 0 to 9, its global median value remains remarkably steady at a constant four points throughout the entire 1981–2005 period. Obviously this statistic obscures some important variation both within and across countries; in order to give a more complete picture of how states' performance on this measure varies, I present a series of mini-graphs, or sparklines (Tufte, 2006), in Figure 5.2 showing how each state's score varies over the 1981–2005 period.

The Models

In this chapter I test for the existence of an IGO-based diffusion effect using the same framework as before. This involves constructing a diffusion

Figure 5.2 Trends in women's rights scores among all countries in the data.

Note: The x-axis for each sparkline represents the years 1981–2005, while the y-axis represents the country's score on the *Women's Rights* variable.

variable, *IGO Context*, that captures the average level of respect for the relevant variable (i.e., gay rights or women's rights) among each state's IGO partners at each point in time.[11] As in Chapter 3, in the first instance I calculate this by assuming that all states make an equal contribution to establishing the human rights cultures of the IGOs to which they belong, and that all IGOs are equally influential over their member states. At the next stage I'll follow the protocol I had used in Chapter 4 to relax these assumptions.

Recall from Chapter 3 that *IGO Context* is a variable whose values lie on the same scale as the human rights indicator on which it is based and whose values can be interpreted as the average of the relevant human rights practices found among a state's IGO partners. In the case of the dichotomous measure of gay rights legislation, the level of *IGO Context* will therefore be bound between 0 and 1, and its exact value can loosely be thought of as the *proportion* of a state's interaction partners that have adopted the norm. For instance, in 2005 India had an *IGO Context* with respect to legalization of homosexuality of 0.57, whereas the corresponding value for Uganda was 0.47. This suggests that, on average, India received more progressive examples of gay rights policy from its IGO partners in 2005 than did Uganda.[12]

As before, I test the IGO-based diffusion effect by regressing each of the dependent variables on the relevant *IGO Context* measure in the presence of relevant covariates. However, the different nature of my measures of gay rights and women's rights calls for different types of regression analysis in each case. In the case of the gay rights models, the dependent variable is a dichotomous indicator of whether the state has legalized homosexual acts. However, given that states that have enacted a progressive piece of legislation with respect to gay rights are generally very unlikely to repeal that legislation, I am interested only in modeling the transition to (rather than the maintenance of) more progressive gay rights policies.[13] I therefore use an event history model that has time-to-legalization of homosexual sex as its dependent variable. Moreover, given that the data involves a number of time-varying covariates and that I want to avoid making any assumptions about how the probability of adoption of these laws changes over time, I use a simple discrete-time logit specification where the unit of analysis is the country-year and where the cases representing each country-year following adoption of the laws are excluded (see Box-Steffensmeier and Jones, 2004: Ch. 11). This ensures that country-year observations are included in the data used to estimate the model only for the period of time during which the country is "at risk" of experiencing the event (which, in this context, means adoption of the relevant legislation).

For the models of *Women's Rights*, the dependent variable is ordinal in nature, with possible scores ranging from 0 to 9. While ordered probit or logit models are in principle more appropriate for ordinal variables, in cases where the number of levels is high a simpler OLS model tends to produce substantively similar results. I therefore present the results of OLS models but I show in Table 4 of the online appendix that the results

Table 5.1 **Models of gay rights and women's rights.**

	Gay Rights	Women's Rights
IGO Context	11.45	0.28
	(0.00)	(0.00)
GDP per capita	0.27	0.01
	(0.21)	(0.35)
Polity 2	0.08	0.01
	(0.07)	(0.00)
New Democracy	0.50	−0.03
	(0.33)	(0.53)
Regime Durability	−0.01	0.00
	(0.03)	(0.02)
Population Density	−0.00	−0.00
	(0.51)	(0.82)
Trade Dependence	−0.01	0.00
	(0.27)	(0.72)
FDI Dependence	0.02	−0.00
	(0.60)	(0.96)
Conflict	−0.58	−0.12
	(0.36)	(0.00)
Lagged DV		0.81
		(0.00)
N	1841	2496
AIC	250.82	5456.54

Note: P-values are shown in parentheses below each coefficient estimate.

presented in Table 5.1 are similar in sign and statistical significance to those obtained using an ordered probit model. In the models of women's rights, I include a one-year lagged dependent variable in an attempt to minimize the bias that results from serial correlation among the levels of the dependent variable.

To ensure consistency with the results of the previous chapters, I begin with a baseline model that includes the same battery of covariates that I used in the models of physical integrity rights.[14] I then examine the impact of including some additional variables that recent work has found to be associated with trends in gay rights. However, because the measures of gay and women's rights are more focused on the passage of legislation than was the measure of physical integrity rights used in Chapter 3, I include an additional variable in the baseline model called *New Democracy* that indicates whether the state has undergone a transition to democracy within the previous five years,[15] or, in the case of newly-independent states, whether the state is democratic and less than five years old. Presumably, recently formed democracies will be more willing than others to establish their liberal credentials by enacting relevant legislation, a pattern which has been noted with respect to the greater willingness of new democracies to bind themselves to international human rights treaties (Moravcsik, 2000).[16] Empirical studies by world society scholars of the adoption of women's suffrage have also suggested that newly-created states are more likely to take advantage of the window of opportunity that the act of independence creates for the enactment of global cultural norms (Ramirez, Soysal, and Shanahan, 1997; Paxton, Hughes, and Green, 2006).[17]

For both the gay rights and women's rights models, I lag all of the independent variables by one year to ensure that the covariates always reflect levels of the variables that exist prior to the point in time at which the dependent variable is measured. The women's rights data are limited by the availability of the CIRI variables. Available data on gay rights policies cover a much longer period, but, because of limitations in the availability of data for GDP per capita, the regression models for the gay rights and women's rights models cover the period 1960–2005 and 1981–2005 respectively.

5.3 Results

The results of these models are shown in Table 5.1. Again, I have presented the p-values in parentheses below each coefficient estimate instead of its standard errors. In the case of both the gay rights and the women's rights models, we can see that the estimated effect of *IGO Context* appears to be positive and statistically significant. Moreover, a series of cross-validation trials shows that the inclusion of the *IGO Context* variable results in a consistent increase in the out-of-sample predictive power of the models.[18]

To give a sense of the substantive size of the IGO-based diffusion effects, Figure 5.3 consists of a series of marginal effect plots that show how variation over the range of the relevant *IGO Context* variable affects the expected levels of the outcome variable. (In these graphs, the values of

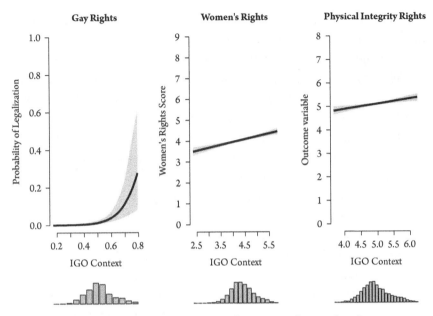

Figure 5.3 Effect that variation over the range of *IGO context* has on the relevant outcome variable.

Note: In each case the values of all other covariates are held constant at their median levels. The grey bands represent the 95% confidence intervals. Below each graph is a histogram showing the distribution of the relevant *IGO Context* variable within the data.

all other covariates are held constant at their median levels.) For instance, from the graph shown in first panel of that figure—representing the gay rights model—we can see that the probability of a state adopting the relevant legislation in a given year remains very low until the value of *IGO Context* exceeds about 0.6 (i.e., the point at which 60% of its IGO partners have legalized homosexual acts.) From that point on the probability of legalization begins to increase sharply as the value of *IGO Context* continues to increase.[19] A closer look at the underlying data suggests that when *IGO Context* is varied over its interquartile range, the probability that an "average" state changes its policy in a single year increases from 0.006 to 0.026—more than a four-fold increase.

Comparing these effects to that of the *Women's Rights* model is somewhat difficult due to the fact that two very different types of regression models are used. (Recall that the gay rights models are event history models implemented in a logit framework, whereas the women's rights model is a simple OLS model that includes a lagged dependent variable.) This makes an apples-to-apples comparison of the *IGO Context* coefficients impossible to do, but it is nevertheless interesting to note from the middle panel of Figure 5.3 that the diffusion effect implied by the women's rights model is slightly larger than that for physical integrity rights: an increase over the interquartile range of its *IGO Context* variable (while holding all other covariates at their median levels) leads the expected value of *Women's Rights* (on the 0–9 point scale) to increase from 3.96 to 4.14. The corresponding figures for physical integrity rights suggest an increase (on the 0–8 point PIR scale) from 5.02 to 5.09.

In a separate series of robustness tests, I modified the model of gay rights to include controls for two other variables that, according to recently published work, can have a statistically significant impact on the adoption of gay rights legislation. Asal, Sommer, and Harwood (2013) report that states with a common law tradition are more likely to continue to outlaw homosexual acts, while Ayoub (2014) finds that European states that are more closely connected to transnational networks of LGBT organizations are more likely to pass legislation protecting LGBT rights. The results of these tests—details of which are provided in Table 5 of the online appendix—show that the *IGO Context* variable remains statistically significant when included in models that include a dummy variable for a British legal tradition and in those that include a count of the total number of human rights INGOs active in the state.

Alternative Diffusion Pathways

As noted in Chapter 3, an alternative explanation for any effect of *IGO Context*—whether in the context of women's rights, gay rights, or any other dependent variable—is that the observed correlation is in fact due to other, non-IGO related, processes of interaction that facilitate norm diffusion among states. In other words, the argument would be that states that engage in frequent interaction with one another outside of IGOs (perhaps as a result of simple geographical proximity) would be more likely to adopt the same policies as their neighbors *and* would be more likely to belong to the same IGOs in the first place. In that case, IGO ties would appear to be responsible for the correlation between the women's rights practices of one state and those of its interaction partners when in actual fact the underlying mechanism has nothing to do with IGOs. It might instead involve, for example, the fact that geographically proximate states are exposed to similar cultural influences and/or tend to have large movements of people taking place between them.

In order to account for the possibility that the positive coefficient for *IGO Context* could be capturing some other sort of (non-IGO related) diffusion process, I adopt the same two-pronged approach used in Chapter 3. I first re-estimate the models in the presence of three additional covariates that are designed to capture alternative channels of diffusion. These consist of (1) a geographical spatial lag that is simply the mean of the relevant gay rights or women's rights variable among the 10 geographically closest states; (2) a cultural spatial lag that reflects the average gay rights/women's rights scores found among the states that share a common language, religion and/or colonial heritage with the focal state (see details in Section 3.3); and (3) a *global* average of the relevant gay rights/women's rights variable (designed to capture more universal influences on a state's policies).[20]

The results obtained when re-estimating the models of gay rights and women's rights in the presence of these additional control variables are shown in Table 6 of the online appendix. These results show that the estimated effect of *IGO Context* remains positive and statistically significant in both models. As was the case in Chapter 3, in each case I am again able to show that these models perform better in terms of their out-of-sample predictive power than the corresponding models that lack the *IGO Context* variable.

Although these results suggest that the effect of *IGO Context* is robust to the inclusion of these alternative channels of diffusion, one drawback of this approach is that the various spatial lags are likely to overlap to a significant extent. An alternative solution is to try sequentially replacing the *IGO Context* variable with each of the alternative spatial lags and pit these models against each other in a head-to-head test of their predictive power. This is the procedure I employed in Section 3.3, as recommended by Zhukov and Stewart (2013).

The results of this analysis are presented in Table 5.2. In the case of the gay rights models, the model that contains the *IGO Context* variable outperforms all other spatial lags across the 100 cross-validation trials, thereby lending further support to the IGO-based diffusion hypothesis. However, in the women's rights models, I find that while the model with *IGO Context* outperforms the models with the *Common Culture* and *Global Norm* variables, this is not true in the case of the model with the geographic spatial lag (*Neighborhood Effect*). In this particular case (see

Table 5.2 **Out-of-sample predictive power of models that replace *IGO Context* with alternative spatial lags.**

Non-IGO Diffusion Pathway	Outperformed by IGO Context?	
	Gay Rights	Women's Rights
Neighborhood Effect	Yes (94:6)	No (0:100)
Common Culture	Yes (90:10)	Yes (100:0)
Global Norm	Yes (94:6)	Yes (100:0)

Note: The numbers in parentheses indicate the number of times that the model was outperformed by the model containing IGO Context in a series of 100 cross-validation trials.

the cell highlighted in grey), the model with the geographical spatial lag outperforms the model with *IGO Context* in all 100 cross-validation trials.

What do these findings imply for our study of IGO-based diffusion of gay rights and women's rights? The results with respect to gay rights make a clear case for the importance of IGO-based diffusion. While the finding with respect to geographic diffusion of women's rights casts some doubt on the extent to which shared IGO membership is responsible for the observed convergence in women's rights policies, this finding is not in itself sufficient to exclude the role played by IGOs. Indeed, in a subsequent test, I find that adding *IGO Context* to the model of women's rights that contains the *Neighborhood Effect* spatial lag results in a consistent (93:7) improvement in its out-of-sample predictive power. In this case, the estimated coefficient of *IGO Context* is again positive with a p-value of around 0.02. Taken together, these results suggest that while geographical or cultural channels of diffusion are likely to play some role in the transmission of gay and women's rights, IGO-based diffusion is likely to still have a significant independent effect.

Testing Sender, IGO, and Receiver Effects

The results for gay rights and women's rights that I have presented so far use the simple form of the *IGO Context* variable. Recall from Chapter 3 that I constructed this in a way that assumes that (1) all states make an equal contribution to establishing the human rights culture of the IGOs to which they belong; (2) all IGOs are equally influential when it comes to changing the behavior of their member states; and (3) all states are equally receptive to the signals they receive from their IGO partners.

Because these are clearly very restrictive assumptions, I shall now follow the procedure used in the previous chapter to study the effects that relaxing each of these assumptions has on the apparent transmissibility of the norms through the IGO network.

I begin by testing for the presence of what I shall call sender effects. Recall from Chapter 4 that this is the idea that some states may have a greater potential to influence their fellow IGO members than others. For example, rather than assuming that all member states have an equal impact on the human rights culture of an IGO like the OAS, I can adapt the model to account for the fact that the United States is likely to have far greater influence over the OAS than do states like Panama or the Dominican Republic. I do this by recalculating the *IGO Context* variable in a way that weights the influence of each state by either its GDP or its democracy score. The results of these tests—details of which are provided in Section 7 of the online appendix—suggest no sender effects for the gay rights models, but they do suggest that richer or more democratic states have greater influence over the transmission of women's rights. These findings for women's rights are therefore similar to those of the physical integrity rights models discussed in the previous chapter.

As was the case with the models of physical integrity rights, I again found no compelling evidence to suggest that IGOs with a human rights mandate are more effective at inducing convergence among their members than are other types of IGOs. The results are mixed and appear to be sensitive to the choice of coding scheme used to identify IGOs with a human rights mandate (see details in Section 4.2). This again lends support to the argument that it is membership in the larger IGO network—rather than membership in certain critical types of IGOs—that matters most for norm diffusion.

Finally, I tested for the presence of what I call receiver effects. This involves asking whether some states are more receptive than others to the signals or pressures they receive from their fellow IGO members. Recall from Chapter 4 that I found that richer states tend to be *more* receptive to IGO-based based pressures than poorer states. I had suggested that this result is more consistent with an acculturation mechanism than one that depends upon the stronger states coercing the weak into changing their policies. In the case of both gay rights and women's rights, I again find the same result: at higher levels of GDP, the estimated effect of *IGO Context* is stronger in both models (see Figures 3 and 4 in the online appendix). However, the evidence in support of a moderating effect of the other receiver variables considered in Chapter 4—namely, democracy, human rights INGOs, and the total number of IGOs—is less compelling than it is for physical integrity rights.

5.4 Discussion

This chapter began by laying out a number of arguments as to why norms that are more clearly enumerated in international law ought to diffuse more easily through IGO networks than norms that lack such a foundation. The results, however, have not supported that hypothesis: the norm concerning the legalization of homosexuality appears to have diffused successfully through IGO networks in spite of the fact that it lacks support in any of the major human rights instruments. Although it is difficult to directly compare the effects of the *IGO Context* variables in these two very different models, the substantive effects presented in Figure 5.3 suggest that IGOs play a significant role in the diffusion of both norms.[21]

The finding that IGO-mediated norm diffusion takes place in a way that does not appear to depend upon the legal status of the norm provides further evidence in support of the acculturation mechanism discussed earlier. If, for the reasons discussed at the beginning of this chapter, states have an interest in adopting norms that are deemed more legitimate in the eyes of the international community, then we should find that states are more likely to adopt the women's rights standards than the gay rights standards of their fellow IGO members. In other words, if the international political rewards on offer for protecting women's rights are significantly higher than the equivalent rewards for protecting gay rights, then states should be more likely to pay the domestic political costs of doing so. Instead we find that, in general, both types of norm diffuse relatively easily through IGO ties, suggesting that the mechanism involved is more likely to involve a process of socialization than a straightforward calculation of costs and benefits on the part of the states involved.

An alternative explanation for these findings may be that even without a strong foundation in international law to support the adoption of gay rights, some IGOs have nonetheless taken a strong stand on this issue and have exerted pressure on their member states to make the necessary reforms. The most prominent example of this is the Council of Europe which, following the 1981 decision of the ECtHR in *Dudgeon v.*

United Kingdom, has effectively prevented European states from outlawing private homosexual acts among consenting adults (Fellmeth, 2008: 819). However, the tests of IGO effects carried out in Section 5.3 suggest that the IGO-mediated diffusion effect is not enhanced when we restrict the analysis to subsets of IGOs that have a specific human rights mandate.

What about the characteristics of the states themselves? Surprisingly— yet consistent with the results of the previous chapter—the balance of evidence suggests that richer, more powerful states are actually more receptive to these norms (regardless of their degree of legalization) than are poorer states. This poses a challenge to much of the existing literature on norm diffusion that has assumed that powerful states are better positioned both in terms of their ability to influence others and to resist outside influences. For instance, the mechanism of norm transmission proposed by Keck and Sikkink (1998) involves transnational advocacy networks enlisting powerful states to bring pressure to bear on the target states. One clear implication of this is that more powerful states are better placed to resist external pressures, and are therefore less likely to change their behavior. Indeed, in a study of states' decisions to adopt policies protecting women against domestic violence, Hawkins and Humes (2002) argue that states that are poorer or less stable tend to be more susceptible to the effects of international socialization than richer, more stable states.

However, the findings I present here and in the previous chapter suggest that richer, more powerful states are actually more receptive to IGO-based signals with respect to human rights. Once again this is at odds with a mechanism that relies on states applying pressure on their IGO partners; rather, it would seem to be more consistent with a story in which richer states have a greater capacity to learn from and implement policies that have been adopted by other states.

The results of this chapter lend further weight to the view that IGOs play an important role in norm diffusion—a function that has been largely overlooked in debates about the impact of IGO membership. As noted at the beginning of the chapter, the study of gay rights is especially interesting in light of the fact that it is a category of human rights that currently enjoys relatively little recognition in international law. But the study of gay rights is also interesting for another reason: while most people living in the Western world tend to assume that sooner or later all states will adopt progressive policies with respect to gay rights, some recent events in states such as Uganda, Nigeria, Russia, and India have suggested a troubling counter-movement. If these events develop into a larger movement to claw back some of the hard-fought victories of the gay rights movement, an interesting question for future research to consider is whether IGO-based socialization is perhaps complicit in this process. After all—and as the results of Section 3.3 had indicated—there is no reason to expect that a process of acculturation in IGOs should be restricted only to the transmission of progressive norms (Goodman and Jinks, 2013: Ch. 4).

6

Cause or Effect?

6.1 Introduction

The previous chapters have demonstrated the existence of a strong correlation between the human rights practices of a given country and those of its fellow IGO members. They have also shown that this convergence effect is apparent across a number of different types of human rights issues. But while the statistical models have included temporally lagged covariates, it is nonetheless possible that this correlation is at least in part due to states selecting themselves into IGOs whose members have similar human rights practices to their own—in other words, the homophily argument set out in Chapter 2. To the extent that this could be true, the proposed norm-diffusing effect of IGO membership may be smaller than the results of the previous chapters suggest.

In this chapter I evaluate the validity of that alternative explanation by building a model of states' decisions to join other states in co-membership of IGOs. In doing so I report two key findings. The first is that when states decide whether to join IGOs they generally do *not* take into consideration the human rights practices of the organizations' existing members. This lends further support to the view that the correlation we observe between states' human rights practices and those of their fellow IGO members is the result of a social influence effect, rather than a homophily effect.

At the same time, I use the analysis in this chapter to shine more light on the factors motivating states to join IGOs in the first place. This leads to the second key finding, namely that cultural similarity plays a surprisingly important role in states' IGO-joining behavior. I find that states that are similar to each other on a number of different cultural dimensions (religion, language, and/or colonial heritage) appear to be significantly more likely to form IGO ties with each other. This is an especially interesting finding that forces us to think beyond purely functional explanations of interstate cooperation. I interpret this result as suggesting that states that share common cultural traits are more trusting of each other's international commitments and are therefore more likely to enter into international regimes with one another.

6.2 IGOs and Human Rights Conditions

Of the approximately 300 IGOs that are currently in existence, the vast majority appear to make no serious effort to restrict membership to states with good human rights records (see Duxbury, 2011). With the exception of a few high-profile cases—for example, the EU's reluctance to conclude accession talks with Turkey due in part to its poor human rights standards or the Commonwealth's refusal to re-admit South Africa until after the apartheid regime ended in 1994—most IGOs try to include as many states as possible that are relevant to the mission of the IGO.

For example, the Council of Europe—Europe's chief human rights organization whose judicial arm is the ECtHR—includes almost every European state among its 47 members. Included among these are states like Ukraine and Russia, which joined the organization in 1995 and 1996 when their CIRI PIR scores were only 4 and 3, respectively. At the time of their joining, their scores were significantly lower than those of the existing members; in 1994, the year prior to Ukraine's accession, the member states of the Council of Europe had a median PIR score of 8, which is the highest possible score on the index.

Another illustration of the surprising indifference of IGOs to the human rights performance of their member states is provided by the case of South Africa under the apartheid regime. In spite of the fact that South Africa had effectively been expelled from the Commonwealth, was facing severe economic sanctions and was prohibited from participating in many international cultural and sporting events during that period, the IGO data show that its pattern of IGO memberships remained comparable to those of its peers. To illustrate this point more clearly, the upper panel of Figure 6.1 shows how the total number of IGO memberships held by South Africa during the period from 1965 to 2005 compares to those of other states. In this figure, the grey dots represent the total number of IGO memberships held each year by the 10 states that were closest to South Africa in terms of their GDP per capita that year.[1] (Keep in mind that GDP per capita tends to be a very strong predictor of a state's total number of IGO memberships.[2]) The upward sloping line represents South Africa's total number of IGO memberships each year. As the position of the line relative to the dots indicates, South Africa's total number of IGO memberships was similar to those of its economic peers even during the height of the global anti-apartheid campaign in the 1980s and early 1990s. After the apartheid regime finally came to an end in 1994, South Africa's total number of IGO memberships did undergo a notable increase, although even at this stage the increase remained broadly in line with those of its economic peers.

What is also striking is the fact that despite the very strong opposition of other African states to South Africa's apartheid regime, South Africa's neighboring states continued to share a large number of IGO ties with South Africa. As the lower graph in Figure 6.1 shows, South Africa

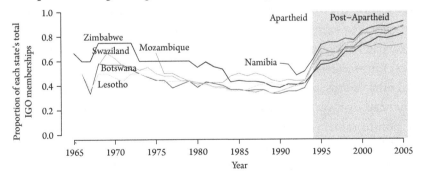

Figure 6.1 South Africa's IGO ties, 1965–2005.

was a co-member of around 40% of the IGOs to which its neighbors belonged during the apartheid era. As one would expect, this proportion began to increase significantly after the end of the apartheid regime. Nevertheless, the fact that the extent of shared memberships was so high during the pre-1994 period despite its neighboring states' abhorrence of the apartheid regime suggests that the need to maintain international cooperation by remaining within the IGOs was still strong enough to trump these concerns, a point that Audie Klotz notes in her discussion of social sanctions against South Africa (Crawford and Klotz, 1999: Ch. 10).

Further examination of the IGO data reveals that, in general, states show a very high degree of inertia with respect to their IGO memberships. States do not appear to continually re-evaluate their IGO memberships, and once they join, they tend to retain their memberships for the life of the IGOs. For example, the IGO data reveals that the United States and Iraq belonged to 27 of the same IGOs in 1989—the year before the outbreak of the first Gulf War—but still belonged to 27 common IGOs in 1992, one year after the war had ended. (Their joint membership in all but one of these 27 IGOs remained constant over this period.[3]) Clearly, IGO memberships are relatively "sticky"; once you're in, it's fairly unlikely that you'll ever leave.[4]

When it comes to building a model of state-IGO ties, it would therefore seem inappropriate to model these ties in a way that implicitly assumes that states are continually re-evaluating their portfolio of IGO member- ships in light of current events (cf. Boehmer and Nordstrom, 2008). To illustrate this point more clearly, Table 6.1 provides a list of all the states that left a sample of 12 of the most prominent IGOs in the period 1990–2000. (Note that this consists only of the states that left IGOs and not those whose membership was temporarily suspended.[5]) As these results show, the only states that departed from these IGOs are the ones that ceased to exist following their breakup or incorporation into other states. In all of these cases, the successor state(s) re-joined the IGO more or less immediately.[6]

In other words, a state's decision to join a particular IGO is likely to be influenced by a very different set of factors from those that influence its decision to remain within that IGO. Given that the rate at which states leave IGOs tends to be very low, what is likely to reveal more about states' associational preferences is their decision to join IGOs in the first place. Put differently, if we suspect that states might choose to associate to a greater degree with other states that have similar human rights practices

Table 6.1 **States that left prominent IGOs in the period 1991–2000.**

IGO	State
ASEAN	None
Council of Europe	None
European Union	None
World Bank	South Yemen (1991); West Germany (1991)
International Labour Organization	East Germany (1991); West Germany (1991); North Yemen (1991); South Yemen (1991)
International Monetary Fund	North Yemen (1991); South Yemen (1991); West Germany (1991)
NATO	None
African Union	None
OECD	None
World Health Organization	North Yemen (1991); Czechoslovakia (1993)
World Trade Organization	None
United Nations	Czechoslovakia (1993)

to their own, we should expect to find a stronger correlation between the human practices of the state and those of its *recently-acquired* fellow IGO members than between the human rights practices of the state and those of its pre-existing fellow IGO members. For this reason I construct a dependent variable that reflects only the *new* state-IGO ties that form in a given year. This variable, which will be described in more detail in Section 6.3, is simply a count of the number of new IGO ties that form between state i and state j in a given year. By regressing this variable on a measure of the similarity between the human rights practices of these two states, we can test the hypothesis that states are more likely to form IGO ties with states that have similar human rights practices to themselves.

6.3 Methods

Constructing the Dependent Variable

For the purpose of this analysis, I construct a network variable that I refer to as *IGO Flows*. It indicates which new state-to-state relationships have formed as a result of states joining IGOs. I construct it in three stages.

Table 6.2 **Extract of the *Membership* matrix for 1991.**

	UN	*WHO*	*IMF*	*NATO*	*AsDB*
Afghanistan	1	1	1	0	1
Belarus	1	1	0	0	0
China	1	1	1	0	1
France	1	1	1	1	1
Mongolia	1	1	1	0	1
Russia	1	1	0	0	0
Taiwan	0	0	0	0	1
USA	1	1	1	1	1

First, I begin with a sociomatrix that indicates which states belong to which IGOs by the end of any given year. I refer to this as the *Membership* matrix. Table 6.2 shows an excerpt of the *Membership* matrix for the year 1991. In this matrix the rows represent the countries and the columns the IGOs.[7] Each cell in the matrix is populated with either a 1 to indicate that the state belongs to the IGO in that year or 0 if it does not. From the first two columns of the table we can see, for example, that of the eight countries in this sample, all but Taiwan belonged to the UN and the World Health Organization (WHO) in 1991.

Second, I create a sociomatrix for each year that identifies the new state-IGO relationships that form in that particular year. I call this the *New Joiners* matrix. The corresponding values of the *New Joiners* matrix for the above sample of countries and IGOs for 1991 is shown in Table 6.3. In this case, an entry of 1 in the cells indicates only that the state has joined the IGO in that particular year. (States that were already members of the organization before the beginning of 1991 will therefore be coded as 0.) Here we can see that, for example, during 1991 Belarus joined the UN and the WHO, while Mongolia joined the International Monetary Fund (IMF) and the Asian Development Bank (AsDB).

Finally, I take the *New Joiners* matrix and multiply it by the transpose of the *Membership* matrix.[8] The state-state matrix that results (after having removed the values along the diagonal) indicates which new state-state ties have been formed via IGOs in that particular year. In keeping with the distinction between stocks and flows that is commonly used when discussing patterns of foreign direct investment, I refer to this matrix as *IGO Flows*. This matrix (for each of the years between 1982 and 2005) will become the dependent variable used in the analysis in this chapter.

Table 6.3 **Extract of the *New Joiners* matrix for 1991.**

	UN	WHO	IMF	NATO	AsDB
Afghanistan	0	0	0	0	0
Belarus	1	1	0	0	0
China	0	0	0	0	0
France	0	0	0	0	0
Mongolia	0	0	1	0	1
Russia	0	0	0	0	0
Taiwan	0	0	0	0	0
USA	0	0	0	0	0

Table 6.4 **Extract of the *IGO Flows* matrix for 1991.**

	AFG	BLR	CHN	FRN	MON	RUS	TAW	USA
AFG	0	0	0	0	0	0	0	0
BLR	2	0	2	2	2	2	0	2
CHN	0	0	0	0	0	0	0	0
FRN	0	0	0	0	0	0	0	0
MON	2	0	2	2	0	0	1	2
RUS	0	0	0	0	0	0	0	0
TAW	0	0	0	0	0	0	0	0
USA	0	0	0	0	0	0	0	0

The corresponding section of the *IGO Flows* matrix for 1991 is shown in Table 6.4. Note that this is an asymmetrical matrix: each *i,j* cell in this matrix therefore indicates the number of new IGOs that state *i* has joined to which state *j* already belongs (or is simultaneously joining) in a particular year.[9] For example, the {BLR, AFG} cell shows that Belarus joined two IGOs in 1991 of which Afghanistan was already a member, whereas the {AFG, BLR} cell shows that Afghanistan did not join any new IGOs in 1991 of which Belarus was already a member.

Accounting for Dyadic Dependence

As explained above, the dependent variable used in this chapter, *IGO Flows*, is a directed dyadic variable. Dyadic models are commonly used in IR; for example, tests of the democratic peace theory involve asking whether two states are less likely to go to war with each other if both states are democracies. However, one problem with the way in which these analyses are usually conducted is that they assume that each of the dyads can be treated as independent observations. In other words, Germany's decision to invade Belgium in 1914 is treated as independent of its decision to also invade France that year. This assumption is clearly unrealistic; it would be difficult to imagine Germany invading Belgium had it not also intended to invade France.

This tendency for the status of one dyad to depend upon the status of another related dyad is what network theorists refer to as "transitivity." It is a feature of many different social networks such a friendship ties (e.g., your friend's friend has a higher than average probability of also being one of your friends) or the voting preferences that exist among members of a legislature. It is also likely to play an important role in the formation of IGO ties. To illustrate this point more clearly, consider the example of IGO ties among three countries as illustrated in Figure 6.2. If Country A has many shared IGO memberships with Country B, and if Country B has many shared IGO ties with Country C, then we can expect that the probability of Country A also having stronger IGO ties with Country C would be greater than that of other, unconnected countries like Country D. However, the traditional dyadic regression models used in studies of international relations assume that no dependence exists among the residuals of the dyads in the system and therefore make no provision for the fact that high degrees of transitivity are likely to have significant consequences for the ties that form between states (Ward and Hoff, 2007).

Accounting for dyadic dependence is especially important—perhaps even more so than it is for other types of network models used in IR—when it comes to building a model of the *IGO Flows* variable discussed above. In this case a high degree of transitivity is introduced to the network by design. Consider, for example, the case of Belarus joining the UN and the WHO in 1991. Because all seven of the other states shown in Table 6.4 were already members of both organizations, Belarus' act of joining these organizations simultaneously established two new ties to all seven of these states (see the second row of the table). Joining an IGO therefore automatically induces a set of connections to all existing members of the organization, a feature that leads to a high degree of transitivity within the *IGO Flows* network. This high degree of transitivity is likely to introduce significant bias were we to apply a traditional dyadic regression framework that assumes dyadic independence.

However, recent advances in statistics, coupled with the ever-increasing computational power available to social scientists, have made dealing with the problem of transitivity possible. Hoff, Raftery, and Handcock (2002) proposed a method for modeling dyadic dependence that assumes that the nodes in the network (in this case, the states) exist in some sort of unobserved "latent space," whereby nodes that are close together in that space are more likely to have ties to each other. In this conceptualization, the "space" itself has no substantive meaning—that is, it is not intended to have any connection to the geographical locations of the nodes in the network, or any other such attribute of the nodes—but is merely a modeling device that allows us to organize the nodes in terms of their propensity to form ties to the other nodes in the network. (Hoff and Ward (2004) point out that it can be thought of as analogous to a random effect in a typical regression model.) Thinking of the network in this way directly induces the dependence structure that would otherwise be a "nuisance" for the traditional modeling approach: two states that are positioned close together in the latent space are expected not only to have a tie to each other but also to have ties to other states located nearby. As a result, if we can build a model that accounts for the states' locations in the latent space, we can indirectly account for the dyadic dependence that transitivity induces in the network.

To help describe the basic intuition behind this type of model, Figure 6.3 plots the positions of the same hypothetical countries from the illustration used in Figure 6.2 in a 2-dimensional latent space.[10] In this scenario

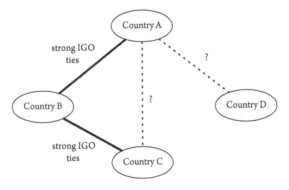

Figure 6.2 Transitivity in social networks.

Note: When transitivity in the network is high, the probability of A having a relationship with C is higher than the probability of A having a relationship with D, all else being equal.

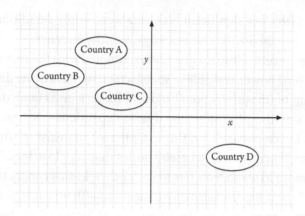

Figure 6.3 Positions of countries A, B, C, and D in a hypothetical 2-dimensional latent space.

Note: Country C is closer to Country A than is Country D, implying that an A-C tie is more likely to form than an A-D tie.

Countries A, B, and C are clustered relatively close together in the latent space, whereas Country D is positioned relatively far away. This implies that, all else being equal, the probability of strong IGO ties forming between the A-B, B-C, or A-C pairs is much higher than the probability of strong ties forming between Country D and any of the other three countries. In other words, if we were to build a model of the probability of ties forming among these four countries, estimating their positions in this latent space would allow us to directly take account of the fact that networks like this tend to have a high degree of transitivity: the probability of strong IGO ties forming between Country A and Country C is higher than it otherwise may be because the strength of their mutual ties to Country B has brought them closer together in the latent space. Country D, on the other hand, is located further away, making it less likely to form ties with Country A.

Capturing this type of dependency is something that would not be possible using a traditional dyadic regression framework where all the dyads are assumed to be independent of each other. In a traditional model, Country A would be considered equally likely to form ties with Country C and Country D, despite the fact that Country A is already tightly connected to Country C via Country B.

By directly modeling this type of dependency in a regression framework, the estimated effects of key covariates on the dependent variable can be shown to be very different than previously thought. For example, in a study of trading relationships among states, Ward and Hoff (2007) use a latent space model to show that, contrary to earlier findings, international conflict has surprisingly little effect on volumes of bilateral trade. They are also able to show that by ignoring the dependency structure that exists among groups of dyads, the standard gravity model of international trade vastly underestimates the volume of trade that takes place among wealthy industrialized countries. By applying a similar approach in re-evaluating the democratic peace theory, Ward, Siverson, and Cao (2007) are able to show that trade and shared membership in IGOs have no consistent effect on reducing the probability of conflict between states.

Details of the Model

In the analysis that follows, I shall be modeling the formation of IGO ties for each year in the period 1982–2005 using the bilinear mixed effects model developed by Hoff (2005). Not only does this model allow us to model dyadic dependencies using the principle of latent space discussed above, it also enables us to separately consider the effects that sender, receiver, and dyadic covariates have on the expected level of the dyadic dependent variable.

The intuition behind Hoff's model can be understood by imagining that the probability of a tie forming between a given pair of nodes in a network is a function of three separate components. As an example, imagine a trade network where state i exports a certain amount of goods to state j. The first component of the model consists of the various characteristics of the state "sending" the tie—that is, the state that exports the goods. This consists of theoretically interesting features of state i—for example, the size of its economy, its level of democracy, etc.—as well as a random effect designed to capture other unobserved characteristics of state i that affect its tendency to export goods to other states. The second component captures characteristics of the "receiving" state, state j, which again consists of both a series of state-level covariates and a random effect. These characteristics describe the general tendency of the state to import goods from others. The third component captures characteristics of the dyad itself. This consists of covariates specific to each particular dyad such as the geographic distance between state i and state j, as well as—most importantly—a measure of the distance that exists between the two states in the latent space (which we can think of as a dyadic random effect). The greater the distance that exists between the two states in the latent space, the less likely they will be to interact with one another.[11] Of course, given that the latent space is unobserved, the positions of the states in this space must themselves be estimated by the model in the same way that one might estimate a random effect for each state in a panel regression model. The concept of latent space is, after all, only used as a convenient means of accounting for the types of dependencies that exist among the dyads in the network, and, as a result, the absolute position of each state in the latent space is not intended to have any substantive interpretation of its own.

The general form of the model can be more formally expressed as:

$$\theta_{i,j} = \beta'_s x_i + \beta'_r x_j + \beta'_d x_{ij} + a_i + b_j + u'_i v_j + \epsilon_{ij}$$

where

$\theta_{i,j}$ is the linear predictor corresponding to the number of new IGO ties formed between state i and state j;

$\beta'_s x_i$ represents the effect of the sender-specific covariates on the baseline probability of state i establishing ties with other states;

$\beta'_r x_j$ represents the effect of the receiver-specific covariates on the baseline probability of state j receiving ties from other states;

$\beta'_d x_{ij}$ represents the effect of covariates specific to the i,j dyad on the probability of a tie being formed between state i and state j;

a_i represents a random effect specific to state i;

b_j represents a random effect specific to state j;

$u'_i v_j$ is the inner product of the coordinates of states i and j in the latent space (this is what allows us to account for dependency among dyads as described in note 11); and

ϵ_{ij} is the error term.

Given that the dependent variable in this analysis is a count of the number of newly formed IGO ties between state i and state j, an exponential link function is used (Long, 1997: Ch. 8). A separate model was estimated for each year in the series 1982–2005 using the Markov Chain Monte Carlo (MCMC) algorithm developed by Hoff (2005).[12] Each model was estimated using 100,000 iterations of the Markov chains, and parameter estimates from every 100th iteration were saved. The first 20,000 estimates were discarded as "burn-in." To facilitate visualization of the latent positions, the models were estimated by assuming a two-dimensional latent space.

Covariates

Recall that the question motivating the analysis in this chapter is whether states tend to join IGOs with similar human rights practices to their own. The key explanatory variable I use is therefore a measure of the similarity between the human rights practices of state i, the state that is joining a particular IGO, and state j, the state that already belongs to that IGO.

I constructed this variable by first calculating the absolute difference between each pair of states' scores on the PIR index for each year. Details of this measure are provided in Section 3.2 (page 61). Given that I am interested in testing a non-directional hypothesis about selection into IGOs on the basis of similar human rights scores, I take the absolute value of the difference between the physical integrity rights index of the two states in the dyad.[13] I then reverse the sign of this variable to ensure that higher values indicate states whose PIR scores are more similar to each other and rescale the variable to ensure that its values lie on a similarity scale ranging from 0 to 100. I refer to this variable as *Human Rights Similarity*. Higher values on this variable therefore indicate a greater level of similarity between the human rights scores of the two members of the dyad. If states do in fact choose to associate with other states whose human rights practices are similar to their own, we should expect to find a positive relationship between *Human Rights Similarity* and *IGO Flows*.

I also control for a number of other dyadic variables that are likely to influence the associational activities of states. One obvious choice is the physical proximity between the two members of the dyad. Given that a majority of IGOs are regional in nature, we can expect states to be much more likely to join IGOs that have geographically proximate states among their members.[14] The distance metric I use is adapted from the great circle distance (in thousands of kilometers) between the states' capital cities compiled by Gleditsch (2002). As with the *Human Rights Similarity* variable, I reverse the values and rescale the variable to turn it into a similarity (in this case, proximity) score that ranges from 0 to 100. I refer to this variable as *Geographic Proximity*.[15] All else being equal, we should expect to find a positive relationship between *Geographic Proximity* and *IGO Flows*.

Given that many IGOs exist to advance the interests of states that share certain cultural traits, I also consider the effect of cultural similarity on states' IGO-joining decisions. For example, the Organisation

of the Islamic Conference (OIC) represents the interests of 57 predominantly Muslim states, while the Organisation Internationale de la
Francophonie (OIF) represents a total of 57 French-speaking states.
Other IGOs have developed on the basis of previous colonial ties. The
most obvious example is perhaps the Commonwealth, an IGO consisting of 53 states that were once (with the exceptions of Rwanda and
Mozambique) British colonies, but other examples include the Organization of Ibero-American States—an IGO that includes most former
colonies of Spain and Portugal—and CABI, a 48-member IGO focusing
on agricultural science, which was originally created as an organization
within the Commonwealth framework but since 1987 has operated as an
independent IGO.

In constructing a measure of cultural similarity, I use the same matrix of
cultural similarity that I had used when considering non-IGO pathways of
diffusion in Chapters 3 and 5. This is a four-point measure constructed by
adding together dummy variables indicating the existence of a common
language, a common religion, or a shared colonial heritage. (For full
details, see the discussion beginning on page 79.) In keeping with the
method used to construct the previous two similarity measures, I rescaled
this variable to place its values on a 0 to 100 scale, where 0 indicates no
cultural ties and 100 indicates the presence of all three types of cultural tie.

I also include variables that capture the degree of similarity that exists
between the joining state and each existing member. These allow us to
test for homophily within the IGO network—that is, the general idea
that actors with similar traits tend to associate with one another.[16] One
possibility is that rich countries are more likely to associate with each
other, as is evidenced by the creation of prominent IGOs such as the
OECD as well as informal organizations such as the G-7/G-8 and the
G-20. Similarly, democratic states may be more likely to associate with
each other than with non-democratic states. I therefore include two
further dyadic variables that I constructed in an analogous way to the
Human Rights Similarity variable: for each pair of states, I first calculated
the absolute value of the difference between the log of its members' GDP
per capita and between its members' Polity 2 regime scores.[17] I then
reversed the sign and rescaled the variables to place them on a 0–100 scale,
where higher values indicate pairs of states whose level of wealth or regime
type are most similar to each other. I refer to these variables as *Wealth
Similarity* and *Regime Similarity*, respectively. As with the *Human Rights
Similarity* variable described above, to the extent that states prefer to form

IGO ties with states that have similar levels of wealth or democracy to themselves, we should expect to find a positive relationship between these similarity measures and the *IGO Flows* variable.

Finally, I include controls for the *monadic* effects of both GDP and regime type. Irrespective of the characteristics of the other partner in the dyad, one could argue that richer, more democratic states are generally more likely to belong to IGOs. Indeed, Beckfield (2003) reports evidence of a positive correlation between a state's level of economic development and its total number of IGO memberships. In their dyadic analysis, Boehmer and Nordstrom (2008) find evidence of a positive relationship between economic development (operationalized as energy consumption per capita) and the number of IGO ties that form between states and between regime type and IGO ties.[18] Here I operationalize these monadic effects using data on GDP per capita (logged) from the *World Development Indicators* and the Polity 2 combined democracy/autocracy score from the Polity IV dataset (Marshall and Jaggers, 2009). I refer to these variables as simply *GDP* and *Regime Type* respectively.[19] These monadic variables refer to the characteristics of the country that is in the act of joining the IGO and are therefore operationalized as sender-specific effects in the equation for the bilinear mixed effects model presented on page 148.

To ensure that all of the variables described in this section reflect levels that exist prior to the levels of the *IGO Flows* dependent variable at each point in time—that is, prior to a state's decision to form a new IGO tie with other states—I lagged all of the covariates by one year. Thus, when we investigate the effect of covariates specific to, say, Mongolia's decision to join two IGOs in which Afghanistan is already a member in 1991 (see Table 6.4), the covariates reflect the characteristics of Mongolia and of the Mongolia-Afghanistan dyad that prevailed in 1990.

6.4 Results

The results of estimating this model for each of the annual cross-sections in over the period 1985–2005 are shown graphically in Figure 6.4.[20] Each of the seven panels in this figure represents one of the covariates included in the model. Within each of these panels I plot a series of ropeladder-style coefficient plots that show how the coefficient estimate (and its 95% credible interval) varies in each of the annual cross-sectional models.

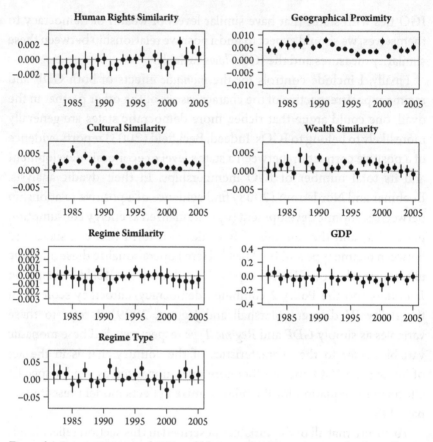

Figure 6.4 Point estimates and 95% credible intervals of the estimates of each coefficient in the year-specific models.

In each panel the horizontal line represents an estimated coefficient of zero; estimates whose 95% credible intervals do not pass that line can therefore be considered to be statistically significant in the classical sense.

The first, and most important, finding to emerge from this analysis is the absence of a consistent effect of *Human Rights Similarity*. The first panel shows its estimated effect hovering around the $\hat{\beta} = 0$ line; in some years the point estimate is positive, while in others it is negative, but in all but five of the 24 annual models the 95% credible intervals include zero. (The results for 1991, 1997, and 2000 suggest a negative coefficient, whereas those for 2002 and 2004 suggest a positive coefficient.) In other words, we see no consistent evidence to suggest that states form IGO ties on the basis of their having similar human rights practices to the existing members (or to those that are simultaneously joining the IGO). These results therefore fail to lend support to the alternative homophily-based explanation for the positive coefficient of *IGO Context* reported in the previous chapters.

Meanwhile, the results reveal a consistently positive effect for both *Geographical Proximity* and *Cultural Similarity*. The effect of geographical proximity is perhaps unsurprising given that states tend to have a greater need to cooperate with their neighbors than with more distant states, but finding a consistently positive effect of *Cultural Similarity* is more striking—especially once we consider that this effect is apparent even after geographical effects have been controlled for.

At the same time, we see evidence to suggest that higher levels of *Wealth Similarity* are in many cases associated with higher probabilities of tie formation, thereby suggesting a homophily effect with respect to wealth. In other words, richer states preferentially join IGOs that consist of other rich states, even after accounting for the effect of all the other variables in the models. The analogous results for *Regime Similarity*, however, show no consistent homophily effect with respect to regime type. When we look at the monadic variables, *GDP* and *Regime Type*, we see no consistent monadic effect of *GDP*, but we do see some evidence to suggest that more democratic states are (when controlling for the dyadic effects of these variables) more likely to join IGOs.

In a separate exercise, I re-estimated the models while including an additional dyadic covariate that indicates the number of shared IGO ties between states i and j that existed in the previous year (i.e., the "stock" of IGO ties). This reveals a very strong positive relationship to the *IGO Flows* dependent variable, although in doing so the effects of the various homophily covariates become more modest. (These results are shown in Section 9 of the online appendix.) This suggests that the best predictor of the formation of new IGO ties between a pair of states is simply the number of existing IGO ties in that dyad. Although this makes the marginal effects of cultural similarity appear much less impressive, this finding is nonetheless consistent with an explanation of IGO formation in which high levels of interaction among specific pairs of states encourage further interaction; in other words, cooperation begets cooperation.

Human Rights IGOs

The results presented above deal with data on all of the different IGOs included in the Correlates of War dataset described in Section 3.2. These results have helped to show that, in general, states are not preferentially associating with other states on the basis of their common human rights practices (at least insofar as their IGO memberships are concerned). But what about human rights IGOs themselves? Despite the fact that the results of Chapter 4 had suggested that the evidence of convergence among states' human rights practices was not any stronger among human rights IGOs than in the wider population of IGOs, it is nonetheless interesting to test whether we see evidence of homophily within this subgroup.

To do so, I re-ran the analysis used in this chapter using only the subset of IGOs that Hafner-Burton, Mansfield, and Pevehouse (2013) identify as IGOs with a human rights mandate. (Recall from Section 4.2 that this list consists of 57 human rights IGOs, 31 of which are identified as emanations of existing IGOs and are therefore not included within the Correlates of War IGO database.) Using membership data on only these 57 IGOs, I constructed a new *IGO Flows* matrix for each year in the 1982–2005 period. I then re-ran the bilinear mixed effects estimation on each of these, using the same set of covariates as before.

Due to the sparseness of the *IGO Flows* matrix that results from working with this smaller group of IGOs, it is not possible to estimate the model for every year in the period. Nonetheless, the results that are available suggest that, once again, states are not selecting into IGOs—even the human rights IGOs—whose existing members have similar human rights practices to their own (see Section 10 of the online appendix for the full results). This is most likely because as discussed earlier in this chapter, even the IGOs that would seem to be the most likely cases for applying human rights-specific membership conditions fail to do so consistently. As a result, these findings lend further support to the view that the convergence among human rights practices within each IGO is driven by a social influence effect, rather than a selection (homophily) effect.

Placebo Tests

Another way to approach to the question of causal inference is to create a placebo test. The logic of placebo tests in political science follows the same logic that applies to the use of placebos in drug trials—that is, when the researcher compares the effect of an active drug to something that looks similar but lacks the active ingredient. The difference in outcomes between the patients who took the actual drug and the patients who (unknowingly) took the placebo can therefore be more confidently attributed to the drug's active ingredient, rather than to some other aspect of the intervention—for example, the patient's belief that the treatment is having an effect.

Applying a placebo test in the context of observational data in political science is obviously more difficult (see Sekhon, 2009), but we can go some way towards applying its logic to this situation by asking whether the convergence effect we observed in Chapter 3 is significantly different from what we might observe using "placebo IGOs." In this context, a placebo IGO could be thought of as one that consists of a similar number of members to the actual IGO, but whose member states have been assigned at random. In other words, we would be treating states as if they belong to IGOs that in actual fact do not exist. Having replaced all the real data on IGO memberships with the fake data created for the purposes of the placebo analysis, I can then recalculate the *IGO Context* variable and test whether its estimated effect in the main regression model used in Chapter 3 is significantly different from that of the actual *IGO Context* variable. If the answer is yes, we have more confidence that membership in the (real) IGOs is having an effect on state behavior, but if the answer is no, we might suspect that the observed convergence in human rights practices is caused by something other than IGO memberships—perhaps a global trend in which states start to develop similar practices.

The results of this exercise are reported in Section 11 of the online appendix. As it turns out, the effect of *IGO Context* in these placebo models is usually negative, suggesting that the human rights practices of states in these placebo IGOs gradually become more *dissimilar* to those of their fellow members of the (fake) IGOs. While it is difficult to know how to interpret these negative coefficients, it is reassuring that they are certainly very different from the strong positive effect of *IGO Context* reported in Chapter 3. The results of the placebo tests, however, start to look different once I try setting up a more realistic scenario by randomly assigning only geographically proximate states to the placebo IGOs. In this case, the effect of *IGO Context* is usually positive—most likely due to the fact that I am picking up the same sort of geographically-based diffusion that I had examined in Section 3.3—but its effect size consistently turns out to be smaller than in the model constructed using the real data. Moreover, the real model outperforms the placebo models in the vast majority (96 out of 100) of cross-validation trials.

Thus, to the extent that one accepts that the concept of a placebo test can be usefully applied in this context, these results add further support to the claim that membership in IGOs is having a causal effect on promoting convergence among the human rights practices of their member states.

6.5 Discussion

The results presented in this chapter reveal two important findings. The first is the absence of a correlation between a state's human rights performance and those of the states with which it forms IGO ties. This finding therefore renders one of the important alternative explanations for IGO-based convergence less plausible—namely, the idea that states are selectively joining IGOs whose existing members have human rights practices that are similar to their own. We can now more confidently conclude that states' IGO-joining behaviors are largely independent of their human rights practices. This lends further weight to the argument that the behavioral convergence reported in the previous chapters is the consequence of states' positions in the IGO network and is not simply the result of a selection effect.

The second interesting finding to emerge from the models estimated in this chapter is that, in contrast to the results for human rights practices, I find evidence to suggest that states tend to form IGO ties with states that are similar to themselves in various other respects. I find that states are more likely to join IGOs where the existing members are geographically proximate, culturally similar, or have a similar level of economic development. In other words, we see strong evidence of homophily on many other dimensions.

Having found some evidence of homophily with respect to these indicators (albeit not with respect to the direct measure of human rights similarity), one might wonder whether this undermines the main causal argument concerning IGO-based diffusion. In other words, could the apparent IGO-based convergence amongst states' human rights practices be confounded by the fact that similar states tend to join the same IGOs in the first place? While the possibility will always remain that some as yet unidentified factor is responsible for both co-membership in IGOs and convergence amongst states' human rights practices, it is important to remember that in Chapter 3 I had found that IGO-based convergence was apparent even in models that controlled for other spatially lagged variables. In constructing these spatially lagged variables, I used weights matrices based on geographical proximity and cultural similarity—variables that we now know to be strongly associated with IGO-joining. This, together with the other evidence presented in this chapter, increases our confidence in the causal nature of the relationship between shared IGO membership and convergence among states' human rights practices.

Nonetheless, this chapter's finding with respect to cultural similarity presents an interesting puzzle of its own. While it is relatively easy to account for the fact that states that are geographically proximate or that share similar levels of economic development are more likely to join the same IGOs, it is not obvious why states would necessarily want to associate with states that are culturally similar to themselves. Of course, some of this might be explained by the fact that culturally similar states tend to be located in the same parts of the world, but given that the model already controls for geographical proximity, cultural similarity is presumably having its own independent effect.

Existing theories of regime formation have little to offer in the way of an explanation for this finding. These theories tend to favor functionalist, rather than cultural, explanations for international cooperation. For instance, Keohane (1984) suggests that international regimes are likely to arise (and be successful) when they can provide opportunities to reduce the transaction costs and information asymmetries associated with interstate bargaining. In an early analysis of IGO participation, Jacobson, Reisinger, and Mathers (1986) interpret this in a way that suggests that richer, more democratic states would be more likely to join IGOs. They argue that states that are more technologically advanced will stand to make significant gains from international cooperation, and that an awareness of these potential gains will cause citizens to put pressure on their leaders to join international regimes (Jacobson, Reisinger, and Mathers, 1986: 149). Their empirical work—as well as that of a number of more recent studies—lends support to this view by finding that richer, more democratic states tend to belong to a greater number of IGOs (see Jacobson, Reisinger, and Mathers, 1986; Shanks, Jacobson, and Kaplan, 1996; Beckfield, 2003; Boehmer and Nordstrom, 2008).

However, these studies have largely neglected other factors such as the presence of a common culture.[21] Why should cultural similarity have any effect on the potential gains from cooperation? One possible explanation is that governments are more willing to trust governments of other states that are similar to themselves. Studies of behavior within networks of individual people have shown that individuals are more likely to give help or lend money to others when both partners to the exchange share a common religion (McPherson, Smith-Lovin, and Cook, 2001: 425–426). For example, in their analysis of responses to a question in the 1985 General Social Survey asking respondents to identify the people with whom they discuss "important matters," Liao and Stevens (1994) find that married men are significantly more likely to mention their wives as their closest confidant if both partners share the same religion. The authors attribute this effect to the experience of socialization in a religious community that causes its members to share a common set of values (Liao and Stevens, 1994: 696).

That cultural similarity might foster greater levels of trust among states, and thereby make them more likely to engage in more extensive international cooperation, is also supported by some anecdotal evidence. For instance, consider the case of Turkey's possible accession to the EU. The idea of a predominantly Muslim state joining the EU has raised concerns among some European conservatives, and has caused Turkish politicians to doubt the sincerity of the EU's willingness to admit Turkey even if it were to meet the formal criteria for accession.[22] Although a large number of confounding variables exist, one could argue that these cultural differences can explain why the EU has been more successful in expanding to include the former communist states of central and eastern Europe than states such as Turkey or even Morocco to the south (see Rumelili, 2004).

An alternative, but still closely related, explanation for the importance of cultural similarity could simply be that states emulate the behavior of other states that are culturally similar. In this case we can think of states as exhibiting a form of herd behavior in their patterns of joining IGOs. Once some influential states join a particular IGO, other culturally similar states do likewise. This mechanism does not directly depend on trust between the cooperating states but is simply a reflection of the fact that states tend to follow the examples of culturally similar others. This is essentially the mechanism that underlies Simmons and Elkins' (2004) surprising finding that states are more likely to adopt similar economic policies to those of the states that have the same dominant religion as themselves. As noted in Chapter 3, they suggest that this result is not due to religion per se but is instead a reflection of the fact that states tend to look to the decisions made by culturally similar others when deciding between competing policy choices (Simmons and Elkins, 2004: 175). States can identify more easily with culturally similar others and are therefore more likely to use the policies of these states to inform their own decision making. Thus, if one state joins a particular international organization, other culturally similar states are more likely to follow its example.

When viewed in the context of constructivist approaches to IR theory, the results of this chapter suggest an interesting two-part role for ideas in the context of the IGO network. Not only does the IGO network facilitate the transfer of ideas and norms among the member states of the individual IGOs (as the results of the previous chapters have shown), but in this chapter we have seen that the very structure of the IGO network itself turns out to be shaped by another set of ideas—that is, the shared culture—of the states that created the IGOs in the first place.

7

Conclusions

7.1 Lessons Learned

What have we learned about the role that the IGO network plays in the diffusion of human rights norms, and what implications does this have for our understanding of the role of IGOs in international politics? In this chapter I shall begin by reviewing what I believe to be the most important ideas to have emerged from the empirical work presented in this book and then go on to discuss their broader implications for theory and policy.

The IGO Network Matters More than its Individual IGOs

The central idea of this book is that IGOs can function as channels for norm diffusion among states. While a number of studies have considered the role of some of the more prominent IGOs in promoting norms among member states (e.g., Finnemore, 1993; Gheciu, 2005a; Johnston, 2008), social scientists have paid relatively little attention to how the larger network of IGOs serves to promote norms among member states. (A notable exception is the world society school, but for the reasons I discuss in Chapter 2, this presents what is actually a very incomplete model of IGO-based diffusion.)

One particularly surprising finding that emerged from Chapter 4 (and that was corroborated by the findings of Chapter 5) is that broadly similar diffusion effects are observed when I use the entire population of IGOs to construct the *IGO Context* variable and when I restrict the sample of IGOs to only those with a human rights mandate. It seems that the ability of the IGO network to act as a vehicle for the transmission of norms is therefore not dependent on a small number of key players in the network such as the EU or the UN.

These results suggest that the norm-transmitting effect of IGOs is not confined to one particular IGO or to one particular class of IGOs. Instead it seems that, when viewed collectively, IGOs of many different types create a web of closely overlapping ties between states. These ties provide multiple pathways for states to influence one another in a way that is analogous to, for example, the multiple opportunities for inter-state commerce that are provided by dense networks of road, rail, sea, and air transportation links in certain regions of the world. No single road or air link may in itself be critical to global trade, but when viewed as a whole a well-connected transportation network is obviously essential to a functioning trade system. Thus, IGOs appear to matter to norm diffusion not because of their individual functions, but rather because of their more general ability to provide a multitude of venues for contact among government representatives.

Social Influence, Rather than Self-selection, is Driving Policy Convergence in IGOs

An important alternative explanation for the convergence in human rights behaviors observed within IGOs is that states choose to associate with states that have similar human rights practices to their own (the homophily argument). In Chapter 6 I tested the hypothesis that states are more likely to join IGOs where the existing members have similar human rights practices to their own. The results, however, were negative: after controlling for the effect of geographical proximity and cultural sim-ilarities (both of which turn out to be surprisingly important predictors of a state's associational behavior), similarities in human rights practices do not appear to be associated with states' decisions to join IGOs. This finding is consistent with the fact that a large proportion of IGOs are regional in nature and tend not to impose any meaningful human rights conditions on their member states.

These results give us confidence in the idea that the effect of the *IGO Context* variable is driven primarily by a process of diffusion rather than selection. States' IGO memberships are generally not endogenous to their human rights behavior, and the positive correlation that we do observe between the trends in the human rights practices of a state and those of its IGO partners can therefore best be explained in terms of behavioral changes on the part of the member states.

Participation in IGOs Promotes Convergence, but not Necessarily Improvements, Among States' Human Rights Standards

Studies of norm diffusion generally assume that states are headed in the direction of improving their human rights standards but vary in the rate at which they make these improvements. In other words, they implicitly assume a kind of ratchet effect whereby states' human rights standards either improve or simply remain unchanged as a result of their interactions with other states. What attracts much less attention is the possibility of negative social influences as a result of the diffusion process—in other words, the possibility that a state that resides in a bad "IGO neighborhood" might actually experience a decline in its human rights standards as a result.

In Chapter 3 I tested this hypothesis using a method designed to uncover asymmetries in a diffusion process (Konisky, 2007). The results suggested that the IGO-based convergence effect is actually a combination of both positive and negative influences: states exposed to positive influences therefore experience an improvement in their human rights practices at the same time that states exposed to negative influences experience a decline in their standards. Presumably states are not only inspired to improve their human rights standards in order to emulate those of their peers, but they are also liable to let these standards slip when surrounded by less positive role models. Overall, states are becoming more similar to their IGO partners, whether for better or worse. As I shall discuss below, this finding has important implications for debates over whether to engage with or further isolate norm-violating states.

Acculturation, Rather Than Material Inducements or Persuasion, is most Likely to be Driving Convergence in Human Rights Practices

If IGO-mediated norm diffusion is mainly the result of coercion or material inducements—in other words, if states change their behavior only because they are compelled to do so by their IGO partners—then we should expect to find that more powerful states are better placed to resist these pressures and are therefore less receptive to the norms that prevail within IGOs. One might expect this to explain, for example, why powerful states like the US, Russia, and China have successfully resisted pressure to join the ICC. However, in the models of physical integrity rights, gay rights, and women's rights I did not find any evidence for more powerful states being more capable of resisting international pressures in these areas. Instead, the available evidence suggests that the opposite holds true: richer, more powerful states are actually *more* receptive to the influence of their fellow IGO members.

These results suggest that power matters, but not in the way that realist approaches to IR lead us to expect. Instead they are compatible with a model of international relations that places greater emphasis on the possibilities for acculturation within international institutions (Goodman and Jinks, 2013). An acculturation model would suggest that, rather than being more capable of resisting international pressures, richer states are actually more likely to absorb international norms because they tend to have stronger connections to IGOs. These states tend to have higher levels of representation at a greater number of organizations, creating more opportunities for government ministers to absorb ideas from their international counterparts. In addition, richer states have the infrastructure to implement policy changes more effectively than poorer states. For instance, the governments of richer states are likely to have the regulatory capacity to monitor and enforce policies protecting the rights of women in the workforce much more effectively than would be possible for less developed states. Consistent with this model, I also found evidence to suggest that states that are more democratic or have more active civil societies are generally more receptive to the influences of their fellow IGO members.

7.2 Implications for IR Theory

The findings of this study not only help to establish that international institutions matter—a point that many scholars might argue has already been well established—but that institutions matter in unexpected ways. What this study suggests is that membership in international institutions can have much further-reaching effects on their member states than their titles or official mandates would seem to suggest. As well as solving collective action problems with regard to specific issues such as economic integration, collective security, and environmental protection, IGOs can potentially play a more general role in international politics by providing venues in which states can influence each other's domestic practices across a wide range of issue areas.

Showing that these types of socialization effects occur within IGOs provides further evidence to support that idea that the effects of international interactions on behavioral change depend upon who the parties to the interaction are and not simply the total amount of interaction that takes place. While this point may sound obvious, most studies of the effects of economic and social globalization have tended to use aggregate measures of globalization, such as the total number of IGOs (or INGOs) to which a state belongs. This is a point that has been shown to be important in recent studies of trade-based diffusion, where the question of with *whom* each states trades turns out to be as, if not more, important than the question of the total amount of trade that each state engages in (Prakash and Potoski, 2006; Greenhill, Mosley, and Prakash, 2009). Moreover, in the specific context of IGOs, this particular point challenges the contention of the world society school that international organizations connect states to a single set of norms that collectively constitute "world culture" (Meyer et al., 1997; Boli and Thomas, 1999). Rather than serving as a repository of a single global set of norms, this study has shown how IGOs can influence the behavior of states by acting as bridges between the norms and practices of different groups of states.

Moreover, this study has demonstrated the value of adopting more nuanced models of international diffusion. Most studies of diffusion in international politics include spatially lagged variables that take account of the varying connections that each state has to the others in the system, but in doing so they flatten the differences that exist among the ability of states to influence (and be influenced by) their interaction partners. By taking account of characteristics of the "sender" and "receiver" states in the IGO network, I have been able to show how different aspects of state power can affect their influence within the network.

This study also makes an important contribution to the question of why states form particular IGO connections. Although a very large literature has developed around the question of the efficacy of international regimes, and many detailed case studies have addressed the question of why particular states have or have not joined particular IGOs, very little is understood about the factors determining the breadth of IGO ties at the dyadic level. By studying the formation of new IGO ties between pairs of states, Chapter 6 has shown that states' levels of economic and political development are relatively poor predictors of the formation of new IGO ties. Instead, states appear to be far more likely to form IGO ties with states that are similar to themselves in terms of culture or level of economic development or with states with which they already share a large number of IGO ties. These findings suggest that the formation of IGO ties cannot be explained by rationalist explanations alone, but that the formation of these ties also depends upon the cultural affinity that exists between the cooperating states.

Having argued that participation in large networks of IGOs can have a significant impact on the development of states' human rights practices, an important question to consider is what this means for the future development of human rights at the global level. Do the results of this study suggest that the increasing institutionalization of the international system will lead to better human rights standards? Unfortunately, there is no simple answer to this question. While a small number of individual IGOs (e.g., the EU) are likely to have had an impact in improving human rights, the larger IGO network can perhaps be more accurately thought of as serving simply as a conduit for the diffusion of norms among its member states. This suggests that increasing levels of interconnectedness will not necessarily cause states' human rights practices to improve but will instead lead them to converge towards some sort of average. Of course, whether convergence towards that average is good or bad for human rights will depend upon the role that other factors play in shaping states' human rights practices: if states' human rights practices are on the whole improving over time—as recent work by Fariss (2014) suggests—then we have grounds to believe that the IGO-based diffusion of human rights could be a force for good.

However, what complicates this story is that the IGO network contains important structural characteristics that scholars of international institutions often lose sight of when attending to important global institutions such as the UN or IMF. Rather than causing states to become uniformly more connected to one another, the rapid growth in the number of regionally focused IGOs is causing certain forms of connections among states to form at the expense of others. By studying the evolution of ties with the IGO network, Beckfield (2010: 1047) concludes that "the world polity more closely resembles a regionalized world than a singular small world." What this means is that, for better or worse, the IGO-based diffusion of human rights is likely to become more salient at the regional level than at the global level—a claim that finds some support in the results presented in Chapter 4. IGO ties could therefore facilitate the diffusion of superior human rights standards in one tightly connected region and at same time promote the diffusion of more lax standards in another (see Beckfield, 2010: 1054).

Thinking of IGO-based diffusion in this way has important implications for the ongoing debate among policymakers about whether a strategy of engagement or a strategy of isolation is the better way to deal with norm-violating states like Russia, Iran, or North Korea. At least as far as our participation in IGOs alongside these states is concerned, these results generally favor engagement. Indeed, the finding that IGOs can also serve as conduits for the diffusion of less progressive models of human rights suggests that isolating a norm-violating state could actually be dangerous: expelling them from IGOs whose members care about human rights might cause these norm-violating states to undergo an even greater decline in their standards. Future work will need to address the question of how this form of engagement can be managed in a way that increases the probability of bringing about desired changes in the human rights practices of the target states.

Appendix

METHODS APPENDIX

A.1 Diffusion Simulations

Consider the following very simple model of IGO-based diffusion that mirrors the basic structure of the model used in this book. The model assumes that the human rights performance of a state is a linear function of:

1. the average human rights standards of its fellow IGO members in the previous period multiplied by a coefficient D;
2. its own human rights standards in the previous period multiplied by a coefficient L; and
3. a normally-distributed random error, $N(0, e)$, designed to capture exogenous changes in the state's human rights practices.

To keep this example very simple, let's assume that we have a system consisting of only 5 states, all of which belong to the same IGO. Let's also assume that at t_0—that is, before any IGO-based diffusion has taken place—the states vary widely in their human rights performance. Specifically, let's assume that at t_0 the first state has a score of 0 on the PIR index, the second has a score of 2, the third has a score of 4, the fourth has a score of 6, and the fifth has the maximum available score of 8. I shall then run the model over hundreds of iterations and observe how the human rights practices of each of these states evolves.

In the first scenario, Scenario 1, I assume a modest IGO-based diffusion effect $(D = 0.05)$, a high degree of temporal dependence $(L = 0.95)$ and no exogenous variation $(e = 0)$. As the graph in the upper left-hand

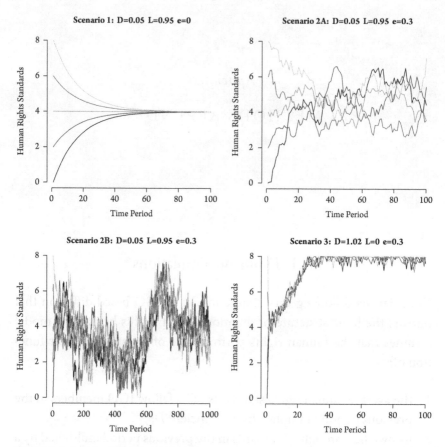

Figure A.1 Simple diffusion simulations.

panel of Figure A.1 shows, the five states' human rights practices gradually converge towards their mean. (As a result this rather unrealistic scenario does indeed lead to an "end of history" with respect to human rights.)

In the second scenario, Scenario 2A, I assume the same values of D and L, but this time I make the scenario more realistic by introducing an exogenous source of country-specific variation by setting $e = 0.3$. Here we again see evidence of convergence, but the converge effect is often masked by the role that the random variation is playing in determining each state's human rights practices.

The next scenario, Scenario 2B, is simply an extension of Scenario 2A. Here the parameters are exactly the same, but I have allowed the simulation to run for a much longer period of time. As the graph shows, the exogenous variation introduced to each state's human rights scores at each point in time causes their individual scores to embark on a "random walk," but the IGO-based diffusion effect serves to keep the human rights performance of all five states broadly in line with each other. This describes the type of outcome that, I argue, is most consistent with the results of the statistical models examined in this book.

By way of contrast, the last scenario, Scenario 3, illustrates an altogether different process. In this case I have created a self-reinforcing feedback loop by setting the diffusion coefficient to a number greater than 1. I have also introduced a small degree of exogenous variation in each state's human rights score. As the results show, having a value of D greater than 1 causes the states' scores to rapidly converge and then steadily move towards the maximum available score.

A.2 Cross-Validation

This project departs from existing studies of norm diffusion by not only considering the statistical significance of the *IGO Context* variable, but also by asking whether it makes a positive contribution to the predictive power of the model. In many social science applications variables can be found to be statistically significant simply because the model has been "overfitted," meaning that the model describes idiosyncratic features of the data used to generate the model without capturing the underlying data-generating process (Beck, King, and Zeng, 2000). Given that the amounts of data available to IR scholars is restricted by the relatively small number of independent countries that currently exist in the world, it is especially important that we avoid drawing inferences about international processes on the basis of statistically significant regression coefficients alone (Ward and Hoff, 2007; Ward, Greenhill, and Bakke, 2010). One way to insure against this risk is to test whether a model estimated using one set of data improves our ability to successfully predict outcomes in another set of data. Models that perform better under these conditions are likely to more accurately capture the true relationships that were responsible for generating the data in the first place (Schrodt, 2002).

One way to test a model's predictive power is therefore to estimate models using only a limited portion of the available data, while holding aside another portion of data for model testing. For example, if we had time-series cross-section data on all countries over the period 1981–2000, we might want to estimate a model using the data for the 15-year period from 1981–1995, and then assess the ability of that model to correctly

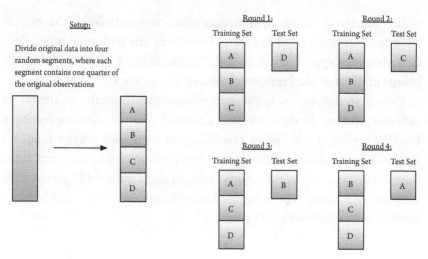

Figure A.2 Four-fold cross-validation procedure.

predict outcomes in the five-year period from 1996–2000. The problem with this approach, however, is that we would in effect be depriving ourselves of the opportunity to incorporate information from the 1996–2000 period into the original models. Given the significant costs associated with collecting many types of data in international relations, this would be a hard sacrifice to make.

A more efficient alternative is to use what is known as a cross-validation procedure. Cross-validation techniques—which are now a standard feature of the applied statistics literature—involve repeatedly partitioning the data into "training" and "test" sets, estimating the model using the training set, and then using that model to predict the outcomes in the test set. The better the model, the smaller the difference will be between the values of the actual and predicted outcomes in the test set. This procedure is repeated for alternative partitions of the data, thereby ensuring that each segment of data is used in both the model building and model evaluation stages. We can therefore think of this as a solution to a methodological problem that allows us to have our cake and eat it too; essentially we can build a model using all available data, while also collecting information about the ability of that model to make out-of-sample predictions.

Throughout this study I use a four-fold cross-validation procedure. As is illustrated by Figure A.2, this involves randomly dividing the available data into four equally sized segments, re-estimating the original model using a data set comprised of three of these four segments, and then assessing the predictive accuracy of the predictions made for the fourth segment. I repeat this process for a total of four separate rounds, each time using a different combination of three segments as the training set while setting aside the fourth as a test set. This ensures that I end up generating predictions for each observation in the original dataset.

I then assess the accuracy of these out-of-sample predictions by comparing the actual values of the dependent variable in the data with the predicted values generated by the model. There are many possible ways to do this, and the choice will depend in part upon the type of model used. For the analyses of physical integrity rights in Chapter 3 and of women's rights in Chapter 5, I use a simple linear model that allows me to measure predictive power by simply calculating the mean square error (MSE) of the out-of-sample predictions (i.e., $\frac{1}{n}\sum(y-\hat{y})^2$, where $\hat{y}$ represents the predicted level of the dependent variable and y the actual level of the dependent variable for each observation).

In the case of the logit models used for the event history analysis of the adoption of gay rights policies in Chapter 5, I measure the models' predictive power using the same cross-validation procedure described at the beginning of this section. For these models, the prediction metric is the average of the "expected Percent Correctly Predicted" (ePCP) statistic generated in each iteration of the cross-validation procedure (Herron, 1999). The ePCP statistic essentially provides a measure of how successful a model of categorical outcomes (like a logit model) is at assigning probabilities to the "correct" outcome category. In other words, a high ePCP score tells us that, on average, the model is assigning high probabilities of an outcome of 1 to the observations that are actually known to have an outcome of 1, and vice-versa.

Ultimately, for the purpose of this analysis I am interested in assessing the relative performance of different models—for instance, testing whether a model whose *IGO Context* variable has been constructed in a particular way does a better job than competing models at predicting outcomes. But because the relative performance of different models often turns out to be sensitive to the way in which the data is randomly partitioned into the four segments in the first stage of the process, I have chosen to iterate the cross-validation exercise over multiple draws of the data in order to construct some measure of the uncertainty around the cross-validation results. I do this by cycling through 100 random partitions of the data, each time performing the four-fold cross-validation described above and assessing which of the models under consideration performs best in terms of its out-of-sample predictive power. The result is therefore a score ranging from 0 to 100 of the number of times in which one particular model outperforms its alternatives.

The R functions I wrote for comparing multiple models using this particular cross-validation routine are available for download in the replication archive.

NOTES

Chapter 1

1. For some interesting examples of the application of a network perspective to the study of IGOs, see Pevehouse (2005); Hafner-Burton and Montgomery (2006); Maoz (2011).
2. Strictly speaking, MNCs represent a type of INGO, although the term INGO tends to be used only to refer to non-profit organizations.
3. This study is therefore concerned with IGOs, and not with human rights treaties. The study of the impact of human rights treaties has generated a fascinating literature in recent years. For some of the more important recent contributions, see Neumayer (2005); Simmons (2009); Hill (2010); Cole (2012); Lupu (2013); Fariss (2014).
4. A number of subsequent studies have lent empirical support to this insight. For example, in a study of negotiations over trade liberalization, Davis (2004) finds that opportunities for issue linkage between liberalization in the agricultural sector and liberalization in other industrial sectors is a strong predictor of whether the talks ultimately succeed or fail. She finds that negotiation agendas that force debate on a number of different sectors as part of an all-or-nothing package of liberalization (as was the case in the Uruguay Round of negotiations on the General Agreement on Tariffs and Trade (GATT)) are more likely to result in agreements being reached, whereas those that allow the states to leave discussion of certain sectors off the table are more likely to end in deadlock.
5. On reputation see Mercer (1996); Downs and Jones (2002); Press (2005); Brooks and Wohlforth (2008).
6. For example, during the discussion of North Korea's human rights record as part of its 2010 Universal Period Review, China's contribution was limited to the following (as summarized in the report of the relevant working group):

    China appreciated that the Constitution and laws provide for respect for human rights. It noted that the protection and promotion of human rights are priority tasks of various State organs. DPRK has good educational and health-care systems and strategies are in place for the attainment of the MDGs. China called on the international community to provide humanitarian development assistance and support efforts of the Government to develop economy and improve peoples' life. (UN Doc. A/HRC/13/13, para. 52.)

7. Waltz (1959) has described the types of explanation that privilege domestic politics as the "second image" of international relations, in contrast to explanations at the level of the individual (the "first image") and at the level of the international system (the "third image"). Perhaps the best known example of a second image explanation is the democratic peace theory, which suggests that wars between states are less likely to occur when both parties are democracies.
8. See "Madrid Attacks May Have Targeted Election." *The Washington Post,* October 17, 2004.

9. For a recent experimental study that challenges the notion of a nuclear taboo, see Press, Sagan and Valentino (2013).
10. For a more detailed examination of the ability of IGOs to shape the interests of their member states, see Bondanella Taninchev (forthcoming).
11. On obesity, see Christakis and Fowler (2007); on smoking see Christakis and Fowler (2008); on happiness see Fowler and Christakis (2008); on loneliness see Fowler and Christakis (2008).
12. However, as Noel and Nyhan (2011) show, relying on longitudinal data to exclude the homophily explanation is made significantly more difficult when one accounts for turnover in social networks.
13. See http://thedata.harvard.edu/dvn/dv/briangreenhill.

Chapter 2

1. In keeping with the constructivist view of the mutual constitution of agents and structures (Wendt, 1999: Ch. 4), this model suggests that states create a particular human rights culture within the IGOs to which they belong, and that this culture in turn influences the behavior of their member states with respect to their human rights practices.
2. Although the underlying logic is very different, the argument I advance here can in one sense be thought of as similar to the argument advanced by Julia Gray in her recent book *The Company States Keep* (Gray, 2013). In her study, Gray finds that investors' perceptions of a state's sovereign risk is influenced in part by the reputations of that state's interaction partners—specifically, the fellow members of the economic IGOs to which it belongs. While Gray is primarily concerned with the signaling role that membership in IGOs play—rather than in thinking of IGOs as sites of socialization—my argument is similar to hers in the sense that it is the practices of the member states, rather than the official policies of the IGO itself, that condition the effect that IGO membership will have on a state.
3. The concept of the *IGO Context* can therefore be thought of as analogous to the spatially lagged variables used in studies of policy diffusion; the key difference is that instead of reflecting the average human rights practices of a state's geographic neighbors, this quantity reflects the average human rights practices of a state's fellow IGO members (see Beck, Gleditsch, and Beardsley, 2006).
4. See Cichowski (2004) for an interesting analysis of how the EU's main judicial body, the ECJ, has come to include questions of individual human rights as an important part of its agenda.
5. In one of the early studies of socialization in international relations, Ikenberry and Kupchan (1990) argue that norm diffusion is most effective when a state can use its material power to force another state to change its behavior. This change in behavior tends to be followed by a change in beliefs on the part of the coerced state. According to Ikenberry and Kupchan, the most prominent examples of this are the successful democratization of Germany and Japan in the aftermath of World War II.
6. See "Report assails collusion in Europe with CIA," *International Herald Tribune*, November 29, 2006.
7. See http://www.hrw.org/news/2011/02/14/restoring-protection-lgbt-people-against-extra judicial-executions and http://ukhumanrightsblog.com/2010/12/21/general-assembly-vote -on-extrajudicial- killings-and-gay-rights/, accessed March 16, 2015.
8. In addition, I also weight the degree of influence by the size of the IGO in order to account for the fact that IGOs with fewer members presumably enable individual member states to exert greater influence over each other. The code to generate these maps and their underlying data is available in the replication archive.
9. The system for classifying IGOs on the basis of their institutional capacity developed by Boehmer, Gartzke, and Nordstrom (2004: 37–38) involves the following categories: "Minimal" IGOs are those that have very limited organizational structure and whose decisions do not create binding obligations for their member states. "Structured" IGOs have larger bureaucracies and more clearly codified decision-making procedures, and their decisions are binding upon their member states. "Interventionist" IGOs are those that have far more extensive bureaucracies and formal adjudication systems and have the capacity to impose

sanctions on their member states. Boehmer, Gartzke, and Nordstrom cite the IMF, WTO, and the EU as examples of interventionist IGOs.

10. The ECtHR is not to be the confused with the ECJ. The ECtHR is the court established by the Council of Europe, a 47-member IGO responsible for the promotion of democracy and human rights in the wider European region. The ECJ, on the other hand, is the judicial body of the 28-member EU. Its jurisdiction covers all relevant EU treaties and has therefore traditionally been concerned with issues of commerce among the EU member states, although some scholars have noted that its mandate is evolving into one that resembles a human rights court (Cichowski, 2004).

11. See also Pevehouse (2005). A recent study using network analytic techniques (Torfason and Ingram, 2010) arrives at a similar conclusion: states are likely to become more democratic if they share a large number of IGO memberships with other highly democratic states.

12. I thank Andreas Wimmer for pointing out this distinction to me.

13. See https://www.gov.uk/government/publications/information-pack-for-uk-delegates-to-the-oecd, accessed July 2013.

14. See http://www.nato.int/cps/en/natolive/topics_37356.htm, accessed July 2013.

15. Unfortunately, the term socialization has been used as an umbrella term to describe many different forms of social influence. Many of these socialization concepts—for example, that of Johnston (2008)—are similar to what Goodman and Jinks (2013) refer to as acculturation, but others would fit more naturally within the material inducements or learning/persuasion categories. For example, Ikenberry and Kupchan (1990) use the term socialization to describe, among other things, the change in policies that come about as a result of one state's forceful intervention in the politics of another (e.g., British rule in India). Similarly, Schimmelfennig (2005) proposes a rationalist model of socialization that involves states implementing policy changes in response to IGOs' membership criteria.

16. In the case of the United States, the relevant government agency is the National Institute of Standards and Technology, an agency of the US Department of Commerce.

17. Possible exceptions from the recent War on Terror might include the times when several European states came under pressure from the US to allow their airspace to be used for the extraordinary rendition of terrorism suspects, or when a large number of states adopted anti-terrorism legislation that allowed for longer periods of detention without charge.

Chapter 3

1. This chapter builds upon an earlier article I published in *International Studies Quarterly* on the IGO-based diffusion of human rights (Greenhill, 2010).

2. Pevehouse, Nordstrom, and Warnke (2004) justify their exclusion of these organizations (the so-called emanations) on the basis that they generally cannot be clearly distinguished from the IGOs that created them. In Chapter 4, however, I use data on human rights IGO emanations recently collected by Hafner-Burton, Mansfield, and Pevehouse (2013) to perform a more specific test of the IGO-based diffusion hypothesis.

3. Although the dataset consists of a total of 495 IGOs, there has actually been a significant degree of turnover as new IGOs are established and old ones are dissolved. This means that fewer than 495 are active at present; in 2005, the last year covered by the current version of the dataset, the number of active IGOs was 330.

4. In 2005 the UN had 191 members.

5. For more on the state-level factors that correlate with varying participation in IGOs, see Beckfield (2003).

6. In 2005, these three states belonged to 16, 19, and 20 different IGOs respectively.

7. In 2005, the 10 states that belonged to more than 100 different IGOs were, in descending order: France, Germany, the United Kingdom, the Netherlands, Italy, Denmark, Finland, Spain, Sweden, and Belgium.

8. When information from the two sources conflicted, the Amnesty International data took precedence. See the CIRI Coding Manual (2008).

9. In a subsequent analysis of these coding patterns, Cingranelli and Richards were able to confirm that abuses of these four categories of human rights tend to be hierarchically related

(i.e. the states that engage in the more severe categories of abuse are generally also engaging in the less severe categories of abuse at the same time) and can therefore be meaningfully aggregated into a single composite measure of respect for physical integrity rights (Cingranelli and Richards, 1999).

10. The color schemes used for the maps and figures in this book were chosen from the selection of palettes developed by Harrower and Brewer (2003).

11. As shall be discussed later, Fariss (2014) provides an interesting critique of the measurement standards implicit in the CIRI indices.

12. For a detailed discussion of the relationship between democracy and human rights, see Davenport and Armstrong (2004) and Hafner-Burton and Ron (2009).

13. I am grateful to Beth Simmons for suggesting this.

14. An interesting question to ask is what baseline these statistics should be compared against. One possibility is to generate a series of "placebo" IGOs that are equal in size to the actual IGOs, but whose patterns of membership have been randomized. (For instance, the placebo for NATO might consist of Belarus, Cambodia, and Egypt in place of Canada, Mexico, and the United States.) When I calculate the equivalent change over the 1981–2005 period in the standard deviation of these placebo IGOs, I find that, over multiple iterations, the overall average decline is between 10–12%—that is, evidence of a more general degree of convergence among states' PIR scores that is significantly smaller than the 19% decline observed among the members of the actual IGOs.

15. See Ward and Gleditsch (2008) on spatial modeling techniques. For a discussion of ways in which spatial modeling techniques can be applied in the context of non-geographical forms of ties between states, see Beck, Gleditsch, and Beardsley (2006).

16. For examples of this type of operationalization, see Bearce and Bondanella (2007); Cao (2007); Ingram, Robinson, and Busch (2005).

17. Moreover, the edges (or ties) in this type of network are said to be "undirected," meaning that the relationship defined by the edges is assumed to be symmetrical. In other words, if A is connected to B, then A can influence B while B can also influence A. While this simplifying assumption may be appropriate in the case of states' shared IGO memberships, it would be harder to defend in the case other types of relationships (e.g., trade or aid relationships) that tend to be highly asymmetrical.

18. Beckfield (2010) also employs a bipartite conceptualization of the IGO network in his study of the changing structure of the global IGO network. For a more general discussion of bipartite vs. unipartite networks, see Wasserman and Faust (1994: 299–302).

19. Recalculating IGO Context in a simpler way that includes the score of the focal state in the calculation of each IGO's human rights culture produces very similar regression estimates.

20. Note that as the IGO-means (i.e., the human rights cultures) are calculated from the perspective of each country, each IGO will have a slightly different value. So, from the perspective of the United States, the IGO-mean for NAFTA consists of the average scores of Canada and Mexico, whereas from the perspective of Mexico it consists of the average scores of the United States and Canada.

21. See, for example, Vreeland (2008).

22. Specifically, a regime transition is defined as a change of three or more points in the country's Polity score that takes places within a period of three years or less (Marshall and Jaggers, 2009).

23. I thank Michael D. Ward for encouraging me to think about regression output in this way.

24. Conversely, a negative coefficient on a spatially-lagged variable would indicate some sort of repulsion process—that is, a process in which states deliberately differentiate themselves from the states to which they are most closely connected. While this might occur in some social contexts—for example, where corporations choose to locate their production plants far apart from each other in order to serve a larger possible market (see Garretsen and Peeters, 2009; Kao and Bera, 2013)—it is difficult to imagine why an analogous process might occur in the context of IGO-based diffusion of human rights practices.

25. See, for example, Amnesty International (2014).

26. Rather than stratifying the data into subsets with either higher or lower levels of the dependent variable relative to the spatially lagged variable (as I have done here), Konisky (2007) suggests estimating the model on the full data while interacting the spatial lag with an indicator of which

subset each observation belongs to. Estimating the models using that approach produces very similar results.

27. Distances between countries are measured in terms of the shortest distance between their capital cities, which were obtained from the dataset developed by Gleditsch (2002). Including a spatial lag provides a more nuanced measure of regional influences than is commonly done in studies that simply estimate a separate intercept for a few discrete (and often somewhat arbitrarily defined) regions. See Ward and Gleditsch 2008: Ch. 2. On a practical level, it means that we can explicitly model the fact that a northern European state like Norway is subject to a very different set of international influences than states like Greece or Malta at the southern end of the continent.

28. Data on the languages, religions, and colonial heritage of each country were obtained from the *CIA World Factbook*. In the case of the language variables, only the official language(s) (or where inapplicable, the primary language) was used to identify the language group(s) to which each state belongs. In the case of the religion variable, only the religions with which more than 30% of the population identified were recognized for the purpose of identifying religious ties between states. The categories I used for the purpose of identifying religious ties between states were Christianity, Islam, Hinduism, and Buddhism. I ignored sectarian differences within each of these major religions.

29. I also find that, in the multiple models created to account for the uncertainty inherent in the Fariss data, including *IGO Context* leads, on average, to an improvement in the out-of-sample predictive in 73 out of 100 cross-validation trials.

30. Smith and Wiest (2012) coded these data at two or three-year intervals for the period relevant to this study using information from the *Yearbook of International Organizations*. I used linear interpolation to fill in the data for the intervening years. In counting the number of INGOs, I considered only those that Smith and Wiest (2012) identify as having a general human rights goal.

31. This produces an estimated *IGO Context* coefficient of 0.19 with a p-value of 0.003.

32. This is the same metric I had used when discussing Hungary's changing sources of IGO-based influence in Section 2.2.

Chapter 4

1. Based upon 2012 levels of GDP (at purchasing power parity) as reported in the *CIA World Factbook*.

2. I also kept in place all of the same covariates designed to account for other non-IGO based influences on a state's human rights practices.

3. On the concept of soft power in IR, see Nye (2004).

4. To avoid attaching negative weights to non-democratic states, I added 10 points to each state's Polity 2 score. This produces a democracy scale that ranges from 0 to 20 instead of -10 to 10.

5. Although this may sound as if the dependent variable is appearing on both sides of the regression equation, it is important to keep in mind that because the *IGO Context* variable is lagged by one year, the weighting scheme is also lagged by one year. This means that we are still asking whether a state's *PIR Score* at time t is influenced by its *IGO Context* at time $t - 1$; the only difference is that we are now constructing *IGO Context*$_{t-1}$ in a way that gives greater influence to states with higher levels of *PIR Score*$_{t-1}$.

6. The model that uses the dichotomous democracy measure outperforms the baseline (unweighted) model in 99 out of 100 cross-validation trials, while the model that uses the continuous measure of democracy outperforms the baseline in all 100 trials. When directly compared against each other, the model with the continuous measure outperforms its dichotomous counterpart in 91 out of 100 trials.

7. This model outperformed the baseline in only 2 of the 100 cross-validation trials.

8. According to the World Bank's website:

> Although its policies, programs and projects have never been explicitly or deliberately aimed towards the realization of human rights, the Bank contributes to the promotion of human rights in different areas, e.g., improving poor people's access to health, education, food and water; promoting the participation of indigenous peoples in decision-making and

the accountability of governments to their citizens; supporting justice reforms, fighting corruption and increasing transparency of governments.

(http://web.worldbank.org/WBSITE/EXTERNAL/EXTSITETOOLS/0,,contentMDK: 20749693 pagePK: 98400 piPK:98424 theSitePK:95474,00.html, accessed July 21, 2014)

9. The full list of 18 IGOs consists of: Organisation Internationale de la Francophonie, the Andean Parliament, the African Union, the Central European Free Trade Association, the Council of Europe, the Commonwealth Secretariat, the Community of Portuguese-Speaking Countries, the European Training Foundation, the International Bureau of Education, the International Criminal Court, the Intergovernmental TV and Radio Corporation, the North Atlantic Treaty Organization, the Organization for Security and Cooperation in Europe, the Central American Integration System, the United Nations, the United Nations Educational, Scientific and Cultural Organization, and the World Tourism Organization.

10. More specifically, I recorded the number of hits produced by running a search for articles containing the IGO's full name and the term "human rights," using the Lexis-Nexis database of global newspaper articles for 2013. I then took the natural logarithm of these counts (plus one) in order to produce a more uniform distribution of IGO weights.

11. The only possible exception is the model produced using the first approach (my own search for the mention of the term human rights in the organizations' aims), which outperforms the baseline model in 56 out of 100 cross-validation trials. The other three models almost never outperform the baseline model.

12. I thank Jon Pevehouse for this suggestion.

13. These data were obtained from the directory of permanent missions to the UN published by the UN's Protocol and Liaison Service.

14. According to this logic, the increased exposure to the practices of other states need not make the richer states more receptive only to positive influences on their human rights standards; we might also expect them to be more receptive to negative influences too. Indeed, as discussed in Section 3.3, the IGO-based diffusion of human rights standards is likely to consist of a mixture of upward and downward influences.

15. Observant readers will notice that this graph suggests that when the value of logged GDP falls below 20 (corresponding to a total GDP of about US$500 million), the estimated effect of *IGO Context* is actually negative and statistically significant at the 0.05 level. However, this can most likely be dismissed as an artifact of the data used to estimate the model, rather than compelling evidence of a negative convergence effect among these very poor states. This is so for two reasons: First, only around 1.5% of all country-year observations used to estimate the model have a low enough GDP to fall into this category. Second, re-estimating the model without these observations produces a very similar overall result, thereby confirming that these low-GDP observations do not exert undue influence over the slope of the line estimated in the graph.

16. See Chapter 3, note 30, for a discussion of my treatment of the data from Smith and Wiest (2012). Interestingly, the number of human rights INGOs is not as strongly correlated with the Polity 2 measure of democracy as one might expect; the correlation coefficient is only 0.55.

17. As noted in the robustness checks discussed in Chapter 3, a more basic model that includes the number of human rights INGOs in addition to *IGO Context*—but without the interaction term—produces a similar estimate of the diffusion effect. At the same time, however, it suggests that states whose citizens participate in a greater number of human rights INGOs have *worse* performance on the PIR index. The cause of this negative correlation is an interesting question for future research. It could perhaps be explained by poor human rights standards creating a greater demand for INGO attention (i.e., a selection effect), or because a greater presence of human rights INGOs makes detection or publication of human rights violations more probable (see Fariss, 2014).

18. In the cross-validation trials, all of these interaction models represent a consistent improvement in terms of out-of-sample predictive power relative to the baseline model.

19. It is worth noting that this is unlikely to result from democracy being confounded with measures of material power. As Table 4.1 shows, democracy has only a relatively weak positive correlation to the measures of GDP used in this analysis.

Chapter 5

1. An alternative explanation for any difference between the transmissibility of women's rights and gay rights might be that, regardless of their status in international law, gay rights are simply too recent a development for there to be much evidence of an IGO-mediated diffusion effect. However, as is illustrated by Figure 5.1, there has been a significant increase in the number of states that have adopted progressive policies with respect to gay rights. This chapter will examine to what extent IGO ties can help to explain these patterns of adoption after controlling for a number of different domestic and international factors that may explain a state's policies in this area.

2. Indeed, the Saudi government is careful to frame its policies towards women in terms of its compliance with a local interpretation of universal human rights principles. For example, on the website of its embassy to the United States the Saudi government claims that

   > We believe that the comprehensive concept of human rights should be based on the real-ization that human communities have special characteristics, cultures, beliefs and religions, which must be acknowledged and respected. The Kingdom respects this international norm and adheres to the noble objectives that call for the protection of human rights and preservation of human dignity. (http://www.saudiembassy.net/issues/human-rights/default.aspx, accessed March 16, 2015.)

   Elsewhere on the website the government takes pains to point out various rights that women enjoy in Saudi Arabia, as well as achievements that women have had in occupying ministerial roles (see "What about Muslim Women?" at http://www.saudiembassy.net/about/country-information/Islam/understanding_Islam.aspx and "Women appointed to top jobs at Ministry of Education" at http://www.saudiembassy.net/archive/2007/news/page788.aspx).

3. Hathaway (2002) makes a similar argument with respect to what she calls the "expressive" role of treaty ratification.

4. For a critique of the role that reputation plays in international relations, at least from the point of view of international security, see Mercer (1996); Downs and Jones (2002); Press (2005); Brooks and Wohlforth (2008).

5. The public order defense has however been challenged by the 1994 opinion of the UN Human Rights Committee in *Toonen v. Australia* (Fellmeth, 2008: 820).

6. The data used in this chapter were obtained from the 2011 version of the report, available online at http://old.ilga.org/Statehomophobia/ILGA_State_Sponsored_Homophobia_2011.pdf (accessed June 29, 2011).

7. As shall be discussed in Section 5.2, the event history model of legalization of homosexuality used in this study explains variation in the time taken for states to legalize homosexual acts within the 1960–2010 period. States that had not officially outlawed homosexuality in the first place are therefore excluded from the model, and cannot bias the results in the same way that they would if included in, say, a simple logit or probit model of legalization status in each year.

8. The data on women's political rights and women's economic rights cover the period 1981–2009, while the data on women's social rights cover the period 1981–2007. However, due to limitations in the availability of IGO membership data, the regression analyses in the following sections do not extend beyond 2005.

9. It is important to note that while CEDAW requires states to remove barriers to women's political participation, it does not require that they implement quotas regarding women's representation in political offices.

10. Other examples of non-democracies with high scores on the CIRI measure of women's political rights include Czechoslovakia in the late 1980s and Eritrea in 2004.

11. For full details on the construction of *IGO Context* please refer to Section 3.2.

12. Although a single comparison is obviously insufficient to demonstrate the importance of *IGO Context*, it is worth noting that India went on to decriminalize homosexuality in 2009, whereas Uganda signed its notorious "Anti-Homosexuality Act" into law in February 2014. However, as at the time of writing both of these developments have faced significant reversals: in December 2013 India's Supreme Court overturned the 2009 decision that had decriminalized homosexual acts, and in August 2014 the Ugandan Constitutional Court invalidated the recently-signed "Anti-Homosexuality Act."

13. As I shall be discussing below, the same logic does not apply to the women's rights models.

14. The list consists of *GDP per capita, Regime Durability, Population Density, Democracy, Trade Dependence, FDI Dependence,* and *Conflict.* (For full details, see pages 70–72.)

15. Transitions to democracy were identified with respect to the Polity 2 score. A positive score that had been preceded by a score of zero or less in any of the previous five years was taken to indicate a democratic transition.

16. Moravcsik's explanation for the willingness of newly-established democracies to embrace the European Convention on Human Rights (ECHR) is based on the theory that the leaders of these states have a strong incentive to "lock-in" recent democratic reforms. Binding a state to a powerful international human rights regime would presumably make it much more difficult for future governments to dismantle these democratic reforms. In the case of women's rights or gay rights, however, the mechanism is likely to be very different: newly-democratic states will presumably want to adopt such legislation as part of a more general normative embrace of progressive reforms (e.g., South Africa legalized homosexuality in 1998), even though doing so is likely to have only a limited effect on tying the hands of future governments.

17. It is worth noting that the results for physical integrity rights presented in Table 3.1 of Chapter 3 are robust to the inclusion of the *New Democracy* covariate. The results of these robustness tests are presented in Table 3 of the online appendix.

18. In both the gay rights and women's rights models, the inclusion of the *IGO Context* variable led to an improvement in the model's out-of-sample predictive power in all 100 cross-validation trials. See Appendix A.2 for details of the cross-validation procedure.

19. Keep in mind that because this is a logit model, the relationship between each of the independent variables and the probability of adoption necessarily has a non-linear form.

20. In the case of the women's rights model, this reflects the average level of the composite measure of women's rights found among all states in that particular year. In the case of the gay rights model, this variable is the cumulative number of states that have passed the relevant piece of legislation by the end of each year.

21. Interestingly, in their study of human rights in Latin America, Lutz and Sikkink (2001) make a similar observation. They note that while a highly legalized treaty system exists with respect to states' obligations under the Convention Against Torture, a much less formal regime exists to protect citizens' rights to democratic institutions of governance. Yet they find that norms concerning democracy appear to have diffused more successfully than those concerning the non-use of torture.

Chapter 6

1. These were drawn from all states in the world, not just African states.

2. See Beckfield (2003).

3. By the end of the Gulf War, the United States and Iraq no longer shared membership in one of the original 27 IGOs (the International Natural Rubber Organization), but acquired joint membership in one other (the World Customs Organization).

4. By suggesting that states are unlikely to break their existing IGO ties in response to changes in their partner states' human rights performance, this in itself helps to make the endogeneity problem less acute. However, the possibility remains that states choose only to form *new* IGO ties with states that, at least at the time of joining, tend to have similar human rights practices to their own. It is this aspect of the endogeneity problem that is the primarily concern of this chapter.

5. Using an original dataset on suspensions of states from IGOs, von Borzyskowski and Vabulas (2014) find that instances of what they refer to as "political backsliding"—cases that can include but are not limited to instances of major human rights violations—only leads to suspensions from IGOs in very rare cases (typically fewer than two suspensions per year in the entire dataset.)

6. Similar results were found when I considered a sample of less prominent IGOs. In Section 8 of the online appendix, I provide a list of states that left from a randomly selected sample of 10 IGOs during the same period.

7. The following abbreviations are used for the IGOs: United Nations (UN), World Health Organization (WHO), North Atlantic Treaty Organization (NATO), and Asian Development Bank (AsDB).
8. This matrix uses the following three-letter country codes from the Correlates of War dataset: Afghanistan (AFG), Belarus (BLR), China (CHN), France (FRN), Mongolia (MON), Russia (RUS), Taiwan (TAW), and United States (USA).
9. This operationalization of the *IGO Flows* variable does not distinguish between a situation in which state i joins an IGO in which state j is already a member and one in which state i and state j simultaneously join a new IGO. While it would be interesting in future work to separately consider each of these pathways to shared IGO membership, for the purposes of this exercise I employ a more parsimonious model that simply reflects the decision of state i to form a new IGO tie with state j through either of these pathways.
10. Note that the latent space need not be restricted to only two dimensions.
11. In practice, this distance can be calculated by simply calculating the inner product of the vectors of coordinates of the positions of states i and j in the latent space: the further apart these sets of coordinates are, the lower this proximity measure will be. For example, if Country A in Figure 6.3 is located at a position with the coordinates $(-2, 3)$ and Country C is located at a position with the coordinates $(-1, 1)$, the inner product of these vectors is given by $(-2 \times -1) + (3 \times 1) = 5$. If Country D, being significantly further away from A, is located at position $(4, -3)$, the inner product of these vectors is equal to $(-2 \times 4) + (3 \times -3) = -17$. This much lower value for the A-D relationship relative to that of the A-C relationship implies a reduced probability of a tie being formed.
12. The R programs used to estimate this type of model are available for download at http://www.stat.washington.edu/hoff/code.php.
13. For the purpose of calculating these differences, I treat the 9-level PIR index as if it were coded on an interval scale. Values of zero were imputed for dyads where one or both countries have missing data on the CIRI PIR index.
14. Of the 495 IGOs in the Pevehouse, Nordstrom, and Warnke (2004) dataset, I identified 307 as having a distinct regional focus.
15. I replaced missing values for dyads involving the micro-states of Kiribati, Nauru, Tonga, and Tuvalu with the corresponding distances to Samoa, given that it is located relatively close to these islands.
16. For a discussion of the importance of homophily in networks of individuals, see McPherson, Smith-Lovin, and Cook (2001). In the international realm, Lee and Bai (2013) investigate the role that various forms of similarity among states plays in the formation of free trade agreements.
17. As with the *Human Rights Similarity* variable discussed above, I replaced missing values for each of these two dyadic variables with zeros.
18. However, in light of the constraints imposed by the traditional dyadic regression model, Boehmer and Nordstrom test for the existence of these general relationships by employing the so-called weak-link assumption. This involves testing for the existence of a correlation between the number of IGO memberships and the *lower* of the two democracy (or development) scores found among the members of each dyad. Unlike the traditional dyadic model, the bilinear mixed effects model employed here has the advantage of allowing the user to directly specify dyadic and monadic covariates and therefore avoid having to make the often questionable weak-link assumption (see Ward, Siverson, and Cao, 2007: 588).
19. I imputed missing values for *GDP* using the first-quartile GDP per capita value for each particular year, given that the states with missing values are mostly small island states such as Fiji or Tuvalu. However, missing values for *Regime Type* were replaced with the global average Polity 2 score for each year.
20. Unfortunately, the bilinear mixed effects model does not accommodate time-series network data, so in most applications a series of cross-sectional models are estimated instead (see Hoff and Ward 2004; Ward and Hoff 2007; Ward, Siverson, and Cao 2007)—although for an alternative approach to dealing with time-series data in this framework, see Ward, Ahlquist, and Rozenas (2014).

21. Beckfield (2003: 413) does, however, consider membership in the various civilizations defined by Huntington (1996) as an explanatory variable, but finds little evidence of this affecting their levels of IGO membership.

22. See "Turkey Restates Determination to Join the European Union," *The New York Times*, June 26, 2009; "Cold on Turkey," *The New York Times*, September 10, 2009.

BIBLIOGRAPHY

Abrams, Dominic, Margaret Wetherell, Sandra Cochrane, Michael A. Hogg, and John C. Turner. 1990. "Knowing what to think by knowing who you are: Self-categorization and the nature of norm formation, conformity and group polarization." *British Journal of Social Psychology* 29(2):97–119.

Amnesty International. 2014. "USA: Another year, same missing ingredient." *Amnesty International Reports* AMR 51/032/2014.

Apodaca, Clair 2001. "Global economic patterns and personal integrity rights after the Cold War." *International Studies Quarterly* 45(4):587–602.

Asal, Victor, Udi Sommer, and Paul G. Harwood. 2013. "Original sins: A cross-national study of the legality of homosexual acts." *Comparative Political Studies* 46(3):320–351.

Aveyard, Paul, Rachna Begh, Amanda Parsons, and Robert West. 2012. "Brief opportunistic smoking cessation interventions: A systematic review and meta-analysis to compare advice to quit and offer of assistance." *Addiction* 107(6):1066–1073.

Axelrod, Robert. 1984. *The Evolution of Cooperation*. Basic Books.

Ayoub, Phillip M. 2014. "Contested norms in new-adopter states: International determinants of LGBT rights legislation." *European Journal of International Relations*, doi: 1354066114543335.

Ayoub, Phillip M. forthcoming. *When States Come Out: Europe's Sexual Minorities and the Politics of Visibility*. Cambridge University Press.

Baldez, Lisa. 2014. *Defying Convention: US Resistance to the UN Treaty on Women's Rights*. Cambridge University Press.

Barnett, Michael N. and Martha Finnemore. 2004. *Rules for the World: International Organizations in Global Politics*. Cornell University Press.

Baylis, John, Steve Smith, and Patricia Owens. 2014. *The Globalization of World Politics: An Introduction to International Relations*. 6th ed. Oxford University Press.

Bearce, David H. and Stacy Bondanella. 2007. "Intergovernmental organizations, socialization, and member-state interest convergence." *International Organization* 61(4):703–733.

Beck, Nathaniel, Gary King, and Langche Zeng. 2000. "Improving quantitative studies of international conflict: A conjecture." *American Political Science Review* 94(1):21–35.

Beck, Nathaniel, Kristian S. Gleditsch, and Kyle Beardsley. 2006. "Space is more than geography: Using spatial econometrics in the study of political economy." *International Studies Quarterly* 50(1):27–44.

Beckfield, Jason 2003. "Inequality in the world polity: The structure of international organization." *American Sociological Review* 68(3):401–424.

Beckfield, Jason. 2010. "The Social Structure of the World Polity." *American Journal of Sociology* 115:1018–1068.

Bob, Clifford. 2012. *The Global Right Wing and the Clash of World Politics*. Cambridge University Press.

Boehmer, Charles, Erik Gartzke, and Timothy Nordstrom. 2004. "Do intergovernmental organizations promote peace?" *World Politics* 57(1):1–38.

Boehmer, Charles and Timothy Nordstrom. 2008. "Intergovernmental organization memberships: Examining political community and the attributes of international organizations." *International Interactions* 34(3):282–309.

Boli, John and George M. Thomas. 1999. *Constructing World Culture: International Nongovernmental Organizations Since 1875*. Stanford University Press.

Bondanella Taninchev, Stacy. forthcoming. "Intergovernmental organizations, interaction, and member state interest convergence." *International Interactions*.

Box-Steffensmeier, Janet M. and Bradford S. Jones. 2004. *Event History Modeling: A Guide for Social Scientists*. Cambridge University Press.

Brambor, Thomas, William R. Clark, and Matt Golder. 2006. "Understanding interaction models: Improving empirical analyses." *Political Analysis* 14(1):63–82.

Brooks, Stephen G. and William C. Wohlforth. 2008. *World out of Balance: International Relations and the Challenge of American Primacy*. Princeton University Press.

Bruce-Jones, Eddie and Lucas Paoli Itaborahy. 2011. *State-sponsored Homophobia: A World Survey of Laws Prohibiting Same Sex Activity between Consenting Adults*. International Lesbian and Gay Association.

Bunch, Charlotte 1990. "Women's rights as human rights: Toward a re-vision of human rights." *Human Rights Quarterly* 12(4):486–498.

Campbell, John L. 2002. "Ideas, politics, and public policy." *Annual Review of Sociology* 28:21–38.

Campbell, R., F. Starkey, J. Holliday, S. Audrey, M. Bloor, N. Parry-Langdon, R. Hughes, and L. Moore. 2008. "An informal school-based peer-led intervention for smoking prevention in adolescence (ASSIST): A cluster randomised trial." *The Lancet* 371(9624):1595–1602.

Cao, Xun 2007. *Convergence, Divergence, and Networks in International Political Economy*. Ph.D. Thesis, University of Washington.

Cao, Xun 2009. "Networks of intergovernmental organizations and convergence in domestic economic policies." *International Studies Quarterly* 53(4):1095–1130.

Cao, Xun. 2010. "Networks as channels of policy diffusion: Explaining worldwide changes in capital taxation, 1998–2006." *International Studies Quarterly* 54(3):823–854.

Carter, David B. and Curtis S. Signorino. 2010. "Back to the future: Modeling time dependence in binary data." *Political Analysis* 18(3):271–292.

Chayes, Abram and Antonia Handler Chayes. 1993. "On compliance." *International Organization* 47(2):175–205.

Checkel, Jeffrey T. 2005. "International institutions and socialization in Europe: Introduction and framework." *International Organization* 59(4):801–826.

Christakis, Nicholas A. and James H. Fowler. 2007. "The spread of obesity in a large social network over 32 years." *New England Journal of Medicine* 357(4):370–379.

Christakis, Nicholas A. and James H. Fowler. 2008. "The collective dynamics of smoking in a large social network." *New England Journal of Medicine* 358(21):2249–2258.

Chwieroth, Jeffrey M. 2009. *Capital Ideas: The IMF and the Rise of Financial Liberalization*. Princeton University Press.

Cichowski, Rachel A. 2004. "Women's rights, the European Court, and supranational constitutionalism." *Law & Society Review* 38(3):489–512.

Cingranelli, D.L. and D.L. Richards. 1999. "Measuring the level, pattern, and sequence of government respect for physical integrity rights." *International Studies Quarterly* 43(2):407–417.

Cingranelli, David L. and David L. Richards. 2004. "The Cingranelli-Richards (CIRI) Human Rights Dataset." http://www.humanrightsdata.com/.

Cingranelli, David L. and David L. Richards. 2008. *The Cingranelli-Richards (CIRI) Human Rights Data Project Coding Manual*. CIRI.

Ciorciari, John D. 2012. "Institutionalizing human rights in Southeast Asia." *Human Rights Quarterly* 34(3):695–725.

Cole, Wade M. 2012. "Human rights as myth and ceremony? Reevaluating the effectiveness of human rights treaties, 1981–2007." *American Journal of Sociology* 117(4):1131–1171.

Crawford, Neta and Audie Klotz. 1999. *How Sanctions Work: Lessons from South Africa*. Palgrave Macmillan.

Davenport, Christian. 2007. "State repression and political order." *Annual Review of Political Science* 10:1–23.

Davenport, Christian and David A. Armstrong. 2004. "Democracy and the violation of human rights: A statistical analysis from 1976 to 1996." *American Journal of Political Science* 48(3):538–554.

Davis, Christina L. 2004. "International institutions and issue linkage: Building support for agricultural trade liberalization." *American Political Science Review* 98(1):153–169.

De Boef, Suzanna and Luke Keele. 2008. "Taking time seriously." *American Journal of Political Science* 52(1):184–200.

Downs, George W. and Michael A. Jones. 2002. "Reputation, compliance, and international law." *The Journal of Legal Studies* 31(S1):S95–S114.

Duxbury, Alison. 2011. *The Participation of States in International Organisations: The Role of Human Rights and Democracy*. Cambridge University Press.

Farer, Tom J. 1997. "The rise of the inter-American Human Rights regime: No longer a unicorn, not yet an ox." *Human Rights Quarterly* 19(3):510–546.

Fariss, Christopher J. 2014. "Respect for human rights has improved over time: Modeling the changing standard of accountability." *American Political Science Review* 108(2): 297–318.

Fellmeth, Aaron X. 2008. "State regulation of sexuality in international human rights law and theory." *William & Mary Law Review* 50:797.

Finnemore, Martha 1993. "International organizations as teachers of norms: The United Nations Educational, Scientific, and Cutural Organization and science policy." *International Organization* 47(4):565–597.

Finnemore, Martha and Kathryn Sikkink. 1998. "International norm dynamics and political change." *International Organization* 52(4):887–917.

Finnemore, Martha. 1996. "Norms, culture, and world politics: Insights from sociology's institutionalism." *International organization* 50(02):325–347.

Forsythe, David P. and Baekkwan Park. 2009. "United Nations Human Rights Council." *Encyclopedia of Human Rights* Oxford University Press.

Fowler, James H. and Nicholas A. Christakis. 2008. "Dynamic spread of happiness in a large social network: Longitudinal analysis over 20 years in the Framingham Heart Study." *BMJ: British Medical Journal* 337:a2338.

Frank, David J., Ann Hironaka, and Evan Schofer. 2000. "The nation-state and the natural environment over the twentieth century." *American Sociological Review* 65(1):96–116.

Garretsen, Harry and Jolanda Peeters. 2009. "FDI and the relevance of spatial linkages: Do third-country effects matter for Dutch FDI?" *Review of World Economics* 145(2):319–338.

Gheciu, Alexandra 2005a. "Security institutions as agents of socialization? NATO and the 'New Europe.'" *International Organization* 59(4):973–1012.

Gheciu, Alexandra. 2005b. *NATO in the New Europe: The Politics of International Socialization after the Cold War*. Stanford University Press.

Gilardi, Fabrizio. 2010. "Who learns from what in policy diffusion processes?" *American Journal of Political Science* 54(3):650–666.

Gilardi, Fabrizio. 2014. "Four ways we can improve policy diffusion research." *Working Paper*. http://www.fabriziogilardi.org/resources/papers/Gilardi-Improve-Diffusion.pdf.

Gleditsch, Kristian S. 2002. "Expanded trade and GDP data." *Journal of Conflict Resolution* 46(5):712.

Gleditsch, Kristian S. and Michael D. Ward. 2006. "Diffusion and the international context of democratization." *International Organization* 60(4):911–933.

Gleditsch, Nils Petter, Peter Wallensteen, Mikael Eriksson, Margareta Sollenberg, and Håvard Strand. 2002. "Armed conflict 1946–2001: A new dataset." *Journal of Peace Research* 39(5):615–637.

Goffman, Erving. 1961. "On the characteristics of total institutions." *Asylum: Essays on the Social Situation of Mental Patients and Other Inmates*. Anchor Books.

Goldstein, Judith L., Douglas Rivers, and Michael Tomz. 2007. "Institutions in International Relations: Understanding the effects of the GATT and the WTO on world trade." *International Organization* 61(01):37–67.

Goodman, Ryan and Derek Jinks. 2013. *Socializing States: Promoting Human Rights Through International Law*. Oxford University Press.

Gourevitch, Peter 1978. "The second image reversed: The international sources of domestic politics." *International Organization* 32(4):881–912.

Gray, Julia. 2013. *The Company States Keep: International Economic Organizations and Investor Perceptions*. Cambridge University Press.

Gray, Mark M., Miki Caul Kittilson, and Wayne Sandholtz. 2006. "Women and globalization: A study of 180 countries, 1975–2000." *International Organization* 60(02):293–333.

Greenhill, Brian, Layna Mosley, and Aseem Prakash. 2009. "Trade-based diffusion of labor rights: A panel study, 1986–2002." *American Political Science Review* 103(04):669–690.

Greenhill, Brian. 2010. "The company you keep: International socialization and the diffusion of human rights norms." *International Studies Quarterly* 54:127–145.

Gruber, Lloyd 2000. *Ruling the World: Power Politics and the Rise of Supranational Institutions*. Princeton University Press.

Guzman, Andrew T. 2008. *How International Law Works: A Rational Choice Theory*. Oxford University Press.

Haas, Ernst B. 1980. "Why collaborate? Issue-linkage and international regimes." *World Politics: A Quarterly Journal of International Relations* 32(3):357–405.

Hafner-Burton, Emilie M. 2005a. "Right or robust? The sensitive nature of repression to globalization." *Journal of Peace Research* 42(6):679–698.

Hafner-Burton, Emilie M. 2005b. "Trading human rights: How preferential trade agreements influence government repression." *International Organization* 59(3):593–629.

Hafner-Burton, Emilie M. and Kiyoteru Tsutsui. 2005. "Human rights in a globalizing world: The paradox of empty promises." *American Journal of Sociology* 110(5):1373–1411.

Hafner-Burton, Emilie M. and Kiyoteru Tsutsui. 2007. "Justice lost! The failure of international human rights law to matter where needed most." *Journal of Peace Research* 44(4):407–425.

Hafner-Burton, Emilie. 2009. *Forced to Be Good: Why Trade Agreements Boost Human Rights*. Cornell University Press.

Hafner-Burton, Emilie M. and Alexander H. Montgomery. 2006. "Power positions: International organizations, social networks, and conflict." *Journal of Conflict Resolution* 50(1): 3–27.

Hafner-Burton, Emilie M., Edward D. Mansfield, and Jon C.W. Pevehouse. 2013. "Human rights institutions, sovereignty costs and democratization." *British Journal of Political Science* 45:1–27.

Hafner-Burton, Emilie M. and James Ron. 2009. "Seeing double: Human rights impact through qualitative and quantitative eyes." *World Politics* 61(2):360–401.

Hanieh, Adam. 2013. "Bahrain." In Amar and Prashad (eds.) Dispatches from the Arab Spring: Understanding the New Middle East. University of Minnesota Press, 63–88.

Harrower, Mark and Cynthia A. Brewer. 2003. "Colorbrewer.org: An online tool for selecting colour schemes for maps." *Cartographic Journal* 40(1):27–37.

Hathaway, Oona A. 2002. "Do human rights treaties make a difference?" *Yale Law Journal* 111(8): 1935–2042.

Hawkins, Darren and Melissa Humes. 2002. "Human rights and domestic violence." *Political Science Quarterly* 117(2):231–257.

Hawkins, Darren and Wade Jacoby. 2010. "Partial compliance: A comparison of the European and Inter-American Courts of Human Rights." *Journal of International Law & International Relations* 6:35–85.

Herron, Michael C. 1999. "Postestimation uncertainty in limited dependent variable models." *Political Analysis* 8(1):83–98.

Hill, Daniel W. 2010. "Estimating the effects of human rights treaties on state behavior." *Journal of Politics* 72(04):1161–1174.

Hoff, Peter D. 2005. "Bilinear mixed effects models for dyadic data." *Journal of the American Statistical Association* 100(469):286–295.

Hoff, Peter D., Adrian E. Raftery, and Mark S. Handcock. 2002. "Latent space approaches to social network analysis." *Journal of the American Statistical Association* 97(460):1090–1099.

Hoff, Peter D. and Michael D. Ward. 2004. "Modeling dependencies in international relations networks." *Political Analysis* 12(2):160.

Huntington, Samuel P. 1996. *The Clash of Civilizations and the Remaking of World Order*. Simon and Schuster.

Hurd, Ian 2003. "Legitimacy and authority in international politics." *International Organization* 53(02):379–408.

Ikenberry, G. John and Charles A. Kupchan. 1990. "Socialization and hegemonic power." *International Organization* 44(3):283–315.

Ingram, Paul, Jeffrey Robinson, and Marc L. Busch. 2005. "The intergovernmental network of world trade: IGO connectedness, governance, and embeddedness." *American Journal of Sociology* 111(3):824–858.

Jacobson, Harold K., William M. Reisinger, and Todd Mathers. 1986. "National entanglements in international governmental organizations." *American Political Science Review* 80(1):141–159.

Johnston, Alastair Iain 2008. *Social States: China in International Institutions, 1980–2000*. Princeton University Press.

Johnston, Alastair Iain. 2001. "Treating international institutions as social environments." *International Studies Quarterly* 45(4):487–515.

Kao, Yu-Hsien and Anil K. Bera. 2013. "Spatial regression: The curious case of negative spatial dependence." *Working Paper*. http://www.maxwell.syr.edu/uploadedFiles/cpr/events/cpr_camp_econometrics/papers2013/Kao_Bera.pdf.

Katzenstein, Peter J., Robert O. Keohane, and Stephen D. Krasner. 1998. "International organization and the study of world politics." *International Organization* 52(4):645–685.

Keck, Margaret E. and Kathryn Sikkink. 1998. *Activists Beyond Borders: Advocacy Networks in International Politics*. Cornell University Press.

Keller, L.M. 2004. "The Convention on the Elimination of Discrimination against Women: Evolution and (non)implementation worldwide." *Thomas Jefferson Law Review* 27(1):35.

Kelling, George L. and Catherine M. Coles. 1996. *Fixing Broken Windows: Restoring Order and Reducing Crime in our Communities*. Simon and Schuster.

Keohane, Robert O. 1984. *After Hegemony: Cooperation and Discord in the World Political Economy*. Princeton University Press.

Klotz, Audie. 1995. "Norms reconstituting interests: Global racial equality and US sanctions against South Africa." *International Organization* 49:451–451.

Koh, Harold Hongju 1997. "Why Do Nations Obey International Law?" *Yale Law Journal* 106:2599–2697.

Kollman, Kelly. 2007. "Same-sex unions: The globalization of an idea." *International Studies Quarterly* 51(2):329–357.

Konisky, David M. 2007. "Regulatory competition and environmental enforcement: Is there a race to the bottom?" *American Journal of Political Science* 51(4):853–872.

Kopstein, Jeffrey S. and David A. Reilly. 2000. "Geographic diffusion and the transformation of the postcommunist world." *World Politics* 53(1):1–37.

Lee, Taedong and Byoung-Inn Bai. 2013. "Network analysis of free trade agreements." *The Korean Journal of International Studies* 11(2):264–293.

Lewis, Jeffrey 2005. "The Janus face of Brussels: Socialization and everyday decision making in the European Union." *International Organization* 59(4):937–971.

Liao, Tim Futing and Gillian Stevens. 1994. "Spouses, homogamy, and social networks." *Social Forces* 73(2):693–707.

Long, J. Scott 1997. *Regression Models for Categorical and Limited Dependent Variables*. Sage Publications.

Lupu, Yonatan. 2013. "The informative power of treaty commitment: Using the spatial model to address selection effects." *American Journal of Political Science* 57(4):912–925.

Lutz, Ellen L. and K. Sikkink. 2001. "International human rights law and practice in Latin America." *International Organization* 54(3):633–659.

Maoz, Zeev. 2011. *Networks of Nations: The Evolution, Structure, and Impact of International Networks, 1816–2001.* Cambridge University Press.

March, James G. and Johan P. Olsen. 1998. "The institutional dynamics of international political orders." *International Organization* 52(4):943–969.

Marshall, M. and K. Jaggers. 2009. "Political regime characteristics and transitions, 1800–2009." *Polity IV Project.* http://www.systemicpeace.org/inscrdata.html.

McPherson, Miller, Lynn Smith-Lovin, and James M. Cook. 2001. "Birds of a feather: Homophily in social networks." *Annual Review of Sociology* 27(1):415–444.

Mercer, Jonathan 1996. *Reputation and International Politics.* Cornell University Press.

Meyer, John W., John Boli, George M. Thomas, and Francisco O. Ramirez. 1997. "World society and the nation-state." *American Journal of Sociology* 103(1):144–181.

Meyer, William H. 1996. "Human rights and MNCs: Theory versus quantitative analysis." *Human Rights Quarterly* 18:368.

Moravcsik, Andrew 2000. "The origins of human rights regimes: Democratic delegation in postwar Europe." *International Organization* 54(02):217–252.

Murdie, Amanda M. and David R. Davis. 2012. "Shaming and blaming: Using events data to assess the impact of human rights INGOs." *International Studies Quarterly* 56(1):1–16.

Mutua, Makau. 2000. "The construction of the African human rights system: Prospects and pitfalls." In Power and Allison (eds.) Realizing Human Rights: Moving from Inspiration to Impact. St. Martin's Press, 143–166.

Nelson, Stephen C. 2014. "Playing favorites: How shared beliefs shape the IMF's lending decisions." *International Organization* 68(02):297–328.

Nelson, Stephen C and Catherine Weaver. forthcoming. "The cultures of International organizations." In Katz Cogan, Hurd, and Johnstone (eds.) The Oxford Handbook of International Organizations. Oxford University Press. St. Martin's Press, 143–166.

Neumayer, Eric 2005. "Do international human rights treaties improve respect for human rights?" *Journal of Conflict Resolution* 49(6):925–953.

Noel, Hans and Brendan Nyhan. 2011. "The 'unfriending' problem: The consequences of homophily in friendship retention for causal estimates of social influence." *Social Networks* 33(3):211–218.

Nye, Joseph S. 2004. *Soft Power: The Means to Success in World Politics.* Public affairs.

OECD. 2013. *Secretary-General's Report to Ministers.* Organisation for Economic Cooperation and Development.

O'Flaherty, Michael and John Fisher. 2008. "Sexual orientation, gender identity and international human rights law: Contextualising the Yogyakarta Principles." *Human Rights Law Review* 8(2):207.

O'Loughlin, John, Michael D. Ward, Corey L. Lofdahl, Jordin S. Cohen, David S. Brown, David Reilly, Kristian S. Gleditsch, and Michael Shin. 1998. "The diffusion of democracy, 1946–1994." *Annals of the Association of American Geographers* 88(4):545–574.

Oneal, John R., Bruce Russett, and Michael L. Berbaum. 2003. "Causes of peace: Democracy, interdependence, and international organizations, 1885–1992." *International Studies Quarterly* 47:371–393.

OPEC. 2013. *Annual Statistical Bulletin.* Organization of the Petroleum Exporting Countries.

Owen, Roger. 2012. *The Rise and Fall of Arab Presidents for Life.* Harvard University Press.

Paul, Thazha V., Deborah Welch Larson, and William C. Wohlforth. 2014. *Status in World Politics.* Cambridge University Press.

Paxton, Pamela, Melanie M. Hughes, and Jennifer L. Green. 2006. "The international women's movement and women's political representation, 1893–2003." *American Sociological Review* 71(6):898–920.

Pevehouse, Jon C., Timothy Nordstrom, and Kevin Warnke. 2004. "The Correlates of War 2 international governmental organizations data version 2.0." *Conflict Management and Peace Science* 21(2):101–119.

Pevehouse, Jon C. 2002. "Democracy from the outside-in? International organizations and democratization." *International Organization* 56(3):515–549.

Pevehouse, Jon C. 2005. *Democracy from Above: Regional Organizations and Democratization.* Cambridge University Press.

Prakash, Aseem and Matthew Potoski. 2006. "Racing to the bottom? Trade, environmental governance, and ISO 14001." *American Journal of Political Science* 50(2):350–364.

Press, Daryl G., Scott D. Sagan, and Benjamin A. Valentino. 2013. "Atomic aversion: Experimental evidence on taboos, traditions, and the non-use of nuclear weapons." *American Political Science Review* 107(01):188–206.

Press, Daryl G. 2005. *Calculating Credibility: How Leaders Assess Military Threats.* Cornell University Press.

Price, Richard. 1995. "A genealogy of the chemical weapons taboo." *International Organization* 49:73–73.

R Core Team. 2013. *R: A Language and Environment for Statistical Computing.* R Foundation for Statistical Computing.

Ramirez, Francisco O., Yasemin Soysal, and Suzanne Shanahan. 1997. "The changing logic of political citizenship: Cross-national acquisition of women's suffrage rights, 1890 to 1990." *American Sociological Review* 62(5):735–745.

Richards, David L., Ronald D. Gelleny, and David H. Sacko. 2001. "Money with a mean streak? Foreign economic penetration and government respect for human rights in developing countries." *International Studies Quarterly* 45(2):219–239.

Rogers, Everett M. 2003. *Diffusion of Innovations.* 5th ed. Free Press.

Rose, Andrew K. 2004. "Do we really know that the WTO increases trade?" *American Economic Review* 94(1):98–114.

Rumelili, Bahar 2004. "Constructing identity and relating to difference: Understanding the EU's mode of differentiation." *Review of International Studies* 30(01):27–47.

Russett, Bruce, John R. Oneal, and David R. Davis. 1998. "The third leg of the Kantian tripod for peace: International organizations and militarized disputes, 1950–85." *International Organization* 52(03):441–467.

Sacerdote, Bruce. 2001. "Peer effects with random assignment: Results for Dartmouth roommates." *The Quarterly Journal of Economics* 116(2):681–704.

Schimmelfennig, Frank. 2005. "Strategic calculation and international socialization: Membership incentives, party constellations, and sustained compliance in Central and Eastern Europe." *International Organization* 59(04):827–860.

Schrodt, Philip A. 2002. "Forecasts and contingencies: From methodology to policy." *Annual Meeting of the American Political Science Association.*

Schwellnus, Guido. 2005. "The adoption of nondiscrimination and minority protection rules in Romania, Hungary, and Poland." In Schimmelfennig and Sedelmeier (eds.) *The Europeanization of Central and Eastern Europe* 51–70.

Sekhon, Jasjeet S. 2009. "Opiates for the matches: Matching methods for causal inference." *Annual Review of Political Science* 12:487–508.

Shanks, Cheryl, Harold K. Jacobson, and Jeffrey H. Kaplan. 1996. "Inertia and change in the constellation of international governmental organizations, 1981–1992." *International Organization* 50(4):593–627.

Sikkink, Kathryn 1998. "Transnational politics, international relations theory, and human rights." *PS: Political Science and Politics* 31(3):517–523.

Simmons, Beth A. 2009. *Mobilizing for Human Rights: International Law in Domestic Politics.* Cambridge University Press.

Simmons, Beth A. and Allison Danner. 2010. "Credible commitments and the International Criminal Court." *International Organization* 64:225–226.

Simmons, Beth A. and Zachary Elkins. 2004. "The globalization of liberalization: Policy diffusion in the international political economy." *American Political Science Review* 98(1):171–189.

Simmons, Beth A., Frank Dobbin and Geoffrey Garrett. 2008. *The Global Diffusion of Markets and Democracy.* Cambridge University Press.

Smith, Jackie and Dawn Wiest. 2012. *Transnational Social Movement Organization Dataset, 1953–2003.* Icpsr33863-v1 ed. Inter-university Consortium for Political and Social Research.

Stahl, Bernhard. 2013. "Another 'strategic accession'? The EU and Serbia (2000–2010)." *Nationalities Papers* 41(3):447–468.

Steglich, Christian, Philip Sinclair, Jo Holliday, and Laurence Moore. 2012. "Actor-based analysis of peer influence in 'A Stop Smoking In Schools Trial' (ASSIST)." *Social Networks* 34(3):359–369.

Strang, David. 1991. "Anomaly and commonplace in European political expansion: Realist and institutional accounts." *International Organization* 45(02):143–162.

Tannenwald, Nina. 1999. "The nuclear taboo: The United States and the normative basis of nuclear non-use." *International Organization* 53(3):433–468.

Thomas, Daniel C. 2001. *The Helsinki Effect: International Norms, Human Rights, and the Demise of Communism.* Princeton University Press.

Torfason, Magnus Thor and Paul Ingram. 2010. "The global rise of democracy: A network account." *American Sociological Review* 75(3):355–377.

True, Jacqui and Michael Mintrom. 2001. "Transnational networks and policy diffusion: The case of gender mainstreaming." *International Studies Quarterly* 45(1):27–57.

Tufte, Edward R. 2006. *Beautiful Evidence.* Graphics Press.

Valentino, Benjamin A. 2014. "Why we kill: The political science of political violence against civilians." *Annual Review of Political Science* 17:89–103.

von Borzyskowski, Inken and Felicity Vabulas. 2014. "The punishment phase: IGO suspensions after political backsliding." Paper presented at the Seventh Annual Conference on the Political Economy of International Organizations, Princeton University from January 16–18, 2014.

Vreeland, James Raymond 2008. "Political institutions and human rights: Why dictatorships enter into the United Nations Convention Against Torture." *International Organization* 62(1):65–101.

Waites, Matthew 2002. "Inventing a 'lesbian age of consent'? The history of the minimum age for sex between women in the UK." *Social & Legal Studies* 11(3):323.

Waltz, Kenneth N. 1959. *Man, the State and War.* Columbia University Press.

Ward, Michael D. and Kristian S. Gleditsch. 2008. *Spatial Regression Models.* Volume 155 Quantitative Applications in the Social Sciences. Sage Publications.

Ward, Michael D. and Peter D. Hoff. 2007. "Persistent patterns of international commerce." *Journal of Peace Research* 44(2):157.

Ward, Michael D., Randolph M. Siverson, and Xun Cao. 2007. "Disputes, democracies, and dependencies: A reexamination of the Kantian peace." *American Journal of Political Science* 51(3):583–601.

Ward, Michael D., Brian D. Greenhill, and Kristin M. Bakke. 2010. "The perils of policy by p-value: Predicting civil conflicts." *Journal of Peace Research* 47(4):363–375.

Ward, Michael D., John S. Ahlquist, and Arturas Rozenas. 2014. "Gravity's rainbow: A dynamic latent space model for the world trade network." *Network Science* 1: 95–118.

Wasserman, Stanley and Katherine Faust. 1994. *Social Network Analysis: Methods and Applications.* Cambridge University Press.

Wendt, Alexander 1999. *Social Theory of International Relations.* Volume 67 Cambridge Studies in International Relations. Cambridge University Press.

Wendt, Alexander. 1992. "Anarchy is what states make of it: The social construction of power politics." *International Organization* 46(02):391–425.

Wild, T. Cameron. 2006. "Social control and coercion in addiction treatment: Towards evidence-based policy and practice." *Addiction* 101(1):40–49.

Wilson, James Q. and George L. Kelling. 1982. "Broken windows." *Atlantic Monthly* 249(3): 29–38.

Zhukov, Yuri M. and Brandon M. Stewart. 2013. "Choosing your neighbors: Networks of diffusion in international relations." *International Studies Quarterly* 57:271–187.

INDEX

acculturation, 44–48, 56, 104, 114–115
Afghanistan, 123, 142, 143, 151
African Union (AU), 31, 105, 141, 178
Amnesty International, 14, 62
Andean Community, 102
Andean Parliament, 178
Arab Labour Organization, 13, 14, 84
Arab Spring, 82, 83, 85
arms control, 50
Asian Development Bank, 142, 143, 180
Association of South East Asian Nations
    (ASEAN), 31, 141
Australia, 30, 109
Austria, 36

Bahrain, 82–90
Bangladesh, 44
Belarus, 142–144
Belgium, 144, 175
Benin, 33
best practice, 9, 43
bilinear mixed effects model, 147, 154, 181
bipartite network, 66, 67
Botswana, 63
boxplot, 69
broken windows theory, 57
Bulgaria, 35
Burma, 32

CABI, 150
Canada, 68, 107
causal inference, 15–18, 55–58
CEDAW, 19, 117, 119, 120
Central American Integration System, 178
Central European Free Trade Association, 178
Chile, 30, 63
China, 49, 93, 96, 142, 143, 162, 173

Cingranelli-Richards Human Rights Data, *see*
    physical integrity rights
civil society, 52
civil war, 42, 71
coercion, *see* material inducement
Cold War, 3, 35, 44, 80
college roommates, 45
common law, 130
Commonwealth, 138, 150, 178
Community of Portuguese-Speaking
    Countries, 178
constructivism, 10, 11, 159
Convention Against Torture, 6, 180
convergence, 3, 15, 18, 59, 165, 167
Council for Mutual Economic Assistance
    (COMECON), 3
Council of Europe, 3, 13, 14, 31, 101, 102, 116,
    134, 138, 141, 178
credible commitments, 41–43, 103
critical mass, *see* tipping point
cross-validation, 79, 95, 97, 100, 104, 107, 128,
    131, 169–171, 178
Cuba, 124
cultural proximity, 20, 45, 79–80, 131–132
culture of anarchy, 10
Czech Republic, 44
Czechoslovakia, 35, 141, 179

Dartmouth, 45
decoupling, 45
democratic peace, 143
Denmark, 109, 175
diplomats, 26–29, 46–51, 56
directed dyads, 143
Dominican Republic, 133
dyadic dependence, 143–147

East Germany, 141